RAIDERS

AND

NATIVES

Raiders and Natives

CROSS-CULTURAL RELATIONS IN THE AGE OF BUCCANEERS

ARNE

BIALUSCHEWSKI

*The University of
Georgia Press*
ATHENS

© 2022 by the University of Georgia Press
Athens, Georgia 30602
www.ugapress.org
All rights reserved

Designed by Kaelin Chappell Broaddus
Set in 10.5/14 Adobe Jenson Pro Regular

Most University of Georgia Press titles are
available from popular e-book vendors.

Printed digitally

Library of Congress Cataloging-in-Publication Data

Title: Raiders and natives : cross-cultural relations in the age of buccaneers /
Arne Bialuschewski.
Description: Athens : The University of Georgia Press, [2022] |
Includes bibliographical references and index.
Identifiers: LCCN 2021038167 | ISBN 9780820361833 (hardback) |
ISBN 9780820361826 (paperback) | ISBN 9780820361819 (ebook)
Subjects: LCSH: Indians of Central America—History—17th century. |
Buccaneers. | Pirates—Central America—History—17th century. |
Pirates—Caribbean Area—History—17th century. |
Indians, Treatment of—Central America—History—17th century. |
Central America—History—17th century. | Spain—Colonies—
America—History—17th century.
Classification: LCC F1434 .B53 2022 | DDC 972.8/03—dc23
LC record available at https://lccn.loc.gov/202103816

Contents

—————— ⚜ ——————

Illustrations and Maps

Acknowledgments

———————— ⚘ ————————

This book was a long time in the making. It is based on years of research and writing. In the course of numerous voyages into uncharted territory, many colleagues and friends guided my way. Above all, I am greatly indebted to Kris Lane, Raynald Laprise, and Kate Zubczyk for their continued support. Kris assisted this project in every possible way from its earliest stages, when it consisted of little more than a vague research proposal. As my research progressed I became acquainted with Raynald who knows the seventeenth-century buccaneers in and out. Many passages of this book are the result of his work rather than mine. Kate endlessly read and edited portions of the text. I am immensely grateful to all of them.

Important references have been provided by Guillaume Aubert, Samantha Billing, David Buisseret, Scott Carballo, William V. Davidson, Jonathan DeCoster, Kevin Dawson, Linford D. Fisher, Carla Gardina Pestana, Jacques Gasser, Gilles Havard, Vitus Huber, James Kelly, W. George Lovell, David F. Marley, Mark Meuwese, Steve Murdoch, John O'Neill, Franz Obermeier, John Paul Paniagua, Andrés Reséndez, and Pascale Villegas. Crucial support and information have also been provided by Alicia Bertrand, Jorge Cañizares Esguerra, Paul Cleveland, Héctor Concohá, Catherine Desbarats, Albert Dreischer, Jason Dyck, Victor Enthoven, Mark Fissel, Felipe Gaitán Ammann, José Miguel García Ramírez, Gundula Haß, Paul Healey, Rosemary A. Joyce, Wim Klooster, Christopher H. Lutz, Alasdair Macfarlane, Adrian Masters, Laura Matthew, Pablo Mauriño Chozas, Kendra McSweeney, Julie Orr, Ernst Pijning, Steven J. Pitt, José Carlos de la Puente, Luis Alberto Ramírez Méndez, James Robertson, Jesus G. Ruiz, Ginevra Sadlier, Danilo Salamanca, David Sheinin, Pablo Miguel Sierra Silva, Tim Stapleton, Arthur Tarratus, John

K. Thornton, Stephen Webre, Patrick Werner, Caroline Williams, David Wilson, and James Wood. Furthermore, Warren O. Bush, Stephen Church, Javier Francisco, Allen Priest, Deborah Shore, and John B. Thomas III have read and edited chapter drafts.

Special thanks go to Mark Hanna, Karl Offen, and Matthew Restall for reading the entire manuscript and providing valuable feedback. Nathaniel Holly and the team of the University of Georgia Press did a superb job bringing this book to light.

At an early stage of research, a Mellon Fellowship at the John Carter Brown Library helped me to examine published primary sources and gain access to secondary literature. After I spent a month at the Beinecke Rare Book and Manuscript Library at Yale, the project received financial support from the Social Sciences and Humanities Research Council of Canada, which enabled me to visit numerous archives and research libraries. In the course of my work I came to appreciate the support of many institutions, particularly the Benson Latin American Collection at the University of Texas at Austin, the Geisel Library of the University of California at San Diego, the Ibero-Amerikanisches Institut in Berlin, the McLennan Library of McGill University, the Special Collections of the McMaster University Library, the Map and Data Library of the University of Toronto, and the Bata Library of Trent University as well as their helpful staffs.

Parts of chapter 2 appear in "Slaves of the Buccaneers: Mayas in Captivity in the Second Half of the Seventeenth Century," *Ethnohistory* 64 (2017): 41–63, and chunks of chapters 3 and 4 appear in "Juan Gallardo: A Native American Buccaneer," *Hispanic American Historical Review* 100 (2020): 233–56.

Note on Terminology

———— ፠ ————

This book is based on research in a variety of languages and cultures. I have tried to keep most terminology as it was used in the seventeenth-century sources. However, ethnic terms required some adjustments. The European terms "Indians" and "Indios" seem outdated and misleading, no matter how common they were in early modern usage. Whenever possible, I have endeavored to find more precise ethnic names. It should be noted that I use the term "Mosquito" instead of "Miskito" or "Miskitu," because the first form was the common spelling in the period under consideration. For the same reason I use "Cuna" instead of "Darienses," which can also be found in Spanish documents, or "Tule," which the modern inhabitants of the San Blas archipelago use. In 2010 "Guna" became the official spelling of the name of the indigenous population of northeastern Panamá. I have retained most spellings of geographical terms as they were and are still used in their respective languages.

RAIDERS
AND
NATIVES

Introduction

⚓

OWARD THE END OF MARCH 1676, THREE UNMARKED VESSELS
with 146 men on board arrived at the mouth of the Río Coco, also
called the Río Wanks or Cape River, in the northern part of Nicaragua's Mosquito Coast. No colonial power exercised authority in
this remote area, and the sparse indigenous population tended to be friendly
to non-Spanish visitors. The motley crew consisted primarily of Englishmen
but also included French and Native Americans. They were led by William
Wright, Jean Tristan, and Bartholomew Sharpe, who would later acquire some
fame for a trans-isthmian foray into the South Sea, now known as the Pacific
Ocean.[1] Determined to take the long and arduous route up the river to Nueva
Segovia, about 450 miles from the coast, the men left their vessels and embarked in a small fleet of dugout canoes and pirogues. A few years earlier, in
November 1669, another gang had attempted to raid this gold-mining region
but was forced to turn around after a ferocious storm caused the loss of four
canoes.[2] This time the fortune hunters were better prepared. The rainy season
was still weeks away, and the men had probably gathered all available information about local conditions. Most importantly, their indigenous accomplices
were ready to help them both live off the land and deal with other natives deep
in Spanish territory.

Driven by insatiable greed for gold, this rogue band paddled day after day
up the meandering Río Coco through the pine savanna and into the evergreen

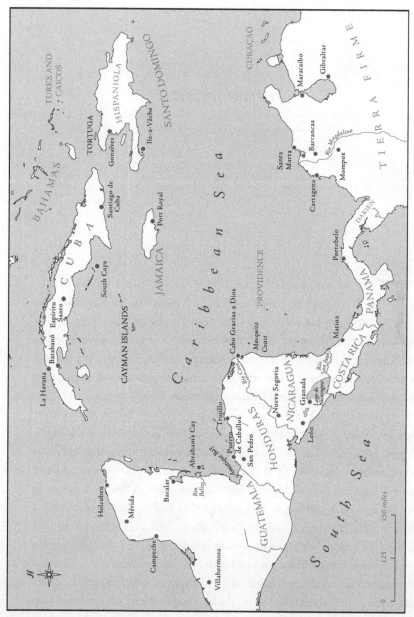

Part of the Caribbean where buccaneers were active.

JENNIFER GREK MARTIN

jungle. When they reached the lush foothills of the interior mountains, cataracts and rapids repeatedly forced the men to haul their canoes and pirogues over land. As a result, it took them several weeks to advance through the wilderness. Although indigenous people dwelling in the region may have seen these strangers, it appears that Spanish authorities were not alerted.[3]

The intruders were probably unaware that they were moving right into a veritable hornet's nest. After the men passed through the forest where Sumu groups lived, they entered lands inhabited by Matagalpas.[4] The latter group had been the focus of Spanish attention for some time, and during the previous decade the area around Nueva Segovia had been a center of native unrest. Hostile Matagalpa bands led repeated attacks on scattered haciendas in the valleys not too far from the town. In order to bring the troublemakers under control, the government dispatched Franciscan missionaries to the region. About 130 indigenous people were relocated to a *reducción*, or a new settlement, near the mission Santa María, some thirty miles north of Nueva Segovia. In exchange for material incentives, they were expected to submit to Spanish rule, adopt Catholicism, and abandon at least part of their cultural practices and identity. This attempt to expand colonial authority into contested territory, however, resulted in total failure. Two rival factions of natives soon fought each other and undermined the entire project.[5] A few years prior to the buccaneers' incursion, several families had left the *reducción* and returned to their traditional ways in their ancestral lands beyond the clutches of the colonial administration.

Once the freebooters reached the headwaters of the Río Coco, they hid their canoes and pirogues and marched for two nights, always trying to remain undetected, through a valley where a number of haciendas were located. There were also a few gold mines in the area, but by the mid-seventeenth century most of the valuable deposits had been exhausted.[6] When the heavily armed gang approached Nueva Segovia, a local man managed to warn officials, who immediately evacuated the several hundred inhabitants consisting of Spaniards, natives, and mulattos.[7] The defense relied in large part on mulattos considered loyal to the colonial regime, but among them they had only five or six muskets. Consequently, the invaders could not be stopped, marching in three groups directly into the center of the abandoned town. They ransacked the buildings, although likely little was left to be looted. The next day the robbers tried to extort ransom, burning the church and two houses to support their demands, which were rejected outright. Realizing it was impossible to acquire the desired plunder, the frustrated intruders decided to return to their vessels. While the men prepared their retreat, the Spaniards deployed about eighty native horsemen, armed with nothing but lances, from nearby haciendas to launch several spoiling attacks and discourage their opponents from advancing any farther. It seems doubtful whether this scare tactic really impressed the marauders. In the end, however, the distressed locals took some revenge by destroying most of the attackers' canoes and pirogues, which forced them to build rafts before they could make the long journey back to the coast.[8] By that point the men probably already had other targets in mind.

B UCCANEERING RAIDS ARE usually presented in the context of international rivalries in the seventeenth-century Caribbean, where French, Dutch, and English gangs infiltrated the Spanish Empire and provided the necessary paramilitary backing for the colonial ventures of their own countries. In fact, many books convey the impression that they are exclusively about European conflicts set in an exotic landscape.[9] Such a Eurocentric focus obfuscates the reality that these raiding gangs—as illustrated by the foray to Nueva Segovia—often operated in regions inhabited by indigenous groups rather than by Spaniards or people of Spanish descent. Both intruders and defenders relied on local support not only during this assault but also in the broader history of buccaneering. The fact that Native Americans had a part in these violent incursions has received virtually no sustained scholarly attention to date. This book presents a new perspective on this chapter of imperial strife by emphasizing cross-cultural relations. Indigenous groups, in various forms and functions, not only participated in but frequently played crucial roles in the course of raids. In a wider context, native populations were among the beneficiaries as well as the victims of hostile intrusions. Closely examining several examples in the Caribbean Rim and along the South Sea coast will lead to a deeper understanding of the fatal struggles that ravaged the periphery of the Spanish colonial empire during this turbulent period.

T HE SITUATION OF THE indigenous people that the raiding gang encountered near the border between Nicaragua and Honduras in 1676 was in many respects typical for much of Central America. After epidemics, social disruption, and violent confrontations with the Spanish conquistadores caused massive population losses in the sixteenth and early seventeenth centuries, large swaths of land remained uninhabited for a long time. Demographic recovery was slow, and repeated disease outbreaks continued to decimate native communities well into the eighteenth century.[10]

Numerous indigenous people who survived the Spanish conquest and its immediate consequences suffered from the imposition of colonial rule in Central America. By virtue of appropriation, the Crown claimed absolute authority in these dominions. Colonization often began as a spiritual and cultural crusade against native religions and traditions, coupled with incessant attempts to reorganize indigenous societies.[11] Furthermore, the population was compelled to pay tribute to the new rulers. Spanish authorities also granted land along with native tribute and labor, known as *encomiendas*, to loyal subjects as rewards for military accomplishments or other merits and services to the Crown. According to this policy, local communities had to supply their *encomenderos* with agricultural products and to provide laborers on a rotating basis to work on the plantations and in other sectors of the colonial economy. Widespread abuses led to unrest in many colonies. The practice of coerced labor expanded dramatically after the discovery of rich silver and gold deposits in various regions of the empire. Mining near Nueva Segovia, as elsewhere, depended at first on the exploitation of Native Americans.[12] Countless workers died in the mines or in ancillary operations. To overcome the resulting labor shortage, the transatlantic slave trade brought an ever-increasing number of Africans to the colonies, adding another element to the already complex intercultural relations.

A recent reinterpretation of Spanish records, along with newly found sources, have led historians to realize that the so-called conquest of the New World relied largely on indigenous allies and auxiliaries.[13] Colonization, however, remained a haphazard affair. From an early stage, the adventurers who crossed the Atlantic in their quest for fame and treasures focused on strategic and, above all, resource-rich regions.[14] In peripheral areas with few goods valued by outsiders for looting, native societies were barely touched by encroachment. The Mosquito Coast and its sparsely populated hinterland offer one such example.[15] That area saw little, if any, contact with Spaniards. Over time, however, the colonial frontier slowly advanced into unconquered territories.[16] This was by no means a peaceful process. Violent clashes and uprisings that claimed many lives were common occurrences in the history of Central America.

CONFLICTS BETWEEN THE indigenous population and reckless colonizers may have been frequent in the New World, but the Spanish Crown focused primarily on European rivalries and wars throughout the early modern period. As early as 1493, a papal bull had fantastically divided the world to prevent strife between the expanding powers of Portugal and Spain. One year later, the Iberian rulers confirmed the partition of the globe in the Treaty of Tordesillas. According to this agreement, all territories more than 370 leagues west of the Cape Verde Islands belonged to Spain.[17] The treaty, however, could not hinder other Europeans from infringing on the Spanish Empire.

For about a century, the nations that challenged Spanish rule in the Americas were unable to establish sustainable colonies in the Western Hemisphere. They engaged in predatory activities—a kind of asymmetrical warfare—aimed at the wealth the Iberians extracted from their overseas territories. Robbery was a widely accepted means for other Western Europeans to catch up with the Spaniards. In this first phase of conflict, non-state actors—of which pirates clearly attracted most attention—were the primary threat to imperial authority in the Caribbean Basin. These irregular forces did not desire conquest and colonization. Instead, they pillaged worthwhile targets and endeavored to make off with rich spoils.[18] As a result of incessant incursions by its enemies, the Spanish Crown, which invested heavily in European wars and depended primarily on the Americas as a source of revenue, was forced to spend an enormous amount of resources to secure its treasure shipments in the New World and across the Atlantic Ocean. At the same time, it neglected the defense of other potential targets in the vast empire, rendering them vulnerable to costly raids. The Spaniards were caught in a struggle they could not realistically win.

In the early stages of colonization, the crucial conflicts took place at sea. Although contemporary Spanish records and modern books use the term "pirates" for nearly all seafaring raiders active in American waters, the reality was far more complex. Piracy is loosely defined as robbery at sea, but most marauding gangs in the Caribbean focused on assaulting ports and towns in coastal areas. Furthermore, in wartime conflicting nations authorized private vessels as corsairs—or privateers, as they became known in the English-speaking world—to prey on enemy shipping. This was a perfectly legal and internationally accepted means to supplement regular forces during hostilities. Recognizing the peculiar form of amphibious warfare in the colonies, privateering commissions issued by English and French governors allowed the holders to apprehend goods and merchandise not only at sea but also "upon ye high Land."[19] In practice, however, many non-Spaniards operated between these two categories—pirates and privateers—seeking the backing of a European prince or a colonial designate, although in remote locations they often knew no limitations in their predatory and violent undertakings. These opportunistic freebooters, marauders, or buccaneers turned out to be a significant factor in imperial endeavors during the late sixteenth century and the seventeenth century.[20] They severely weakened the Spanish Empire, paving the way for the traders, planters, and settlers that followed in the next phase of Western European expansion.

From the Spanish perspective, non-Iberian intruders and indigenous revolts posed the two most serious challenges to imperial rule in the New World. On several occasions, colonial authorities were apprehensive that these two parties would join forces and take up arms against them. In order to break up potential liaisons between their European enemies and native groups, the Spaniards not only launched military campaigns, but they also used a broad variety of measures, as described later in this book, aimed at bringing coastal populations under imperial control. This, of course, caused further resentment and conflicts.

N ATIVE AMERICANS AND freebooters appeared to be natural allies against the Spaniards, but their relations were not necessarily harmonious. A critical moment lay in initial contact, which was always risky. Only under exceptional circumstances did both parties include individuals whose Spanish was sufficient to communicate complex subject matters across cultural boundaries. Time and again the language barrier posed a fundamental challenge to mutual understanding. Besides simple Spanish words or phrases, gestures and hand signs were the sole means to indicate the desire or intentions of each party. Misunderstandings did occur, sometimes with fatal consequences. In most instances, gift exchange helped to smooth relations. Local leaders in general sought iron-cutting tools or firearms. The indigenous people usually offered some food in return. Thereafter, the freebooters communicated their needs in more detail. If they required provisions, which was often the case, problems emerged when they had little to barter or poor natives could not spare foodstuffs.[21] It also may have been difficult to come to terms if the buccaneers wanted strategic information or even asked for support in a raid on Spanish targets. In the course of these interactions, some leaders had to make instant, often fateful, decisions to either assist the strangers or show their loyalty to the colonial regime. Although such cross-cultural encounters must have happened quite frequently, the historical record provides few clues about the exact circumstances that led to the respective outcomes.

Forging ties between Native Americans and Dutch, French, and English marauders was certainly not an easy task, but beneficial connections were undoubtedly formed through both cultural and material exchange. Indigenous people notably profited greatly from iron tools the Europeans brought with them. These devices—chiefly knives, machetes, hatchets, axes, and fishing hooks—were vastly superior to what native populations utilized throughout the precontact period. Coastal inhabitants quickly made effective use of imported manufactures. The fact that iron implements were sometimes traded over enormous distances illustrates their great value.[22] When the Spaniards established their colonial empire, they restricted the availability of such items to loyal groups settled in *reducciones*. In frontier or conflict zones, the cross-cultural trade in iron tools and weapons was generally prohibited. In addition to tools, indigenous populations often highly valued mirrors and nonutilitarian objects such as beads.[23] Itinerant raiding gangs that operated in remote parts of the Spanish Empire were normally prepared to provide locals with at least some desired goods.

The newcomers, in turn, primarily needed to acquire skills to survive and utilize natural resources. Various examples illustrate cultural transference from Native Americans. The term "buccaneer," for instance, derives from the Tupí-Guaraní word *mukem* for a wooden grill used by the inhabitants of Brazil to smoke sliced meat.[24] Since the Europeans only knew how to preserve meat with salt, which was difficult to get in many tropical regions, they were keen to follow the native method. French seafarers corrupted the term into *boucan* and later brought this practice to the Caribbean. The earliest written reference in this part of the globe dates to the late 1620s.[25] The term was subsequently applied to unsettled gangs that adopted indigenous ways and learned to live off the land. In 1653 an eyewitness noted that "boucanniers" frequented the coasts of Hispaniola, from where they launched occasional incursions into other parts of the Spanish Empire.[26] A few years thereafter, this name was used by the English in Jamaica, first referring to French hunters but later also to all non-Iberians who prowled the Caribbean in their quest to profit from the riches of the New World. The French marauders based in western Hispaniola and nearby Tortuga, however, preferred the term *flibustier*, presumably to dissociate themselves from what was regarded as a rather primitive way of life.[27]

Further evidence of cultural adaptation and transmission comes from the famous chroniclers of the buccaneers, Alexandre-Olivier Exquemelin and William Dampier. Besides *boucan*, both authors described several practical features that frontiersmen adopted from native populations. The temporary sheds, for instance, that the hunters built of branches, leaves, and skins when they roamed across Hispaniola were called *ajoupas*. Both name and construction method also derive from the Tupí culture. It appears that multiple French trading voyages to Brazil, including two colonial attempts in the sixteenth and early seventeenth centuries, led to the acquisition of important survival skills that were passed on to successive seafarers who plied Caribbean waters.[28] French adventurers formed small groups that proved to be highly receptive to knowledge provided by indigenous communities. They adapted to local conditions and constantly sought commercial opportunities, challenging Iberian claims over resource-rich regions of the Atlantic World. *Boucan* and *ajoupa* are only two known examples of cultural transmission involving these intruders. Countless other foodways and craft skills must have been lost when settled societies marginalized or absorbed the early pioneers who left no written record.

Although the buccaneers were the only European group to take their name from a Native American term, they were not exceptional in adopting indigenous cultural practices. Many colonists found out in various parts of the growing overseas empires that they would have to rely on local populations to survive in harsh and often unforgiving conditions. Following their arrival at the colonial frontier, migrants sometimes had to abandon a good deal of their cultural identity if they wanted to thrive in the New World.[29] Countless newcomers were highly opportunistic when dealing with the people they encountered. The first Frenchmen who took up residence in the Lesser Antilles in the early seventeenth century, for instance, lived along with Kalinago communities and established a lively cross-cultural exchange. Among other practical things, the French learned from locals how to make *maby*, a refreshing drink brewed of manioc or sweet potatoes. This concoction later enriched rogue bands' daily diet, which was often monotonous and simple.[30]

Europeans also profited from native seafaring skills. Settlers on Saint-Christophe, Martinique, Guadeloupe, and elsewhere learned to build dugout canoes. These traditional watercraft, however, were difficult to paddle and steer, and when untrained men used them in the open sea they were prone to capsizing. Some colonists, therefore, hired indigenous people to help them in coastal waters while others were employed as fishermen. In return, the natives received metal tools and other items that allowed for more efficient handling of their fishing gear.[31]

The era of peaceful exchange from which the newcomers in general benefited more than native societies did not last long, however. When ever-increasing numbers of Europeans began to marginalize the Kalinagos of the Lesser Antilles and came into conflict with them, the latter responded with a form of amphibious warfare against which the colonists had little defense. In their large pirogues, which could carry up to forty armed men as well as sizable cargo, indigenous forces moved swiftly between the islands, employing a hit-and-run strategy against European targets. From 1632 to 1674, for example, Kalinagos living in Dominica launched a series of devastating raids on Antigua, more than a hundred miles away, where an English settlement was struggling to survive.[32] Some buccaneers may have adopted these tactics when they assaulted Spanish towns all along the coastline and major rivers.

Certain native leaders, in turn, learned through their interactions with the newcomers in the course of the seventeenth century that they could use intra-European hostilities to preserve at least some of their political and cultural autonomy.[33] As a theater of almost permanent international conflict, the Caribbean provided the opportunity for diminishing indigenous groups to establish themselves as valued allies or auxiliaries in warfare. In 1664, for instance, six hundred Kalinagos in seventeen pirogues supported an English attack on the French settlement Sainte-Lucie in the Lesser Antilles. Furthermore, during the Second Anglo-Dutch War from 1665 to 1667, in which France and the Netherlands fought the English, native forces played an important role in shifting the balance of power between small colonial militias while at the same time seeking to enhance the scope and effectiveness of their own resistance.[34] But this remained a brief episode in the history of the Caribbean. The rapid expansion of plantations across most islands, along with the massive importation of enslaved Africans, left little space for autonomous indigenous polities, and in the course of the eighteenth century the surviving Kalinago communities ceased to take active part in international strife.

CONDITIONS IN THE Caribbean Rim, particularly in mainland Central America, and along parts of the South Sea shoreline, were quite different for native populations. Although Spain's representatives exercised no or very limited authority in vast swaths of land, opportunities to profit from European rivalries were much rarer than in the Lesser Antilles.[35] Relatively few conflicts between colonial forces and non-Iberian intruders directly affected or involved indigenous people. The instances when natives encountered buccaneers, assisted them during incursions, or even participated in pillages, however, are poorly understood or left untold in the historical literature. Scholars drawing the larger picture of raiding in the seventeenth century must expand their attention into new territory and take these episodes into account.

This book provides a differentiated picture of the relations between Dutch, French, and English freebooters and native communities across various parts of the Spanish Empire. Unlike most Europeans who came to the Americas to establish colonies, seaborne robbers were highly mobile and did not appropriate land for settlement. Therefore, they forged rather pragmatic relationships with their contacts and the environment. Since buccaneers and many indigenous groups faced a mutual enemy—the Spanish colonial regime—some of them sought the support of outsiders to reach strategic goals.

Cross-cultural encounters involving itinerant freebooters were multifaceted and can best be analyzed in their specific contexts. On the Yucatán Peninsula, marauders frequently looted Maya villages and mistreated or abducted coastal inhabitants. Conditions in Central America were quite different. Beginning with the pivotal 1665 sack of Granada in Nicaragua raiding gangs, often assisted by locals, advanced hundreds of miles to pillage targets far inland. On the Mosquito Coast, outlaws forged close ties to indigenous communities, while on Panamá's Darién frontier they competed with the colonial power for the support of native groups. Along the South Sea shore, roving gangs failed to establish peaceful ties to local populations, which contributed to the decline of unregulated raiding toward the end of the seventeenth century. A variety of relations emerged when non-Spanish intruders ventured into unconquered or weakly defended territory. To some degree the interactions between these unequal parties changed behavior patterns, power structure, material culture, subsistence economies, and military strategies on both sides.

For the historian, research on the relations between indigenous groups and non-Iberian freebooters poses a serious challenge. With a few notable exceptions, no written records reveal the native perspective on their encounters with buccaneers. The marauders also tended to provide the authorities—regardless of the nation—with scant information about their ventures, and the surviving accounts of their contacts with indigenous populations are often markedly biased or misleading. Thus scholars rely in large part on the official Spanish correspondence to make sense of the relations between these potential allies against the colonial power. In some cases, however, even the ramshackle and inefficient governing bodies knew very little about major developments within their administrative boundaries. Moreover, after particularly disastrous events, such as a large-scale raid, officials usually tried to save their careers, if not their lives, by downplaying or concealing their own culpability.[36] This occurred frequently in the heyday of the buccaneers.

Considering these limitations, it is necessary to utilize the broadest empirical scope possible for this study. Every scattered piece of information in the colonial archives as well as in the published accounts matters. These sources provide a fascinating insight into the complex interactions that affected or even determined the fate of countless people dwelling in or near the conflict zones of the Caribbean Rim and the South Sea coast in the second half of the seventeenth century.

Chapter 1

THE RISE OF THE
BUCCANEERS

I T TOOK THE SPANIARDS ONLY A FEW YEARS AFTER COLUMBUS'S FIRST
transatlantic crossing to find the treasures every conquistador must have
dreamed of. Transferring this wealth to Europe, however, posed a major and never-ending challenge. Created in 1502, the Casa de Contratación was designed to generate abundant income to the royal treasury in
Madrid. Officials registered, licensed, controlled, and taxed all shipping to
and from the Americas. The centralized commercial bureaucracy also set up
a far-reaching infrastructure to transport the gold and various agricultural
products amassed as tribute from the subjugated indigenous populations of
Hispaniola and elsewhere to Spain. Toward the middle of the century, silver from México and Peru became the most valuable commodity appropriated by the colonial rulers. After the precious metal had been collected—first
robbed, later mined—it was carried overland to the nearest harbor and then
shipped from port to port and across the Atlantic until the treasures reached
Sevilla, the only city where the Crown permitted vessels from America to
unload their cargo.[1] Although settlement, missionary activities, and the establishment of plantations represented important aspects of colonization, by
far the greatest effort was directed to exploiting and transporting the mineral
wealth from the New World to the Old.

The rapid expansion of gold and silver shipments across the Atlantic not
only fed the coffers and ambitions of the royal family in Madrid but also

aroused the greedy attention of many others—adventurers, merchants, nobles—in various parts of Western Europe. Spanish fleets soon became a prime target for raiders. The first assault on a treasure transport occurred in early 1523, when Jean Fleury, commanding a squadron consisting of five vessels, surprised three heavily laden caravels on the high seas somewhere between the Azores and the Iberian Peninsula. The Frenchmen captured two of them and seized a considerable amount of valuables, including jewelry and a variety of exotic goods, that Hernando Cortés had previously plundered from the Aztec capital, Tenochtitlan.[2] Word of this coup spread quickly to coastal Western Europe, inspiring others to launch similar attacks.

In subsequent years many freebooters sailed to the Caribbean. The latter proved to be an almost ideal hunting ground for deep-sea marauders. Currents and the wind patterns, combined with the sailing technology of the period, channeled shipping into certain routes between the numerous islands and cays. Furthermore, the hurricane season beginning in July of each year along with the Atlantic winter storms influenced the scheduling of sail times. Although the galleons developed in the second half of the sixteenth century brought some navigational improvements, Spanish treasure shipments were slow and rather predictable, and pirates soon figured out where and when they could intercept. It is unknown exactly when the first raiders appeared in the New World, but the earliest recorded assault took place in November 1536, when French marauders seized a Spanish vessel off the north coast of Panamá.[3] This began a long history of pillage and plunder in the Caribbean.

Reacting to these attacks, the Spaniards introduced a convoy system designed to protect shipping lanes between various parts of their vast overseas empire. As early as 1526, treasure vessels were ordered to sail in fleets, and additional ordinances required all merchant ships to be armed, adhere to a specific schedule, and call at only a few designated colonial ports. In 1537 naval vessels began to escort the galleons across the Atlantic. By 1566 a wide-ranging network of convoys connected different ports with the transport routes of valuable goods. The *flota de Indias* departed from Sevilla in April with merchandise bound for Veracruz, where treasures from México and the Philippines were laden. Another convoy for Portobelo and Cartagena de Indias followed in August. The galleons then congregated in the fortified port of La Habana in Cuba. In May or June, after all business had been completed and the precious cargo loaded on board the vessels, a large convoy sailed back to Spain.[4]

This schedule, however, frequently could not be kept, and countless problems occurred in the shipment of commodities from one port to another. Time and again vessels fell prey to freebooters.

In the first half of the sixteenth century, a pattern of pillage emerged. Fortune hunters sailed from Western Europe to the Caribbean, where they raided Spanish shipping and harbors. Marauders then made their way back to their home port to unload their loot.[5] Investors received their shares, while local economies profited from the infusion of silver, gold, and valuable merchandise. For coastal populations, such ventures were often a rare opportunity to acquire substantial wealth.

SEAFARING NATIONS AT WAR with one another during the early modern period generally issued commissions, or letters of marque, to shipowners or captains, permitting them to raid enemy shipping and seize lawful prizes. What became known as privateering was an inexpensive way to make use of armed vessels without having to spend scarce funds on large navies. It pressured antagonists to deploy forces for the protection of merchant shipping, and, if successful, disrupted commerce leading to the acquisition of resources that otherwise would have strengthened the enemy's economic and financial viability.[6]

Arising from a maritime tradition that originated in the late Middle Ages, privateering was a strictly regulated business. Upon return from a successful voyage, the loot had to be declared in a prize court or, in French colonies, with the governor. A certain percentage of the proceeds were then paid to the authorities, and after this deduction the remaining amount was to be distributed among the shipowners, officers, and crew. However, many privateers violated or circumvented these regulations. The legality of their actions often depended on diverging interpretations of whether the timing, location, and targets of raids fell within the terms of their commissions. The dividing line between privateering and piracy was frequently blurred, and cycles of war and peace—communicated with a considerable delay in the colonies—made it difficult to determine the exact legal status of freebooters. In times of war, the demand for privateers surged, whereas in periods of peace marauders found themselves without a source of income.[7] Many continued to engage in raiding, especially in the seventeenth-century Caribbean, where international conflicts never seemed to be resolved. Privateers who operated outside the terms of their commission became pirates and were, at least in theory, subject to capital punishment. Legal mechanisms for sanctioning seaborne robbers beyond the boundaries of the emerging nation-state were still in their infancy, however, and colonial authorities sometimes lacked the will to bring pirates to trial.[8] As a result of these factors, the Caribbean turned out to be an utterly lawless zone, and perpetrators operating on this legal frontier generally showed little respect for imperial claims.

For the Spanish Crown, it did not matter whether its European enemies held a valid commission to assault its vessels in wartime. The authorities adhered to the Treaty of Tordesillas and regarded all non-Iberians who appeared in the Caribbean to seek a living or establish colonies as pirates. This policy led to a de facto permanent state of war in the region.[9] Among the Western Europeans who defied Spanish rule in various parts of the Americas, it was first French, followed by English, and finally Dutch intruders who challenged and undermined the long-standing policy of exclusion.

French seafarers arrived in the Caribbean in the early sixteenth century, and during the protracted wars with Spain beginning in 1520, freebooters assaulted shipping along the new sea-lanes. The Crown legitimized plunder by freely issuing privateering commissions. Furthermore, local magnates from the Atlantic coast and the hinterland provided capital and access to markets where the raiders could dispose of their spoils. Among the seized cargos were not only treasures but also tobacco, sugar, indigo, and other highly valued agricultural products. Small port towns such as Dieppe, Honfleur, Dunkerque, and Le Havre in Normandy, along with Biarritz and Bayonne in the Basque country, owed much of their prosperity to the fruits of these sponsored raids. Although many Frenchmen targeting the treasure fleets were Huguenots and therefore fiercely anti-Spanish, some Catholics participated in such ventures as well. The lure of Spanish wealth enticed all segments of society. The peace treaty of 1559, however, ended hostilities in Western Europe and led to a slump in raiding. Moreover, in the following years, colonial ventures in Brazil and Florida absorbed a significant amount of resources. Despite this, fortune hunters from France's Atlantic periphery never fully abandoned their attacks on shipping and port towns in the Americas.[10] French incursions posed the most persistent threat to Spanish holdings in the far-flung empire.

The English began to move into the Caribbean during the conflict with Spain in the latter half of the sixteenth century. The Tudor kings initially formulated imperial aspirations in the early years of the century, but they did not have the resources to challenge Iberian claims in the New World. This changed under Queen Elizabeth between 1558 and 1603, when the Crown pursued what has been succinctly characterized as "a highly aggressive para-naval policy towards Spain."[11] The adventurers of the period, chiefly hailing from fishing communities of the southwest of England, infiltrated American waters and became involved in contraband and the slave trade. After a few transatlantic voyages, their knowledge of the Caribbean enabled them to maintain themselves in the region for two or three years at a time. On their return to England, participants in these ventures used their newly acquired navigational skills to steer other vessels to promising destinations in the New World or passed on their expertise to those inspired to follow suit. Driven by lust for Spanish silver and their private wealth accumulation while ostensibly acting in service of the English Crown, these seafarers blurred the line between legitimate raiding of enemy shipping and outright piracy. When relations between England and Spain deteriorated after 1568, these men lost all restraints and assaulted their enemies whenever the opportunity arose. In the course of this conflict, the most daring and successful raiders, notably Walter Raleigh and Francis Drake, acquired the status of national heroes.[12] Despite frequent setbacks and failures that led to considerable loss of life, hundreds of English vessels crossed the Atlantic to loot targets in the Spanish Empire.

As the long Anglo-Spanish war came to a close in 1603, Dutch sea rovers became the principal threat to shipping in the Caribbean. The United Provinces of the Netherlands remained at war with Spain until 1648, and hostilities had gradually spread from land to sea. The Dutch regarded privateering as an effective means to disrupt the inflow of wealth from the Americas on which Spanish military expenditure in Europe in large part depended. Established in 1621, the West-Indische Compagnie issued many commissions, carrying the Dutch war of independence to the New World. The company was a peculiar construct that connected raiding with overseas trade and colonizing activities.[13] Shipowners, mostly from Zeeland in the south of the Netherlands, also undertook individual privateering voyages to the Caribbean and South America. Driven by a combination of patriotism with mercenary motives, notables from

Middelburg, Vlissingen, Amsterdam, and other cities invested in predatory ventures, which turned out to be very profitable at times. In contrast to similar actions taken by other Western European nations, it appears that Dutch privateering did not lead to so many abuses because the authorities strictly enforced adherence to the commissions.[14] Nevertheless, Dutch attacks caused massive losses to Spanish shipping.

At the same time, Spain experienced a prolonged period of crisis. The situation was predicated by a decline in the inflow of silver from the Americas that began in the early seventeenth century. Instead of scaling down unnecessary expenditure and gaining efficiency with far-reaching reforms, the Crown renewed efforts to subdue the rebels in the Netherlands and waged war in France, which eventually led to military disaster. As a result, the Habsburgs not only lost control of Portugal and had to recognize the independence of the Netherlands after the Thirty Years' War but were also severely compromised in other international conflicts.[15] Mounting problems in Europe soon had repercussions on the other side of the Atlantic, where Spain's enemies exploited any weakness and expanded their predatory activities in various parts of the New World.

Probably the most spectacular and costly loss in the Caribbean was due to a Dutch privateering attack. In September 1628, Piet Hein, with thirty-one vessels and four thousand soldiers in the service of the West-Indische Compagnie, waylaid a treasure fleet off the northwest coast of Cuba. They assaulted fifteen galleons and engaged the Spaniards in a running fight. The Dutchmen boarded some of the vessels in the open sea while forcing others into a bay to seize them. After days of looting, the valuable cargo of silver, gold, pearls, indigo, and sugar was transported to the Netherlands, where the enormous influx of wealth caused inflation.[16] For the Spanish Crown, this loss represented a devastating blow. The commander of the pillaged fleet was brought to trial for dereliction of duty, found guilty, and executed. In the next few years, the convoys consisted in large part of heavily armed ships.[17] Consequently, transatlantic trade experienced a slump, and as Spanish authorities focused on improving the defense of their treasure fleets, minor port towns and coastal shipping, particularly at the periphery of empire, became more susceptible to raids.

Throughout the early modern period, Spanish officials not only worried about foreign assaults, they were also concerned about illicit trade. According to mercantilist principles, the economic function of the colonies was to gener-

ate a surplus of wealth for export to the motherland, where the main beneficiaries were the Crown, the aristocracy, and the clergy. Trade across the Atlantic was strictly regulated and limited, rendering it difficult for settlers to sell
enough of their locally produced sugar, cacao, tobacco, sarsaparilla, dyes, and
other goods to purchase all the imports they desired or needed. Moreover, this
policy severely curtailed trade between the colonies, and high taxes along with
logistic problems further hindered commerce within the Spanish Empire. The
feeble state of economic development encouraged coastal populations outside
the major ports to forge ties through middlemen—often people of African descent—with foreign contraband traders, mostly Dutch merchants.[18] The latter
conducted business in a far more efficient manner than their Iberian counterparts and generally offered manufactured goods for a lower price. In return, the
traders obtained agricultural products and hides that were greatly sought after in Europe. Various Spanish attempts to curb such connections failed. Most
notably, the governor of Santo Domingo forced the inhabitants of Hispaniola's northern and western shore in 1605 and 1606 to abandon their settlements
and move to the eastern part of the island.[19] This ill-advised policy left a huge
flank of the colony open to hostile penetration. In the following years, the unprotected stretch of coast attracted all kinds of outcasts from various Western
European countries, particularly from the Netherlands and France.

This vexed state of affairs allowed the emergence of the buccaneers. In contrast to their predatory predecessors, who crossed the Atlantic to participate
from the riches of the New World and then returned to Europe, this new
breed of rovers was based solely in the Caribbean. Motley groups of adventurers lurked on the western and northern littoral of Hispaniola, taking temporary residence in deserted settlements along the shore. In the nearby rolling savannas, they found herds of domesticated animals—goats, sheep, hogs, cattle,
and also horses—that became feral after the Spanish colonists had left. This
livestock provided a means of sustenance and income for small hunting parties bearing their characteristic long muskets and assisted by dogs that chased
down the game.[20] While the hides were sold to traders, the meat was preserved
in a traditional way from which the buccaneers derived their name. Spanish expeditions against these intruders remained largely unsuccessful. On occasion
some of these hardy, sharp-shooting, avaricious, and opportunistic frontiersmen turned their hunting and survival skills to raiding. An assault on a coastal
town or enemy shipping required a modest capital outlay—a small vessel and

A buccaneer in Hispaniola. Alexandre-Olivier Exquemelin,
De Americaensche Zee-Roovers (Amsterdam: Jan ten Hoorn, 1678), 22.

firearms with ammunition were usually sufficient—and often promised considerable returns. Access to supplies and knowledge of local conditions enabled rogue bands to advance into neglected parts of the Spanish Empire, where they found sparsely defended targets.

Although freebooters sought to operate under the cover of a privateering license, for many, legal considerations were probably of minor importance. In general, robbers were active where and whenever the potential gains seemed to outweigh the risks. This was always a subjective matter. In a region marked by low life expectancy and high mortality due to hurricanes, accidents, and a host of tropical diseases, the risk of being captured by Spanish forces or killed in an ambush may have appeared negligible.[21] From the individuals' perspective, therefore, it was often worth taking a gamble by participating in a daring assault if a large profit was at stake. Of course, for some marauders visions of treasures would have been hard to resist under any conditions, and the fact that most buccaneers lived in an all-male environment only increased their willingness to resort to violence in the pursuit of material goals.

D URING THE FIRST HALF of the seventeenth century, hordes of intruders—contraband traders as well as raiders—severely weakened Spain's ability to defend its extensive imperial holdings in the New World. In the wake of these uncoordinated incursions, other maritime nations began to establish colonies in the Americas. After a number of costly failures and setbacks, the growth of tobacco plantations in Virginia beginning in 1612 provided the model for profitable staple production that boosted further colonization. In the following years, much effort was focused on the Caribbean islands with no Spanish presence. Between 1624 and 1632, English colonists landed in Saint Christopher—later shared with the French—Barbados, Nevis, Antigua, and Montserrat. Furthermore, in 1629 Providence Island, off the east coast of Nicaragua, was occupied. At about the same time, the Dutch built trading posts on Tobago and Curaçao off the South American mainland, then known as the Tierra Firme, which had been the focus of Dutch intrusion since the turn of the century. The French afterward took possession of Guadeloupe, Martinique, and half a dozen smaller islands in the Lesser Antilles.[22] Although most of these early colonies were situated at the periphery of the Caribbean Basin, they provided a foothold for further expansion into strategic areas of the Spanish Empire. By the 1630s this part of the globe had become fiercely contested, with several Western European nations endeavoring to seize a share in the wealth that had made Spain the world's leading power.

While all colonizing efforts during this period had been approved by their respective governments, only a select few received any direct financing or material support. As the Spanish Crown did from the earliest stages of overseas expansion, French, English, and Dutch central authorities sought imperial possessions, but they lacked sufficient resources to achieve this goal. In this state of affairs, it was usually left to private entrepreneurs to carry out the ambitious visions of their rulers.[23] They did so with hopes of large returns. Investors speculated to cash in on the growing metropolitan demand for tobacco and sugar, as well as other staple crops such as cotton and indigo. However, unrealistically high expectations frequently led to disappointment. Whoever the protagonist in Europe, it turned out to be very difficult to establish economically viable colonies in the New World, and much capital was lost in failed ventures. Distinctions between locations in terms of climate, soil, and natural resources as well as what they might be capable of producing often remained to be discovered. Many problems, moreover, were caused by the individuals in charge of the colonizing process at the fringe of the empire. Spanish officials embezzled or stole a considerable portion of the treasures that they were supposed to transport to Sevilla, while disillusioned French, English, and Dutch colonists turned to raiding and other illicit endeavors as a major source of income.[24] Both activities undermined Spanish imperial authority, and the latter led to a multitude of conflicts in the Caribbean and beyond.

In search of opportunities to enrich themselves, non-Iberian intruders operated almost all over the Caribbean Sea. The many islands and cays provided refuge to hide from possible pursuers or to make repairs, careen, and refurbish their vessels. Hispaniola, however, was the focal point of most outlaw activities. The native population had long disappeared, and vast stretches of coast remained outside Spanish control. Perhaps the first temporary base for roving gangs in the Caribbean emerged at Cap Tiburon, at the southwestern tip of Hispaniola, where the Spaniards had never settled. It offered good anchorages and rich hunting grounds. French frontiersmen—many of whom had come from Brazil—were probably conversant with this area by the turn of the seventeenth century. The nearby Ile-à-Vache later served as a meeting point where freebooters gathered before setting sail for a raid.[25]

In late 1629 and early 1630, two groups of French and Englishmen, who had been expelled from Saint Christopher by a fleet coming from Spain, sought refuge in Tortuga, a small island off the uninhabited northwest coast of Hispaniola. The first settlers began to plant tobacco while others came to Tortuga to cut valuable dyewood that grew in coastal areas. The rocky northern side provided protection from the Spaniards, and in the following years scores of vagrants from the Netherlands, the British Isles, and particularly France frequented the anchorages on the southern shore—the best sheltered, Basse-Terre, became the site of the largest settlement.[26] Although the main focus of the colonists was on agricultural production, the island also served as a base for smugglers and raiding parties. It appears that the early marauders primarily seized slaves from Portuguese vessels and later turned to other sources of wealth. Despite repeated attempts, Spanish forces failed to expel the intruders. In 1635 Spanish troops, guided by an Irish dissenter, launched a large-scale assault. They killed 195 men and burned down their habitations, but others took up their position as soon as the troops had left. Further military operations aimed at regaining control of the increasingly fortified island in 1636 and 1654 also met with little or only temporary success. Fiscal pressures in combination with an ensuing surge of English attacks prompted the Spaniards in 1655 to withdraw for good from this stretch of coast and abandon all plans to reintegrate the region into their empire.[27] In the following years, French settlers and hunters used this colony as a hub for assaults on Spanish holdings.

Freebooters needed a safe haven in the Caribbean where they could return after incursions into the Spanish Empire. Here the men repaired and refitted their vessels, exchanged information, and gathered crews for new ventures. Above all, buccaneers relied on access to markets to trade spoils for supplies, naval stores, firearms, ammunition, provisions, alcohol, and additional necessities. They found these markets in the fledgling economies of the English, Dutch, French, and later Danish port towns in the Caribbean and, to a lesser extent, in mainland North America. Opportunistic merchants were keen to obtain hides along with looted gold, silver, and other valuables for whatever the marauders desired.[28] Since robbers were usually under time constraints and had little choice to sell their booty elsewhere, buyers likely used their bargaining power to acquire plunder at a good price. One can assume that the trade in prize commodities was a highly lucrative business, and part of the contraband doubtlessly ended up on vessels bound for Europe.

Although bands of buccaneers were often multinational and detached from European affairs, political developments on the other side of the Atlantic strongly influenced the pattern of raiding in the Caribbean throughout most of the seventeenth century. English assaults on Spanish targets received a boost after the overthrow of the Stuart monarchy on the British Isles in 1649. Oliver Cromwell was fiercely anti-Catholic, and in the summer of 1654 a combination of religious, economic, and strategic motives prompted his regime to develop the Western Design, aimed at seizing control of at least part of the Spanish Empire.[29] In early 1655 an English fleet consisting of thirty-eight vessels with some 2,500 soldiers on board crossed the Atlantic. The commanders were determined to capture a major colony. However, an attempt to invade Santo Domingo on the southeastern side of Hispaniola failed disastrously. The troops, already severely weakened and decimated by disease, then sailed to Jamaica, where they met with little Spanish resistance. Although the campaign was deemed a failure at the time, the conquest of this island in the heart of the Caribbean turned out to be one of the most significant achievements of the Cromwellian regime.[30] It quickly became a key strategic asset and paved the way for the rise of the English colonial empire toward the end of the century.

Jamaica was well suited for trade and plunder, yet for years the condition of the settlement was precarious. England lacked the resources to conquer remote parts of the island, where a few Spaniards held out until 1660, and to defend its colony adequately against a possible counterattack.[31] In order to secure this new imperial outpost, the military government encouraged settlers to come to Jamaica. Many men who had joined the English invading force in Barbados and Saint Christopher in 1655 stayed to seek their fortunes in this infant colony. Proven combatants were crucial to its defense. In the following years, hundreds of outcasts from the motherland supplemented these early residents, but mortality among all newcomers was very high.[32] In an attempt to divert Spanish resources toward defending their holdings rather than attacking the intruders, the navy launched a series of assaults on port towns of the Tierra Firme. Río de la Hacha, Santa Marta, Tolú, Coro, and Cumaná were all seized, looted, and the fortifications torn down. Of course, besides strategic motives, material gain was a major incentive for the commanders. Within a short time, Jamaica became the center for extensive predatory operations against the Spanish Empire. Although the early raids exclusively involved naval vessels, from about 1659 such ventures were increasingly carried out by privateers, sometimes with dubious commissions.[33]

Even during the peace period following the interregnum, privateering continued using the pretext that Spanish imperial policy deemed unarmed English traders criminals. It was generally believed that only force would persuade the Spaniards to open their ports to foreigners. Beginning in 1661, Charles II endorsed this aggressive policy by allowing Jamaican governors to proclaim war after a peremptory effort to establish trade with the Spanish colonies.[34] Furthermore, royal authorities endeavored to dissolve the remaining Cromwellian military units by encouraging veterans to raid enemy shipping and harbors. Numerous men were keen to emulate this example rather than seek employment in the agricultural sector or elsewhere on the underdeveloped island. In 1662, at a time when Jamaica had just over 3,600 settlers, twelve armed vessels with a total of 740 crew members anchored off the south coast ready to assault Spanish holdings, and more "Private men of War" joined these informal forces in the next few years. By 1670 their number had risen to about 1,500, and for many plunder was their only source of income.[35]

S AILORS AND DISCHARGED SOLDIERS clearly formed the core of early Jamaican marauding gangs, but little is known for certain about the origins of other buccaneers. The men based in Hispaniola can be characterized as adventurers who preferred a life under frontier conditions beyond the margins of imperial control to the various forms of economic dependency common both in Europe and in the colonies throughout the early modern period.[36] Many men, English as well as French, who later joined the freebooters, had initially arrived as indentured servants in the New World. By the middle of the seventeenth century, sugar had become the most profitable staple crop in the Caribbean, and large plantations with enslaved Africans rapidly displaced small tobacco farms run with white labor. As a result, scores of impoverished settlers along with their servants were pushed off the land. Others fled from brutal and abusive masters.[37] Rather than returning to Europe, where they would face a grim future, most preferred to stay in America. For single men, the seemingly easiest way to survive economically in this harsh and largely unpoliced environment was to engage in outlaw activity, usually directed against Spain. They developed a strong sense of independence, and while some remained patriots, others' ties to the motherland were limited to their desire to obtain privateering commissions that legitimized assaults on Spanish targets.

Most migrants who had crossed the Atlantic were driven not only by the desire for a fresh start in the New World but also by a deep-rooted hatred for Catholic Spain. The overwhelming majority of the English and Dutch along with many French settlers were Protestants who had grown up in communities that perceived Catholicism as the arch enemy.[38] Throughout the early modern period anti-Spanish resentment was exacerbated by the Black Legend. Popular opinion, fueled by propaganda, framed Spanish conquest and colonization as a murderous process that actively sought to wipe out entire indigenous peoples and cultures. Various publications reminded the readership of a profusion of assumed atrocities that undermined the legitimacy of the Spanish claim to the possession of the Caribbean Islands and Central America.[39] Although raiders typically had no motive other than material gain, it seems likely that the Black Legend fed widespread disdain for Spaniards and provided marauders with a kind of justification for their predatory activities.

While the individual motives for joining an outlaw gang are almost impossible to recover from surviving sources, it is generally easy to overestimate the grievances or push factors that drove people into plain robbery. Over time, as increasing numbers of looters returned to Tortuga or Jamaica with considerable spoils, more men from all backgrounds, including some colorful characters, were attracted by the idea of participating in a profitable raid and joined the core of hardy buccaneers. Successful incursions doubtlessly encouraged further efforts in plundering.

On a macroeconomic level, raiding, along with illicit trade, played a significant role in the development of early English Jamaica. It provided much-needed capital for local businesses before plantations began to generate substantial profits.[40] Therefore, successive governments, supported by the influential merchant elite, tolerated or actively supported freebooters as long as they did not interfere with the Jamaican overseas trade.

From the economic perspective, raiding also fostered the emergence of a peculiar sector that supplied the participants with whatever they desired. Men returning from a successful incursion were known to spend their proceeds freely without much hesitation or long-term consideration. Life was short, and the rough male-dominated environment fostered certain behavior patterns and excesses. The loot was rarely enough to keep any of them prosperous after a short spree. It was exactly this loose way of handling newly acquired wealth that led to the establishment of numerous taverns, alehouses, and brothels in Port Royal, on a ten-mile sand spit sheltering a lagoon on Jamaica's south coast. This cesspool soon evolved from a small fortified settlement into a notorious hangout. Scores of fortune hunters flocked to the town not to participate in a raid but to fleece those who did. Within a few years, Port Royal grew to the largest and probably the richest English town in the entire Caribbean. In 1671, at the peak of the plunder-fueled expansion, almost 2,200 people lived in about eight hundred houses.[41] Until its destruction in a devastating earthquake in 1692, Port Royal served as a haven of opportunity—often the last one—for greedy adventurers and desperate wretches along with their camp followers of both sexes.

The freebooters based in Tortuga or Jamaica were not necessarily sailors. Although all of them must have crossed the Atlantic when they came from Europe, many can be characterized as landlubbers seeking a chance to strike it rich at the expense of the Spaniards. Most of them had likely acquired some seafaring skills, but when they searched for possible targets they did not focus on maritime endeavors. Buccaneers were essentially land forces that used watercraft as vehicles for conducting amphibious warfare against the Spanish colonial empire. They went ashore and sometimes marched enormous distances overland to loot a specific town. Such operations appeared particularly attractive because, unlike plunder seized from prizes at sea, the spoils from land raids did not have to be shared with the authorities as well as the shipowners.[42] During their incursions, the marauders encountered countless native people. Since most Caribbean islands had lost their indigenous inhabitants by the latter half of the seventeenth century, forays into mainland Spanish America may have led to the first direct contact with the New World's native population. Some buccaneers perhaps presumed that the perceived victims of Spanish tyranny would offer their unlimited support. However, cross-cultural relations often turned out to be much more complicated.

Chapter 2

ॐ

MAYAS BESIEGED

THE MOST NOTABLE AND PERSISTENT CONFLICT ZONE ADJACENT to the Caribbean was the Yucatán Peninsula. In the early sixteenth century, Spanish forces conquered many of the highly heterogeneous Maya polities, and the population that had survived violent onslaughts, widespread looting, and the ravages of foreign disease was forced to submit to their new rulers. The exercise of imperial power in this resource-poor region was limited, however. Colonial settlement revolved around the provincial capital, Mérida, in the dry northwestern part of the peninsula where there were also a number of monasteries. The relatively few Spaniards residing in this colony sustained themselves by raising livestock on rural holdings predominantly worked by Mayas from nearby villages. To the south and east of Mérida, effective control of land and native labor became progressively weaker. Scattered indigenous groups living in the dense jungle and swamp regions of southeastern Yucatán and the Petén remained outside the Spanish sphere of influence.[1] In this unconquered territory, a sparse population continued to pursue an economically self-sufficient and politically independent existence.

Maya culture traditionally placed little focus on the sea, although pre-Columbian trade networks not only reached around the long shoreline of the Yucatán Peninsula but also connected the region with various other parts of the Caribbean Basin.[2] The northern littoral of the peninsula was marshy and susceptible to hurricanes, and thus Maya settlements tended to be located in

28

more secure inland areas. The Spaniards, likewise, did not establish any major ports in this part of their empire because there were scant goods to be shipped overseas. Only San Francisco de Campeche on the west coast had acquired some prosperity through the livestock trade as well as the production of cacao and tobacco in its hinterland.[3] The few villages near the seaboard were inhabited almost exclusively by indigenous people. Most were poor fishermen with little to offer other than meager foodstuffs. Despite their poverty, coastal communities became regular targets of predatory attacks from Spain's enemies. In the latter half of the sixteenth century, freebooters sailed along the unprotected shoreline and pillaged one settlement after another.[4]

Such raids became even more frequent in the seventeenth century. Mayas living in the coastal areas were caught in the midst of the conflict between marauders and Spanish authorities. While missionaries and colonial officials exerted pressure on indigenous communities to abandon their cultural identity, adopt Catholicism, and pay tribute to the new rulers, seaborne robbers levied callous violence against the people they encountered whenever it suited their whims.

In august 1633 six ships from the Netherlands, commanded by Jan Janszoon van Hoorn, sailed around the Yucatán Peninsula and eventually arrived off Campeche. To navigate through the region, the Dutchmen employed two Mayas with some knowledge of the coasts, harbors, and pathways. These men were probably captives who realized that their chances of returning to their homes were best served by a successful raid and thus they provided the privateers with the desired information. In any event, the attackers approached the town at night, and while one contingent seized all moored vessels, several hundred men went ashore just south of the port to march through the scrub brush toward their target. At daybreak they reached the outskirts of Campeche, where they encountered the Spanish militia, supported by mulattos and native bowmen. The makeshift defenses were quickly overrun, however, leaving more than twenty Mayas dead and others wounded. As the surviving defenders retreated, one final skirmish occurred in the central square, the plaza, where some locals fought with old arquebuses and swords. They were no match for the intruders with their superior firearms. After all resistance had been exhausted, the attackers began to loot houses, churches, and the

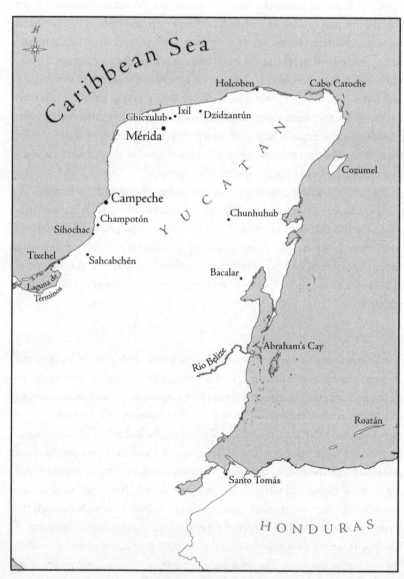

The Yucatán Peninsula.

BEAU AHRENS

convent. This phase was so chaotic that the commanders could barely keep the men under control. In the meantime, most inhabitants fled. Although their indigenous guides had told the Dutch that many natives were ready to join them against the colonial regime, in reality most Mayas took flight along with the Spaniards to seek refuge from the intruders.[5] It took three days for the raiders to ferry all spoils to their vessels and then set sail for the open sea, leaving behind a devastated town.

The indigenous population had good reason to be terrified. Almost three years later, in May 1636, the renegade Diego de los Reyes—better known as Diego el Mulato—appeared alongside two French vessels off Cozumel, where they seized a canoe with Maya fishermen.[6] The gang then went ashore and ransacked their village, stealing chickens, pigs, and fruit. The unarmed inhabitants offered little resistance. After the attackers had burned down the huts, they sailed with a number of captives around the Yucatán Peninsula.[7] Abductions and hostage taking have always been part of the efforts to maximize the spoils of maritime predations. Poor fishermen, however, could not realistically be ransomed for gold and silver. These men were likely abducted because their labor seemed valuable to the freebooters.

The ruthless assaults occurred at a time when native communities entered a long period of crisis. From about 1635 until 1677, the Mayas endured epidemics, locust plagues, crop failures, hurricanes, successive famines, and exploitation by new taxes as well as the imposition of the *repartimiento* system, forcing the indigenous population to exchange labor for often useless Spanish surplus manufactures. The abuse of power was a perennial problem on all levels of colonial administration. Conflicts frequently escalated when native groups attempted to ensure the continuation of their traditional religion, which was increasingly suppressed by local parish clergies and Franciscan friars. Rebellion became the Mayas' foremost form of resistance to the eradication of their cultural identity. It appears that, during the seventeenth century, in no other part of Spanish America did as many insurrections occur as on the Yucatán Peninsula.[8]

Beginning in 1638, indigenous unrest shook the very foundations of imperial rule. Originating on the eastern side of the Yucatán Peninsula, this development was closely connected to raids on coastal populations. Early in the year, a marauding gang assaulted Cozumel and looted a native village. Most Mayas escaped into the jungle, but three or four men fell into the hands of the attackers and were badly mistreated.[9] Almost a year later, a Dutch vessel commanded by Claes Zondergrondt sailed along the nearby mainland coast. Parts of the crew went ashore on various occasions, but no violent encounters are recorded.[10] If these men had advanced to Salamanca de Bacalar, the only colonial outpost in the southeast of the peninsula, they would have discovered deserted houses. Long-standing conflicts had escalated in previous months, and many native inhabitants abandoned the settlements that were under Spanish control. This region became a center of turmoil, which quickly spread to other parts of the province. Officials near the colonial frontier struggled to keep the disgruntled Mayas under control. Occasional attempts at suppression only led to new upheaval and resistance. As a result, more indigenous people fled from conflict zones to seek refuge in the jungle, where the Spaniards exercised no effective authority.[11] Here the natives could preserve at least some of their cultural identity, although living conditions remained difficult.

At the same time, the frequency of small-scale attacks on coastal settlements increased. Most gangs operating in this part of the Caribbean initially targeted Trujillo, the only significant port in Honduras, or scattered trading posts on the province's shoreline, but few generated substantial booty. Given the sparse Spanish presence outside the major towns, colonial records—if they mention these assaults—merely provide a glimpse of the often dramatic events. Nonetheless, the sequence of known raids on the eastern Yucatán Peninsula, despite its poverty, is remarkable. It appears that no coastal town or village was spared from the repeated ravages of Dutch, French, and English freebooters. In early 1642, for example, a rogue band of more than seventy men led by Diego el Mulato and Jean Graveau pillaged dwellings all along the seaboard and on the Bahía de Chetumal.[12] Among the devastated villages were Soite and Cehake, two recently established *reducciones*. Hundreds of indigenous families took flight, but about twenty Mayas were captured and abducted to Roatán, an island thirty miles off the Honduran coast. Here the marauders mistreated the women and coerced the men into helping them clean and repair their vessels. Shortly thereafter, this gang headed back to Bacalar and sacked the town for a second time within only a few months, presumably searching for goods they believed the inhabitants to have previously hidden. The intruders then forced the Mayas to help them carry off the plunder.[13] After that they sailed away.

Although such raids likely yielded inconsiderable spoils—local churches were typically the richest source—freebooters often returned to loot a coastal settlement more than once within a relatively brief period of time. This was partially due to an almost constant need of provisions. The crews were in general much larger than in merchant shipping, which compelled them to frequently resupply during their voyages. Some gangs, moreover, covered huge distances in quest of booty. Coming from Europe, they had crossed the Atlantic and could hardly hope to find any safe haven in the contested Caribbean. Prior to the conquest of Jamaica, only Tortuga and, probably to a lesser degree, Curaçao were ports of call for marauders looking to purchase supplies. Several crews visited Roatán, where the native population was prepared to provide non-Spaniards with shelter and limited amounts of foodstuffs.[14] Outlaws that could not or did not want to pay either went fishing and hunting or robbed the necessities from coastal inhabitants. Undefended native villages, particularly on the Yucatán Peninsula, became prime targets in these efforts. For indigenous communities engaged in small-scale subsistence production, this would have caused not only hardship but perhaps even starvation conditions. It is not documented how many native people died as a result of devastating raids.

The repeated assaults had more tangible consequences. In August and early September 1644, a combined gang led by William Jackson and Henry Taylor roamed the seas near Campeche searching for Spanish merchant vessels. In order to replenish their depleting supplies, raiding parties went ashore at Champotón and nearby Sihochac, where they looted the churches and seized all foodstuffs, mainly consisting of corn. The victims were almost exclusively Mayas. Another target was Tixchel, close to the northeastern end of the Laguna de Términos. Several hundred native families had moved to this mission town to escape instability and unrest in the interior. This did not prevent the freebooters from pillaging the dwellings.[15] In the aftermath of these ruthless assaults, the indigenous people vacated their homes and took up residence in villages at some distance from the shore.

The circumstances on the other side of the peninsula a few years later were slightly different but yielded a similar result. Years of conflict between Mayas and Spaniards in this region had strained cross-cultural relations, and occasional raids exacerbated the situation. In June 1648 marauders seized Bacalar once again, killing one man in a skirmish and wounding three others. The attackers then abducted several women to one of the cays off the mouth of the Río Belize, which served as a resting place. It took two months until a party of eleven Spaniards and fifteen Mayas arrived to rescue the captives. As a result of these dramatic events, the natives abandoned Bacalar and withdrew to another location, Chunhuhub, an old settlement site farther north that they considered more secure.[16] On both sides of the Yucatán Peninsula, many inhabitants fled more than once from Europeans who regarded indigenous populations as little else than sources of supplies.

I N THE FOLLOWING YEARS, freebooters continued to assault coastal settlements, trying to make the best of limited opportunities elsewhere. At that time a demand for slave labor emerged in the Caribbean islands not under Spanish control. By 1641 the residents of Tortuga, led by Jean Le Vasseur, had begun to build a fortification, and a few years thereafter they brought captured natives from the Yucatán Peninsula to the island. In early 1652 a raiding gang even seized the inhabitants of an entire village consisting of about sixty Maya families and took them to Tortuga.[17] It seems likely that most, if not all, were sold to the highest bidder on arrival, as was customary among raiders who claimed legitimacy as privateers. One year later an eyewitness stated that the island had around 150 indigenous slaves—men, women, and also children—but mortality among them was extreme. Some fifty had perished within months, and many more were sick. Others had fled into the woods or were so desperate that they attempted to escape over the water on ramshackle rafts.[18] The overwhelming majority of these natives had been abducted in assaults that eluded the notice of colonial authorities.

When Spanish forces invaded Tortuga in January 1654, they found seventy to eighty Mayas held in slavery. Most of them lived in a small settlement close to the sea. The Spaniards brought these captives to Santo Domingo, where they languished under miserable conditions on a hill near the major town in the southeast of the island. In early 1658 the newly appointed governor of Yucatán, Francisco de Bazán, arrived in Santo Domingo on his way to Campeche. There he learned of these unfortunate individuals and met their cacique—as it turned out, the only Maya who spoke some Spanish—who gave him an account of their ordeal. Bazán offered to take them back to their homes, but the president of the audiencia apparently did not allow him to do so.[19] Even outside the Yucatán Peninsula, the Mayas were victims not only of the buccaneers but also of colonial policies that considered the indigenous population to be nothing more than a cheap labor force.

Assaults on the Yucatán coast with the specific aim of capturing and enslaving natives continued in subsequent years. In July or August 1661, for instance, a group of freebooters sailing along the shore abducted a number of Maya fishermen. The captives faced enslavement in Tortuga, where they were probably forced to fish to acquire foodstuffs for the marauding gangs tarrying on the island.[20] Indigenous slaves provided Basse-Terre's inhabitants with basic services while their reckless masters focused on contraband trade and, above all, raiding.

IN THE EARLY 1660s, one Spanish port in the Caribbean after another was attacked, looted, and demolished. Soon after Christopher Myngs had returned from a successful raid on Santiago de Cuba, preparations for another assault commenced in Jamaica.[21] In February 1663 Myngs sailed with fourteen vessels and over 1,200 men to Campeche. They landed under the cover of darkness on a beach southwest of the town and marched directly to their target, reaching it in the early morning hours. While most locals fled in a panic, the militia hastily assembled for the defense of the town. About 160 Spaniards, augmented by mulattos and free people of African descent, put up spirited resistance. The men fought for three days, primarily from the roofs of houses, but due to a lack of firearms and ammunition they could not repel the attackers, and ultimately the latter prevailed. Among the dead were thirty freebooters and forty-one local defenders. Many more were wounded. The victims included Maya families whose homes at the edge of the town were set on fire. The Englishmen not only plundered houses and churches, they also threw the guns of the fortification into the sea. Furthermore, the raiders seized all Spanish vessels in the harbor. They then released 142 captives, while 34 high-ranking citizens were taken on Myngs's ship and remained there as hostages until the robbers left ten days later.[22] The vessels carried substantial amounts of valuables to Jamaica.

At the time of the assault, several Maya militia units—mostly consisting of bowmen—were in the Yucatán Peninsula, but not near Campeche. It appears that the military command did not have sufficient time to mobilize these forces against the enemy.[23] The failure to fend off the invaders prompted the colonial authorities to improve the defenses of the province.

In the following months, more suspicious vessels were sighted off various coastal stretches of the Yucatán Peninsula. At the same time, the governor ordered the establishment of a string of sentinels along the seaboard and, following a royal decree, the formation of a cavalry unit to confront possible invaders.[24] The new defenses were soon tested. In May or June 1664, another English marauding gang, probably led by John Harmenson, sailed along the northern shoreline. At several points, part of the crew went ashore and ransacked Maya dwellings, including the fishing outposts of the villages Chicxulub and Ixil, which lay farther inland. When about twenty men landed to seize Dzidzantún, some forty-five miles northeast of Mérida, they were ambushed and barely managed to escape with two Spanish and twelve indigenous women as hostages. Back on their vessels, the freebooters made for the small port of Champotón, where they eventually released their captives, presumably to save some provisions.[25]

The attack on the buccaneers near Dzidzantún was carried out by the militia, which was likely acting on intelligence of approaching intruders. However, the existing defenses were strengthened in those years. A network of bulwarks surrounded Campeche and Mérida, batteries protected the town of Campeche, and trenches blocked ways from the coast to the interior. The fortification of Campeche began in 1607 and, like other defenses, was periodically expanded in the following decades. In Mérida a modest fortress was built in 1656. Most of these fortifications were constructed by Mayas, who, under the *repartimiento* system, had to supply materials and labor to build and maintain public works.[26] It is unclear how many people were conscripted for this formidable project, or for how long. At some sites along the northern and western shoreline, watchtowers were erected to discover approaching vessels. These defenses were manned with Mayas.[27] Only a few, if any, villages in coastal areas, on the other hand, received any effective protection. The colonial authorities, which, in theory, should have provided security in exchange for tribute, left a segment of the indigenous population at the mercy of the attackers from overseas.

All defense measures imposed a considerable strain on native groups. The dire situation worsened under Governor Rodrigo Flores de Aldana beginning in July 1664. Even for the corrupt standards of the time, during his tenure the abuse of power and exploitation of the Mayas reached new heights. His excessive *repartimientos*, random requisitions, and other unsanctioned stratagems for extracting wealth from indigenous communities—in part justified by the external threat—were so excessive, and the means officials employed so brutal, that countless Mayas were pushed into resistance. In Mérida, for example, the construction of a citadel in 1667 led to unrest and dozens of court filings. Farther south, natives took flight across the colonial frontier to seek refuge in the unconquered wilderness, then known as the *montaña*.[28]

As a result of the rising tensions and conflicts, in March 1668 a major revolt broke out in Sahcabchén, about twenty miles south of Champotón, not too far from the Gulf coast. More than three thousand Mayas rebelled against the friars and reverted to their traditional culture and religion.[29] The provincial administration in Mérida and the clergy disagreed on the causes of this escalation of unrest. While Governor Flores de Aldana alleged that the natives fled from hostile raids, the bishop and twenty-five Franciscan missionaries cited the governor's repressive policy as a motivating factor.[30] In a quest to divert attention from abuse and exploitation, the administration soon came up with another explanation: certain native leaders were reported to have stirred up peaceful inhabitants of other communities by telling them of ancient prophecies. These tales came to be interpreted as a sign that the natives were no longer subject to Spanish colonial rule and that a new era in the history of the Maya was beginning.[31] The arrival of heavily armed marauding gangs on the nearby shore may have given locals the impression that they could overthrow their oppressors. Indeed, indigenous myths seem to have included stories of forces from overseas coming to the rescue of the subjugated population.[32] However, even if the Mayas knew of European hostilities, at least the coastal inhabitants must have realized that the intruders had their own agenda. There was no anti-Spanish cooperation, and many native people found that their value as slaves outweighed their value as potential allies against the colonial regime.

The surge in conflicts between colonizers and native communities coincided with the emergence of new economic opportunities, which further complicated cross-cultural relations. In 1668 the English government lifted a ban on the import of dyewoods, and in the following years hundreds of buccaneers moved into the Laguna de Términos, where they harvested the trees from which valuable dyes were obtained. Like other extractive businesses in the Caribbean, slavery soon became the basis of economic success. The logwood trade relied to a large degree on enslaved Mayas forced to conduct much of the hard work in the mangrove swamps. Natives felled trees and cut them into pieces, they pulled wood to collection points, and they poled boats through the entangled rivers and creeks. Numerous Europeans lived with native women in small camps. Moreover, indigenous captives—including boys and girls—were taken overseas and sold, along with the lumber, on the colonial markets in North America.[33] It seems reasonable to assume that many of them died soon after their arrival in an unfamiliar and often harsh environment.

THE MARAUDERS ACTIVE in the Caribbean between the 1630s and the 1660s were highly opportunistic. Itinerant gangs seized whatever they required during their voyages. The acquisition of supplies was as important as spectacular assaults on Spanish targets, and for this purpose freebooters sailed along the sparsely protected shoreline of the Yucatán Peninsula to pillage native villages. Dutch, French, and English buccaneers viewed Mayas as little more than sources of supplies. Many indigenous communities fell victim to ruthless raiders. Furthermore, outlaws mistreated and abducted into slavery countless Maya people. These unfortunate individuals were caught in the midst of an international conflict that exacerbated their daily struggles. From within the province, the Mayas were under pressure to abandon their identity and submit to colonial rule, while robbers from overseas appropriated everything that suited their immediate needs. Thus it does not come as a surprise that marauders played a prominent role in the collective memory of the native population. A century after the incursions, Maya groups still mentioned the English as a menace akin to Spanish priests.[34] The freebooters had left a lasting legacy among their victims.

Chapter 3

❦

THE GRANADA RAID

AFTER THE CONQUEST OF JAMAICA IN 1655, RAIDING IN THE CARIB-
bean increased dramatically. The Spaniards were hardly able to protect their holdings against foreign attackers. Most of the targets lay
on the prosperous Tierra Firme coast. Until 1670 gangs based in
Port Royal pillaged Río de la Hacha five times, Santa Marta three times, and
Tolú eight times. Even minor ports such as Cumaná and Coro were repeatedly ransacked.[1] Potential spoils elsewhere were rather limited. The Caribbean
shore of Central America, for example, was relatively poor and the only major
port, Trujillo in Honduras, was abandoned by local merchants after falling victim to five raids within a mere ten years between 1633 and 1643.[2] To strike it
rich, freebooters had to get to the sources of wealth and expand their predatory
activities into regions not devastated by incessant assaults. In the 1660s, therefore, raiding parties began to advance far into the interior, where colonial authorities were scarcely prepared to defend villages and towns.

When non-Spanish intruders made their way through unknown territory
to inland targets, they not only needed guidance but also relied on support in
various capacities and forms. Native populations emerged as a crucial, if not
decisive, factor in a remarkable series of raids that, within a few years, shook
the foundations of colonial rule in parts of the Spanish Empire. The expedition
that laid the groundwork for Henry Morgan's later fame illustrates how raid-

ing parties learned to forge advantageous relations with indigenous groups and individuals.

In NOVEMBER 1664 a multinational gang led by Jacob Fackman, John Morris, and David Maarten, which included Morgan—presumably as Fackman's first lieutenant—departed from Jamaica with about 140 men on three vessels and scoured the coast of the Yucatán Peninsula for easy prey.[3] One night the vanguard in two pirogues approached the port of Campeche, seizing a moored Spanish frigate. With this prize the robbers escaped to the Laguna de Términos, where the entire company stayed for about two months in the tangled mangrove labyrinth.[4] The men likely intended to evade a possible search expedition while they refitted their vessels. During their stay, small parties advanced inland on a regular basis to hunt poultry, deer, and other game.[5] They almost certainly would have encountered dispersed Mayas living in the region, but no details are recorded.

In late February 1665, the freebooters were ready to strike again. They left their hideout and sailed westward along the shoreline right into the mouth of Río Grijalva, in Tabasco, where they captured a few Maya men and forced them to serve as guides. The gang then hid their vessels, leaving behind a small contingent of twenty men, and paddled in a number of pirogues and canoes nearly sixty miles upriver to their intended target, the provincial capital Villahermosa. The shallow Río Grijalva twisted and turned through crocodile-infested wetlands and mangrove thickets. Branches of the river forked off in different directions, sometimes leading to large lagoons. This made navigation difficult, particularly at twilight or night, when the buccaneers preferred to travel in order to avoid detection. Without their guides, the expedition would likely have lost much time reaching their destination. Villahermosa had a population of about fifteen hundred predominantly indigenous people, but early in the year merchants from Guatemala were usually in town to buy and sell cacao for shipment overseas.[6] The capital had already been the target of an English privateering attack in August 1644, at which point native groups from the area seized the opportunity to loot the town while the Spaniards fled. When the raiders arrived, most buildings had already been destroyed by fire.[7] Villahermosa never fully recovered from this assault.

It is not clear whether Fackman, Morris, and Maarten knew of this previous incursion, but this time the Maya guides helped the intruders remain undetected. They entered Villahermosa before daybreak, quickly rounded up the inhabitants, and then ransacked the houses and churches. After that they attempted to extort three hundred head of cattle as ransom for a number of high-ranking captives. When this failed, the robbers retreated to the coast, taking a few hostages with them. In the meantime, Spanish forces had seized the attackers' ships in the mouth of the Río Grijalva, and shortly thereafter five vessels from Campeche arrived and began to land 280 militiamen, including many mulattos.[8] Since the militia, after a rough passage across the sea, was not in a combative spirit, they first dispatched a man with a white flag to their opponents and offered them quarter. But the buccaneers refused to surrender and desperately searched for an escape route. Before they could make a decisive move, a shootout ensued and the militia launched an attack. The operation was poorly executed, however, allowing the marauders to seize two Spanish vessels and set sail for the open sea.[9] This triumph, despite generating little booty, surely emboldened the gang in their resolve to raid further Spanish holdings.

FROM TABASCO THE two prizes commanded by Morris and Maarten sailed for the salt ponds just north of Campeche and then followed the shoreline around the Yucatán Peninsula. On their way they captured and looted a small Spanish barque laden with corn.[10] The crews afterward dropped anchor off the north coast at Holcoben, where thirty men went ashore to raid the village for foodstuffs. The local Maya community did not resist, but twenty-two Spaniards set up an ambush and fired a volley on the intruders. In a subsequent skirmish, the buccaneers killed six of them and wounded seven others. The robbers pillaged the village and continued to Roatán to take on water. The native inhabitants of this island had been deported by Spanish forces in 1650 after Dutch freebooters had used the settlements as a hideout. Thus there were probably no people left to provide supplies. Once the visitors had gathered their own fresh water and firewood, they made a foray to Trujillo. Here the men seized a trading vessel, only to discover that it carried little of value.[11] In order to acquire substantial booty, the commanders needed to find new targets in more prosperous parts of Central America.

Having left Trujillo, the marauders sailed eastward to Cabo Gracias a Dios, the northeastern end of the Mosquito Coast, which had no Spanish presence. Upon arrival they made contact with a native community that welcomed the strangers. In early June 1665, nine indigenous men joined the visitors on board the vessels to participate in a daring incursion. The company planned to paddle up the Río San Juan to raid Granada. They were not the first freebooters to appear in this region. As early as 1640 and 1647, Dutch and French rovers had seized and looted Spanish vessels on the river.[12] While it seems possible that previous raiders reached Lago de Nicaragua, there is no indication that they advanced as far as Granada, on the northwestern side of the large lake. After Friar Thomas Gage had visited this part of the country in 1637, he published descriptions of Spanish wealth—a sharp contrast to the poverty of the native population—and military weakness that probably became common knowledge to English-speaking buccaneers.[13] The journey to Granada, however, was not easy. It was 220 miles from the Caribbean Sea, and a series of earthquakes in 1648, 1651, 1659, and, worst of all, in 1663 had blocked the passage for larger vessels. As a result, the shipping connection between the interior and the coast was severely disrupted.

The freebooters' next stop was Monkey Point, a wide bay behind a peninsula just north of the mouth of the Río San Juan. Here the crews dropped anchor and prepared two canoes and six or seven pirogues acquired from native communities for the long voyage to Granada. Each pirogue carried between fifteen and twenty-five men, their firearms, and little more than a handful of provisions.[14] These small craft enabled the raiders to advance swiftly toward their target and then escape with the loot.

Amphibious hit-and-run warfare was largely unknown in Europe at that time. It appears that such tactics emerged when the buccaneers fused Native American with European military strategies, thereby creating a peculiar form of raiding.[15] However, some marauders were probably not used to paddling and steering watercraft such as canoes and pirogues and therefore had to learn these skills from the Mosquito men they took with them. In the course of this incursion, there must have been a lively exchange of knowledge, and each side undoubtedly profited from these interactions.

Before 130 crew members began their journey up the Río San Juan, both canoes with the heavily armed vanguard went ahead to look for local defenses. A few Spanish sentinels fled after spotting the advance party and thus did not notice the main company following soon thereafter. On their way upriver, which must have taken about a week, the men passed through rolling green hills, dense jungle, and extensive wetlands. Swarms of insects and sweltering heat, frequently interrupted by torrential showers, tested their endurance. Furthermore, the freebooters struggled through a number of rapids caused by the recent earthquakes. When they reached the Lago de Nicaragua, the men silently paddled along the southwestern shore, traveling at night and resting during the day, so that they probably did not see the spectacular volcanic landscape as they approached their target.[16]

At one point on their journey, the marauders met an indigenous man named Juan Gallardo, sometimes called Gallardillo. After working as a pilot on the Río San Juan, he was convicted by the colonial authorities of being involved in a murder, declared a slave of the hospital in Granada, and branded on the forehead. It is not clear under what circumstances he made contact with the strangers, but, full of hatred for the Spaniards, he must have been more than willing to join the raiding party.[17] Gallardo probably offered to lead the intruders into the town, where they hoped to strike it rich.

By all accounts, Granada was an attractive target. Located on a fertile plain, it was surrounded by cacao and indigo plantations as well as cattle ranches. Above all, however, the town served as a commercial center with trade connections both to the Caribbean and the nearby South Sea. It even boasted a shipyard on the lakeshore. Quite a few of the twenty-five hundred residents were wealthy, and Granada's prosperity was in plain view. In addition to seven churches and a cathedral, there was a monastery, the Convento de San Francisco, along with a hospital.[18] The town certainly presented a promising reward at the end of the long and arduous passage from the Mosquito Coast.

Although local authorities had been alerted that a suspicious group was approaching, they made no preparations for a possible attack. The governor was in León, Nicaragua's provincial capital, reporting to royal officials, and most of the officers had gone with him. Entering Granada before dawn, the gang blocked the major streets and quickly seized the arsenal, which contained all of the firearms. The inhabitants were asleep and completely surprised when the raiders woke them by shooting a volley into the air. Some did not have the chance to get dressed before they were forced out of their houses. There was little resistance. The swift operation gave the Spaniards no time to escape or to hide their belongings. In the next few hours, the intruders detained three

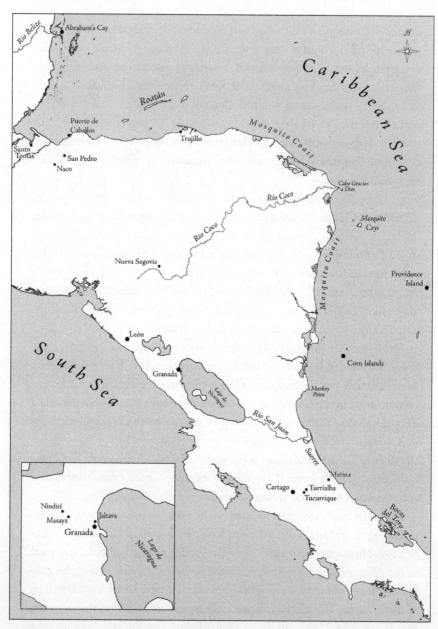

Honduras, Nicaragua, and Costa Rica.

BEAU AHRENS

hundred men in the cathedral and corralled the remaining residents into the central square. A dozen buccaneers guarded them while the rest ransacked houses and churches.[19] Gallardo proved his worth by showing the men where the wealthiest citizens lived. The freebooters afterward tortured some affluent Spaniards until they revealed the location of their valuables. The town's treasurer was even killed, presumably because the robbers suspected that he was hiding money from them.[20]

A few Spaniards managed to flee from Granada and desperately tried to rally resistance in the nearby haciendas and villages but met with little success. Only a handful of men were able or willing to take up arms against the intruders. Most communities in this region consisted of Chorotega families. Under colonial rule they had to supply tribute—usually corn and cotton cloth—and labor to Spanish *encomenderos* or the Crown. Moreover, natives were subjected to various, often very oppressive, exactions. A long history of exploitation and abuse had strained cross-cultural relations. Locals resisted excessive demands, sought ways to escape, and suffered punishment for not complying with orders. All these experiences became part of the collective memory of the indigenous population. Under these circumstances, several hundred Chorotega men from Masaya, Nindirí, and Jaltava resolved to march to Granada, assess the situation, and make contact with the strangers. Led by the native *alcalde mayor*, the district magistrate, of Jaltava, most, if not all, joined the raiders.[21] As it turned out, they were keen to participate in the looting. The arrival of the buccaneers seems to have provided these people, including a representative of the colonial regime, with the opportunity for some form of vengeance for the injustice and hardship that had been imposed on their communities.

From morning until twilight, the invaders and their native accomplices, with Gallardo at the fore, pillaged at will. Nothing was safe from their greed. While the marauders took with them all the gold, silver, and jewelry they could find, the impoverished Chorotega men stole clothing, household items, trifles, and other portable things that seemed valuable to them. The English commanders later reported that some indigenous people wanted to kill all captured Spaniards, particularly the hated clergymen. The natives evidently assumed that the strangers would establish a new order in the region. A combination of wishful thinking and a lack of understanding—in large part due to the language barrier and the haste of the looting—probably led the Chorotegas to misjudge the situation. When the pirogues as well as a Spanish prize seized off the lakeshore were laden with booty and the intruders prepared their retreat, several native men found it too dangerous to return to their homes and, in the words of the commanders, went "up into ye Mountains to secure themselves."[22] Gallardo, along with seven or eight other indigenous people, including a family with children, chose to join the buccaneers and accompany them to their base. After the looters had destroyed all remaining vessels to prevent the Spaniards from pursuing them, they departed with a few community leaders and members of the clergy as hostages. The latter must have considered themselves lucky that the marauders had not left them to the mercy of the natives.

On their way back to the Caribbean, the freebooters took several breaks and went ashore to hunt game as well as cattle. The pirogues were so full of spoils that they could not store sufficient provisions on board. Thus the men released most captives soon after their departure. About fifty miles southeast of Granada, the motley crew stopped at Ometepe, an island consisting of little more than two sizable volcanoes, where they ransacked native villages, taking mostly foodstuffs with them.[23] When the robbers approached the entrance of the Río San Juan a few days later, they left the last remaining hostages behind on the recently seized prize and paddled downriver to the Caribbean coast.

As the raiders were heading for the open sea, colonial authorities in León and Santiago de Guatemala received dramatic reports of the assault on Granada. The accounts, however, probably exaggerated the strength of the attackers, which stoked fears that the intruders would expand their incursion and conquer the entire province. Knowing that he had no armed forces to expel the enemies, the president of the Audiencia de Guatemala dispatched an order to the governor of Costa Rica requiring the deployment of troops and firearms for securing the Río San Juan passage. He specifically asked for indigenous workers to build a palisade until reinforcements arrived.[24] Since the president did not trust any group living in southeastern Nicaragua, he intended to mobilize the nearest group of loyal Native Americans in northern Costa Rica. It is not clear from which specific community these men were recruited, but in October 1665, construction of a wooden structure began about forty miles from the river mouth right above a bend and the first rapid, which was considered the most defensible site. In fact, it took years to complete a ramshackle stockade—rather grandly named the Castillo San Carlos—overlooking the Río San Juan. At about the same time, officials began to conscript indigenous men on a rotating basis to act as sentinels along the river.[25]

The residents of Granada needed quite some time to recover from the shock of the assault. Intercultural relations were tense, and the Spaniards likely watched all natives with suspicion. One can imagine that the authorities put great effort into apprehending the men who had participated in the looting and bringing them to justice. At the same time, the government had to be cautious not to antagonize more indigenous people than absolutely necessary. Royal decrees, therefore, were issued to stop all excesses and abuses that had caused so much resentment in the past. Unrest already undermined colonial rule in the region, so it was not in the interest of the Spaniards to weaken the source of labor and tribute, which made up more than two-thirds of all revenues in Central America.[26] Furthermore, in the following years, the president dispatched missionaries to scattered native communities on the southern lakeshore to convert the families into loyal Christian subjects. The people living near the entrance of the Río San Juan, including the indigenous inhabitants of the Solentiname archipelago, were moved to a *reducción* called Jaén, where they were instructed to plant cacao and artichokes. The success of this undertaking, however, was endangered by internal conflicts and repeated outbreaks of violence.[27]

Most of the buccaneers, meanwhile, returned to Port Royal and spent their ill-gotten gains. Participants in this spectacular incursion told stories in the pubs and taverns to doubtlessly eager audiences.[28] Of course, the robbers embellished their tales of rich pickings in Central America with fabulous descriptions of their achievements. News of lucrative raids quickly spread all over the Caribbean and fired the imaginations of other English, Dutch, and French marauders, who tended to overlook the difficulties in execution. For thousands of men, the looting of Granada became the shining example that they endeavored to emulate. They had little fear of Spanish defenders and knew that native populations could provide crucial support in their predatory ventures.

Chapter 4

༈

NATIVES AND INTRUDERS
IN CENTRAL AMERICA

T HE NEXT FIVE YEARS MARK THE PEAK OF CARIBBEAN RAIDING. Between 1666 and 1671, resolute freebooters led by foolhardy and charismatic commanders assaulted one colonial town after the other, some of which lay hundreds of miles inland. These attacks shaped the legends that are still associated with the names of the buccaneers. The marauders avoided known Spanish strongholds and intended to advance through sparsely defended regions where indigenous groups struggled to make a living. They hoped to get in touch with these people, gain their support, and strike it rich by exploiting the element of surprise. Most gangs, however, failed to repeat the stunning success achieved in Granada in 1665. Many did not even come close to their designated target. The reasons why some incursions were successful and others were not are complex, and any investigation requires a detailed reconstruction of the various expeditions into the heart of the Spanish Empire with a particular focus on how these events included or affected native populations.

M ANY FORTUNE HUNTERS determined to follow Fackman, Morris, and Maarten's example gathered around the veteran mariner Edward Mansfield, who, in November 1665, assembled a considerable force of more than nine hundred men on Jamaica's south coast for another major raid. Since war had broken out between England and the Netherlands, the commander obtained a privateering commission from the governor to attack Curaçao, the most important Dutch colony in the Caribbean. Disregarding the formalities, Mansfield decided to pillage Espíritu Santo in central Cuba instead.[1] The latter target likely promised larger returns, but this venture was evidently not as profitable as expected. Emboldened by the sheer size of his contingent, the marauders resolved to aim for bigger prizes. In February 1666 they cruised with fourteen or fifteen mostly small vessels off Cartagena, and from there they sailed to Portobelo in Panamá. The defenses of both towns, however, appeared too strong so that the men eventually abandoned the idea of launching an assault.[2] During these long days at sea, they must have realized that it was not as easy as anticipated to achieve their dreams of wealth and prosperity. The gang, therefore, adopted a new strategy and sought alternative targets. Some may have felt at this stage that such a force was too large for a successful raid and left the main company. This proved to be an astute decision, as the following events illustrate.

In early April Mansfield's fleet sailed along the Caribbean shoreline of Costa Rica. One night his vanguard went ashore and took a lookout at Bocas del Toro by surprise. The outpost was part of the coastal defense designed to protect the entrance to the Matina valley. About ten years earlier, the Spaniards had begun to cultivate cacao in this region. With few people living in the humid and fever-ridden Atlantic lowlands and the high cost of African slave labor, the government endeavored to move indigenous groups from other parts of the province, particularly Talamanca in the southern plains, to work in the haciendas. All measures to accommodate the growing labor demands met with little success, however, and attempts to expand colonial authority into native lands in 1662 and 1663 failed miserably.[3] When Mansfield's gang of 630 men appeared in the Matina valley, they could not expect to find much wealth. Instead, the freebooters were determined to plunder all the way up to the provincial capital, Cartago, in the mountains farther inland. From there the men planned to advance to the South Sea coast with the hope of pillaging rich targets. During the foray, they sought to form an alliance with indigenous people to help overcome the Spanish defenses.

The first stage of the venture went well. The buccaneers quickly advanced, arriving before daybreak at Matina, a village about ten miles of the coast. Having taken all thirty-five Spanish inhabitants captive, they then proceeded to loot their houses. At one point a dozen Tariaca men joined the intruders, with whom they shared some food, which surely helped smooth relations. Seven locals resolved to accompany the marauders as guides through the mosaic of cacao plantations, riverine swamps, and thick jungle that lay ahead. The next day, however, when the gang seized a hacienda, one native escaped and managed to alert the Spanish authorities farther inland. The new governor, Juan López de la Flor, an able military commander with years of experience in European wars, immediately mobilized the militia in central Costa Rica and dispatched about 330 men—Spaniards as well as people of African descent—against the intruders. The governor ordered his force to take a position in a mountain stronghold just outside Turrialba—roughly ninety miles from the Caribbean shoreline and 2,500 feet above sea level—which controlled the road to the capital. There eighty indigenous bowmen, recruited from a barrio adjacent to Cartago, supplemented the troops.[4] The natives likely formed the backbone of the Spanish defense, since the militiamen had only twenty aging muskets.

The buccaneers, meanwhile, became increasingly exhausted. The men spent much time searching for foodstuffs on their way. In order to obtain badly needed provisions for the large gang, they gave away hatchets, machetes, blades, and clothing that they had previously stolen in Matina. They also promised handsome rewards to all locals they encountered in an attempt to gain their support but met with little success. Most avoided contact with the Englishmen and sought refuge in the wilderness when the strangers approached. Soon their rations ran so low that some hungry freebooters began to butcher horses, mules, and donkeys. Others fell upon native dwellings and robbed them of their sparse supplies, which, of course, alienated the population.[5] There is a good chance that the men spotted plenty of exotic wildlife—parrots, monkeys, hogs—but they appreciated these only as food sources. After Mansfield's gang had passed through the village of Siquirres, deep in the jungle, they entered mountainous terrain to advance to Cartago. It took them a few long days, interrupted by frequent breaks, to reach Turrialba, where the scouting party learned of the colonial forces blocking their way. The marauders realized that they had lost the element of surprise and that it would be almost impossible to succeed as anticipated. Thus they opted to retreat to the coast.[6]

———

Surviving records in Costa Rica shed light on how the government reestablished authority in this province and how it dealt with the local natives who allied themselves with the intruders during the assault. The Tariacas, especially, felt the full wrath of the colonial regime. Right after Mansfield's crew had set sail, a unit of eighty militiamen went to the banks of the Río Matina and captured eleven indigenous men accused of having supported the enemy. Seven were shot dead immediately, presumably in front of the rest of the community. The militia then brought the remaining population of fifty-six men, women, and children to the provincial capital to be distributed over a number of *reducciones*. However, at least some were enslaved and allocated to Spanish officers and other prominent citizens of Cartago. The entire Tariaca village was razed, the surrounding banana, cacao, and fruit trees were cut down, and all other belongings of the inhabitants were confiscated.[7] Nothing remained. The authorities clearly wanted to make an example of this community.

The indigenous population in Costa Rica was traditionally fragmented and localized, with many rivalries and conflicts between the various ethnic groups. While some resented the colonial regime, others competed for privileges and perks from the Spaniards. Therefore, the appearance of the buccaneers provided an opportunity not only for discontented natives to ally themselves with the intruders but also for other inhabitants to benefit from this external threat by contributing valuable—even vital—support to the beleaguered authorities. When news reached Cartago that Mansfield's gang had gone ashore in Suerre in the north of Costa Rica shortly after having departed from Matina, loyal Urinama men volunteered to march under Spanish leadership to Suerre and fight the invaders.[8] No confrontation is recorded, however, presumably because the marauders had left by the time this force arrived.

The experiences with the Tariacas raised some concerns among the government about other indigenous people living in strategic locations. In this context, the Votos communities in the northern plains of Costa Rica, not too far away from the Río San Juan, were also suspected of having been in contact with the enemy. This group had been the focus of the authorities' attention for quite some time. Between 1638 and 1640, three Spanish expeditions to capture natives fleeing from their duties apprehended dozens of men among the Votos.[9] Following the raid on Granada, these people again raised concerns, likely due to intelligence that they had supported the intruders. In June 1666, shortly after news of Mansfield's presence in Suerre had reached Cartago, the militia went to their settlements, detained ninety-six persons, destroyed their huts, and cut down all nearby banana and fruit trees. The Spaniards even did their best to block their trails into the wilderness. The captives were then deported to a new *reducción* near Turrialba to work in the cacao plantations. Shortly after their arrival, however, the government realized that the Audiencia de Guatemala prohibited the relocation of indigenous communities and resolved to reverse this arrangement. Accordingly, toward the end of the year the natives were permitted to return to what was left of their homes. These people must have been furious with the colonial regime. Indeed, even with a military outpost established in their ancestral lands, this group remained a threat to safety near Costa Rica's northern frontier.[10]

At the same time, the authorities endeavored to improve the coastal defenses. A royal decree required the placement of a chain of lookouts with a few watchtowers designed to discover suspicious vessels and alert the militia all along the shoreline. As in the Yucatán Peninsula, it seems that indigenous men were forced to serve as sentinels. In order to lessen the reliance on bowmen, the Costa Rican government tried to acquire a stockpile of muskets over the next few years, but, due to a lack of funds, met with little success. Furthermore, the governor ordered a fortification to be built in Tucurrique, just east of Cartago.[11] This post was meant to protect the way from the coast to the capital as well as to serve as a base for launching future military expeditions into native lands. The Spaniards understood that the indigenous population was key to securing this province.

TREASURE FEVER NOT ONLY affected gangs based in Jamaica but also spread to Tortuga. After having looted Granada in 1665, a small party of raiders appeared on the island and inspired others to seek their fortunes in daring ventures. These men included David Maarten, who had learned of the outbreak of the Second Anglo-Dutch War and avoided Jamaica, and Juan Gallardo, who may have joined him because, as a Spanish speaker, it was easier for him to communicate with French freebooters than with the English. Following his arrival in Tortuga, the native rebel provided the newly appointed governor, Bertrand d'Ogeron, with information about the precarious colonial rule in Nicaragua.[12] In the next few months, Gallardo lived in a hut near Basse-Terre. He befriended two Mayas, both of whom had been captured by French *flibus-*

tiers off Campeche in 1661. After these men had served as slaves on the island for a few years, the marauders evidently realized that the captives could be more valuable as full shareholding members of raiding gangs and released them into freedom. Among other things, they learned to use firearms.[13] From scattered sources it is difficult to assess cross-cultural relations on Tortuga, but it appears that all free residents of this frontier settlement—Europeans as well as Native Americans—were primarily valued for their skills.

In May 1666 at least three indigenous people, Gallardo and the two abducted Maya fishermen, joined Jean François, better known as François L'Olonnais, and Michel d'Aristegui for a large-scale incursion into Lago de Maracaibo, a massive lagoon in western Venezuela.[14] This part of the Spanish Empire had acquired some prosperity through the export of cacao and, due to a lack of effective defenses, beckoned greedy robbers. About six weeks later a fleet of two large ketches and six sloops along with a crew of about four hundred men—many of whom were seasoned hunters—arrived at the entrance of the Lago de Maracaibo. The men stormed a small fortification on an island off the coast and then seized Maracaibo, about twenty miles farther south.[15] When the Frenchmen entered the town they found that most of the twelve hundred residents had fled. The marauders, however, tracked down a number of locals, torturing them until they revealed the whereabouts of other inhabitants along with their valuables. Over the next few days, L'Olonnais's company ransacked one house after another.[16] The governor and many other citizens likely followed the events from the safety of a distant location. They could do nothing other than wait until the invaders left.

After about two weeks in command of Maracaibo, most of the gang sailed across the lagoon to plunder Gibraltar, the center of the cacao trade. Since d'Aristegui and L'Olonnais expected to find the defenses of this port well prepared for an attack, they intended to go ashore near Puerto de las Barbacoas at the mouth of the Río Matatán, just over twenty miles northeast of Gibraltar. From there they planned to advance overland to the target. However, a group of natives, possibly Paraute men led by Spanish officers, were determined to defend this stretch of coast against the marauders. They unleashed one flight of arrows after the other on the approaching boats. These indigenous bowmen were so effective at shooting at their target that the terrified buccaneers quickly turned around and rowed back to their vessels.[17] Being shot at with arrows must have had a devastating effect on Europeans. The Frenchmen did

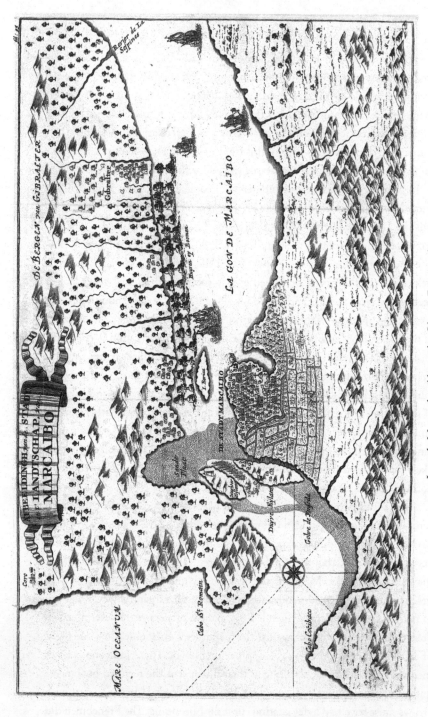

Lago de Maracaibo. Alexandre-Olivier, Exquemelin,
De Americaensche Zee-Roovers (Amsterdam: Jan ten Hoorn, 1678), 94.
COURTESY OF THE JOHN CARTER BROWN LIBRARY.

not know that previous assaults in 1641 and 1642 had prompted colonial authorities all over western Venezuela to mobilize indigenous forces against enemies.[18] Thereafter, the defense of the entire region relied to a large degree on native auxiliaries. Skilled bowmen—along with a few horsemen—stood ready to repel intruders, sometimes far away from their own homes.

Freebooters usually avoided encounters with Spanish forces, but after the failed attempt to circumvent the local defenses, a direct assault on Gibraltar became inevitable. When the attackers' vessels appeared in sight of the town, a fierce artillery shootout emerged. The fighting lasted no less than eight days and nights. It turned out to be the deadliest recorded battle involving buccaneers. In the course of the unrelenting bombardment, both town and vessels were repeatedly hit. About forty crewmen were killed and thirty wounded, but the defenders suffered even heavier casualties. After a few days, corpses littered the streets and damaged buildings of Gibraltar. Among the more than sixty dead was the governor.[19] This must have been a devastating blow to the morale of the locals. As the surviving residents, including many militiamen, fled to the nearby woods and foothills, the marauders went ashore and took control of the town, which they found in a deplorable state. From captives the Frenchmen learned that most of the portable wealth had been removed to the mountains for safekeeping. L'Olonnais immediately sent his vanguard with two forced guides to seek out this hideout and take possession of all riches. When the men reached their target, a ranch about twenty-five miles southeast of the town, they tortured the two Spanish guards until they revealed the exact locations of any concealed valuables.[20]

Although most attention was surely focused on the silver that filled the robbers' coffers, the men also needed sufficient provisions to sustain themselves. Therefore, L'Olonnais sent out armed groups to loot the countryside. One hacienda after the other was ransacked. Among the spoils were several hundred mules that the Spanish landholders used for transporting cacao and tobacco to the port for shipment overseas. Many were butchered while others were kept to carry the plunder to the vessels. In addition to all kinds of valuables, the men stole horses, cows, pigs, poultry, wine, oil, tallow, wheat, flour, corn, and other goods they found useful. Slaves were also captured and brought on board. As a consequence of these losses, all people living in the region—Spaniards as well as scattered indigenous communities—faced considerable hardship.[21] Most inhabitants were reduced to grinding poverty, and the economy remained depressed for years.

Toward the end of July 1666, the freebooters were ready to leave Gibraltar. Since their demands of ransom for the town had not been met, they set fire to the abandoned houses. A nearby shipyard was also burned to the ground before the raiders embarked on their vessels. Two prizes—one would later serve as L'Olonnais's flagship—had been seized in the port to supplement the little fleet that sailed, with all the loot on board, back to Maracaibo.[22] There the intruders demanded a substantial sum of money to leave the town unharmed. The destitute Spaniards camping in the wilderness could not raise the ransom, however, and negotiated a deal to supply the invaders with five hundred head of cattle. It took almost ten days to deliver the cattle, which the marauders slaughtered and preserved on the spot to prevent the meat from rotting in the hot and humid climate.[23] In early September the robbers withdrew to their vessels and endeavored to reach the open sea, but bad weather and contrary winds delayed their departure for weeks.

When the gang arrived at the Ile-à-Vache, off Saint-Domingue's largely uninhabited southwest coast, a dispute arose. Some men planned to divide the loot there, whereas others first wanted to sell the captured slaves and add the proceeds to the shares for every single participant in the raid.[24] The decision was made to sail to Gonaïves, just north of the agricultural heartland of the colony, where, in mid-October, the men waited while a number of African captives were sold on the burgeoning slave market farther south. All of the crew members then received their shares. Gallardo and the Mayas acquired a few remaining slaves.[25] After that the company broke up. Many men returned to Tortuga with considerable spoils.

THIS SUCCESSFUL INCURSION attracted a lot of attention among the non-Spanish outcasts living in and around Hispaniola, and it took only a few months until preparations for the next large-scale raid commenced. In May 1667 L'Olonnais left Tortuga with a massive force of six hundred men on six vessels. They intended to sack Granada and then advance to León. The first leg of the voyage was not long. The crews sailed to Batabanó, a community on Cuba's southwest coast of little more than one hundred native fishermen who supplied La Habana with turtle meat. Spanish authorities watched these people with suspicion as potential allies of hostile intruders, but the Frenchmen were primarily interested in their watercraft. Seagoing canoes were indispensable to paddle up the rivers in Central America and were usually obtained from indigenous populations. L'Olonnais's men not only stole as many canoes as they could get but also carried off some fishermen.[26] Shortly thereafter the freebooters sailed south for Cabo Gracias a Dios. Along the way they seized a Jamaican vessel bound for Cabo Catoche, where her crew intended to cut logwood. On board were two Mayas who had been captured by English buccaneers near Campeche the previous year. These men, together with all other crew members, were forced to accompany the French gang to the Mosquito Coast.[27]

In the following weeks, prolonged periods of calm prevented the marauders from sailing toward the entrance of the Río San Juan. L'Olonnais's large ship and the accompanying five smaller vessels slowly drifted westward along the northern coast of Honduras. With the winds and currents against them, the men spent day after day under an unrelenting tropical sun. In August 1667, when the crews ran dangerously low on provisions, L'Olonnais sent two canoes with heavily armed men up the Río Xagua, just west of Trujillo, where they looted native villages, returning to the ship with corn, hogs, poultry, and other much-needed foodstuffs.[28] In times of scarcity and hardship, the freebooters became ruthless robbers. The victims were once again defenseless communities that may have faced starvation as a consequence of these raids.

In September 1667 a group of nearly 350 buccaneers led by L'Olonnais went ashore near the trading post Puerto de Caballos. They ransacked the warehouse, burned all indigo, and captured two locals who were forced to guide the gang to San Pedro, about thirty miles inland. On their way the men pillaged a number of native dwellings inhabited by the Toplan or Tolupan, then known as Jicaques, leaving behind a trail of destruction.[29] After a while they encountered a unit of Spanish militiamen lying in wait for them, and a brief engagement ensued. The attackers prevailed, but they learned from captives that the colonial authorities had prepared further ambushes. Desperate for provisions, the marauders saw no alternative but to continue their assault, and following several more skirmishes they reached San Pedro. All inhabitants had since fled the town, so the robbers looted the houses and churches without resistance. The spoils in this poor part of the country must have been disappointing, however, and there were likely few foodstuffs to be found. L'Olonnais then dispatched a party of raiders to Naco, a native village in a fertile valley about

L'Olonnais's gang in Central America. Alexandre-Olivier Exquemelin,
*Bucaniers of America: or, A True Account of the Most Remarkable Assaults Committed of Late Years
upon the Coasts of the West-Indies* (London: William Crooke, 1684), pt. 2, 18.

twenty miles farther southwest, to acquire badly needed supplies. Once the men had plundered and burned down Naco, they returned to San Pedro, set all the buildings afire, and then headed back to the Caribbean coast.[30]

In the meantime, some Frenchmen had learned from native fishermen that the inhabitants of Puerto de Caballos were expecting a trading ship from Spain. L'Olonnais decided to retreat with his vessels to one of the many cays or river mouths north of the Bahía de Amatique, from where he planned to launch a surprise assault on this promising target. The marauders' patience, however, was once again tested. After about two weeks in hiding, L'Olonnais sent a scouting party in several canoes to the open sea to watch for sails on the horizon. During this operation, the vanguard captured four indigenous men who had come in a pirogue to trade with the crew of the Spanish ship.[31] The freebooters forced these natives to accompany them, presumably in order to prevent them from alerting the authorities.

Toward the end of November, the marauders' patience paid off. The men first seized the awaited ship off Santo Tomás, and a few days later they discovered a frigate coming from La Habana, which was taken in a fierce battle near Puerto de Caballos. L'Olonnais and his company then sailed with their seven vessels and the two prizes to the mouth of the Río Belize. There was no Spanish presence in this region. Here they needed to refit and careen the vessels. After a few days they reached an island called Abraham's Cay, where they pitched camp and established amicable relations with native fishermen. It was probably helpful that the two Mayas who had stayed with Gallardo in Tortuga were part of the crew, as they almost certainly served as intercultural brokers. They knew how to approach other indigenous people and communicate with them, and they could have fostered enough trust to facilitate further dealings with the inhabitants. In the following weeks, the locals provided the visitors with foodstuffs in exchange for metal tools and raw iron looted from the Spanish prizes.[32] Word of the Frenchmen's presence must have spread quickly among the unconquered people living in this backwater. Native leaders or their emissaries, apparently Mayas from Tipu, came down the river and also made contact with the strangers from overseas. At one point some of these men asked the freebooters to join forces in a campaign against another Maya group, possibly the Itza. They suggested that the inland population was quite wealthy and that the rich colonial towns of Guatemala lay open to pillage once their ene-

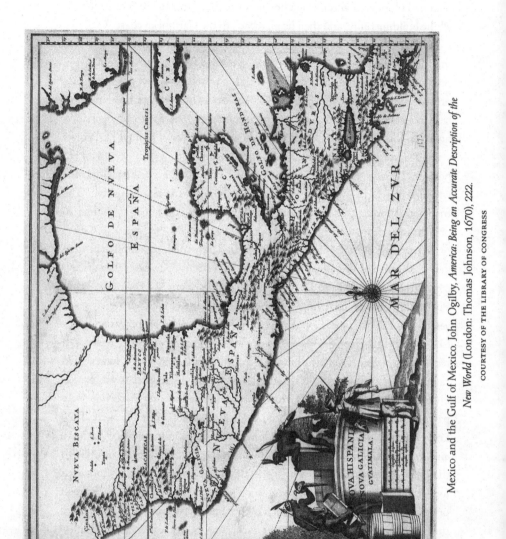

Mexico and the Gulf of Mexico. John Ogilby, *America: Being an Accurate Description of the New World* (London: Thomas Johnson, 1670), 222.

mies had been defeated.[33] However, L'Olonnais was skeptical and decided to reject this proposal. He evidently did not trust the Mayas.

During their five-month stay in Abraham's Cay, the buccaneers made several forays along the coast to Bacalar and up the Río Belize as well as other rivers leading into the dense jungle. They tried to find a way to the provincial capital, Mérida, but even with the help of their Maya interpreters failed to do so. It was reported that the men ended up raiding two native villages from which, besides large quantities of corn and some tobacco, they seized fourteen captives—presumably to extort ransom—who later escaped.[34] The acquisition of a sufficient amount of provisions was probably the foremost concern for this relatively large gang, and when the locals did not provide them with the necessary supplies, the marauders overpowered the Mayas and took whatever they could get. Shortly thereafter they must have left the region.

For l'olonnais and his company, the looting of the two Spanish prizes was certainly not the success they had in mind, and matters worsened in the following months. In June 1668, while the eight vessels under French command lay at anchor off Cabo Gracias a Dios, a storm struck, and the flagship was wrecked on the coast. All of the crew members survived, but about thirty were so discouraged that they decided to stay with the local natives.[35] Six other vessels, meanwhile, took course for the open sea and disappeared beyond the horizon. The core of the gang, led by L'Olonnais, then went aboard their remaining Spanish prize and sailed to the Corn Islands, about forty miles southeast of the cape. Shortly after their arrival, the men also lost this ship on a reef.[36] Before L'Olonnais could raid a worthwhile target, he needed to acquire a new vessel, which proved to be a challenge in this peripheral part of the Caribbean. The men were lucky to salvage seven pirogues from the wreck that they could use to reach the Mosquito Coast.

Toward the end of August, 112 Frenchmen paddled into the mouth of the Río San Juan to seize Spanish trading vessels. Here they encountered a group of nine English freebooters marooned during an earlier expedition. These men lived at the mercy of local natives. Nevertheless, cross-cultural relations must have been so good that they could help the French crew obtain foodstuffs from nearby dwellings. A few days later, the entire company started their advance up the river. Shortly thereafter, however, the vanguard was repulsed by a Spanish militia that had come down from Granada in a small barque. The intruders lost about twenty men, among them L'Olonnais's second-in-command, Antoine Dupuis.[37] The survivors panicked, and most of them retreated in great haste to the coast while others fled into the jungle. Some eighty men in five pirogues made it back to the Corn Islands. There the gang built two large boats from the remains of the wreck.[38] One party tried to get back to Tortuga, while the other, under L'Olonnais's leadership, sailed southeastward along the shoreline of Costa Rica. What exactly happened during this voyage is unclear, but the ruthless robber was finally killed by hostile natives, probably in Bocas del Toro or farther east in Veragua, where there was little Spanish presence.[39] It seems that L'Olonnais had once again—but now for the last time—been too cavalier in his treatment of the people he encountered.

Before L'Olonnais met his end, many raiders had parted ways and sought their own means to acquire the desired booty. In June 1668, while the French vessels were at anchor off Cabo Gracias a Dios, a privateering fleet under the command of Henry Morgan arrived to take in turtle.[40] At that point a number of men, including Gallardo, decided to switch sides. It appears that, after all these failures, they had lost faith in L'Olonnais's leadership. Gallardo, for his part, was probably dismayed to see that the Frenchmen treated innocent natives even worse than the Spaniards did.

M ORGAN'S FLEET WAS headed for Portobelo. The newly appointed admiral of the Jamaican privateers had received information from an indigenous man about the weak defenses of the port, and based on this intelligence he had worked out a plan for a surprise attack. In July 1668 about 420 men switched into a fleet of pirogues and canoes, paddled toward their target, went ashore under the cover of darkness, circumvented the defenses, and seized Portobelo in a bold move. After ransacking houses and churches, the men stayed for two months, during which time they negotiated ransom for returning all captives and not burning down the town, and then safely made their way back to Jamaica. The spoils were enormous.[41] Such success would not have been possible without native support. At this stage every single raid, even if the target was on the open sea, benefited in some way from indigenous participation.

After a few months among Morgan's crew, Gallardo was ready for yet another change. The debauchery in Port Royal, where the English marauders

Buccaneer assault on Portobelo. Alexandre-Olivier Exquemelin,
De Americaensche Zee-Roovers (Amsterdam: Jan ten Hoorn, 1678), 88.

were freely spending their newly acquired riches, presumably did not appeal to him. Gallardo was a restless character. He was a man of action who, with little interruption, joined in one incursion after another. It seems reasonable to suppose that he was still motivated by hatred for Spaniards, but, perhaps more importantly, being part of a heavily armed outlaw gang may have given him a sense of power that he had never felt before. Furthermore, with his indigenous background, his cultural and language skills in combination with experience as a river pilot, Gallardo likely enjoyed a level of respect and recognition during raids that was virtually impossible to achieve elsewhere for Native Americans in the seventeenth-century Caribbean.[42]

GALLARDO NEXT JOINED Laurens Prins, a seasoned rover based in Jamaica. The Dutchman had participated in numerous assaults, and since 1665 he captained his own ship to targets in the Spanish Empire. In May 1669 Prins, together with John Harmenson, left Port Royal, fearing that the governor would revoke their commissions. They sailed via the Cayman Islands to the uninhabited South Cays of Cuba. Part of the crew probably went ashore to hunt and gather supplies on a regular basis. The men also undertook forays to the northwest of the island to prey on coastal shipping near La Habana. At one point they engaged with coast-guard vessels, which led to several fatalities.[43] The marauders waited for months for reinforcements from Jamaica to attack a major port but later abandoned this ambitious plan.

In March 1670 Prins, along with his fellow raiders Thomas Harris and Richard Ludbury, sailed three vessels with a force of 220 men to the mouth of the Río Magdalena, not too far from Santa Marta, which connected the Caribbean with the gold-rich hinterland. Less than two years earlier, right after the Portobelo raid, buccaneers had captured an inhabitant of this port town who mentioned the discovery of a major gold mine, which was rumored to have coincided with a native uprising in Mompox, about 160 miles upriver.[44] Before Prins's men began their advance inland, they evidently wanted to obtain intelligence about the situation. They dropped anchor far off the coast and sent ashore an indigenous man whose task was to spy on the Spanish presence in the region, where a number of unconquered groups lived. The gang may have hoped that a native stranger would not arouse the locals' suspicion, and that if rebels were really in control of the area, the agent could establish good relations. Nevertheless, the man was supposed to be picked up by the marauders after eight days but failed to appear. He had been apprehended by the Spaniards when he reached the trading post Barrancas del Rey, located less than halfway to Mompox.[45] His fate is unknown.

It seems that the disappearance of the native spy left the buccaneers unsure of how to proceed. The commanders ultimately chose to stick to their original plan and advance to Mompox. The town had a royal treasury office, the *cajas reales*, where gold from the surrounding area was collected. But the main attraction for freebooters was the treasure shipments from Honda, about three hundred miles up the Río Magdalena, carrying the royal fifth—the share demanded by the Crown—from Bogotá and elsewhere along with merchant gold. After the gang had found an indigenous man named Felipe, who promised to guide them through the labyrinth of rivers and lagoons, the would-be raiders began their journey on a dozen pirogues. Several natives helped them paddle upriver. Meanwhile, the Spanish authorities had plenty of time to strengthen the defenses along the way to Mompox. The governor of Cartagena ordered all available militia units as well as indigenous forces to seek out and attack the intruders. Near Barrancas del Rey, where the Englishmen had plundered two vessels laden with wine and other goods, the gang was discovered resting on the banks of a river arm, and a group of forty-seven native bowmen—Macayas from the nearby Montes de María—assaulted and killed a few of them, presumably with poisoned arrows. The robbers fled in a panic, leaving behind all provisions, and swiftly paddled back to their vessels. After the men had stolen foodstuffs from villages near the river mouth, a fierce skirmish with twenty-seven militiamen and forty indigenous auxiliaries ensued, which led to casualties on both sides. Eventually, most marauders escaped unharmed, while their guide vanished into the jungle.[46] Disappointed and angered by this failure, the buccaneers chose to loot some better-known targets and follow the example of Fackman, Morris, and Maarten's successful assault on Granada five years earlier.

In early August 1670, at the height of the rainy season, the vessels commanded by Prins, Harris, and Ludbury arrived on the Mosquito Coast. Determined to advance swiftly to their target, the crews set out to paddle up the Río San Juan. Below the Castillo San Carlos that had been constructed in the aftermath of the 1665 raid, the freebooters spotted a frigate, and after a brief engagement the 180 attackers seized the vessel as well as the small fortification.[47]

From a captured officer the men learned that messengers had been dispatched to alert the authorities in Granada. Prins immediately sent his vanguard in a canoe to pursue the Spaniards.[48] A few hours later the main company followed, only leaving behind twenty to thirty men to guard the prisoners and secure their retreat.

When the buccaneers, led by Gallardo, arrived at Granada, they had no problems seizing the town. Only a few skirmishes with the militia, in large part consisting of mulattos, are recorded.[49] It seems that the local defenses had not been substantially improved after the 1665 assault. As a result of the previous raid, the town was now impoverished—many citizens had in fact moved away—and the initial haul must have been rather disappointing.[50] In order to extract additional money, the gang took some inhabitants hostage and extorted ransom from relatives and friends. According to a Spanish account, the Englishmen committed cruelties to bolster their demands.[51] What really happened remains unclear, but the spoils grew considerably in the following days. While the robbers frantically searched the surroundings of the town for the last remaining valuables, one native man, who claimed to have been captured near the mouth of the Río Magdalena a few weeks earlier, escaped from the intruders.[52] He probably had been coerced to paddle the men to their target. Although it is not known whether any indigenous people living in Granada or nearby villages supported this raid, native groups presumably stayed away from further insurgencies because they feared Spanish retaliation once the strangers had departed. The marauders took with them not only bedsheets full of silver and other valuables but also forty-eight enslaved and fourteen free people of African descent. After a few days in command of the town, the men retreated toward the Mosquito Coast. Along their way they looted a number of native settlements.[53] They then left for good.

In august 1670, when freebooters assaulted Granada for a second time within five years, Henry Morgan assembled a formidable force of more than 1,800 men for a raid on Panamá. Toward the end of December, the company landed on the Caribbean shore near San Lorenzo, seized and destroyed the small fortification that overlooked the mouth of the Río Chagres, and then followed the treasure route upstream. After navigating the river as far as possible, they embarked on a seven-day march through the jungle. Although the Spanish forces repeatedly shrank away before this invading host, torrential rain, difficult terrain, and a lack of provisions were daunting obstacles for Morgan's gang. Only at the final advance near their target did the marauders encounter strong resistance, which they overcame.[54]

The buccaneers' march across the isthmus was facilitated by two native guides, and on their way they forced more captives to provide them with information, but the Spaniards also relied to a large degree on indigenous support. About six hundred of the three thousand colonial troops were in fact natives—mostly skilled bowmen—from various parts of the province. This cross-cultural alliance, however, only lasted as long as the indigenous people could hope to profit from it. When it became obvious that Morgan's force was winning the upper hand, these auxiliaries quickly dissipated. Other armed groups came too late to assist in the defense and turned back, adding to the stream of refugees who fled from the advancing horde while part of the city went up in flames.[55] The freebooters not only looted the remains of the buildings but also chased down many of those who had sought sanctuary in the wilderness. Four weeks later, the robbers finally withdrew and returned to the Caribbean coast with their spoils, including hundreds of slaves.

The sack of Panamá was a strategic success that once again exposed the Spanish weaknesses in defending their huge empire, but it was the last major inland raid. In July 1670, after long negotiations, England and Spain agreed to a formal peace treaty ending the state of war in the New World. Although this accord was already in effect before Morgan's men crossed the isthmus, it did not prevent the marauders from attacking and plundering one of the most important port towns in the Spanish Empire. The authorities were furious. In order to restore relations, Morgan was arrested upon his return to Jamaica and, along with Governor Sir Thomas Modyford, brought to England for trial.[56] These measures, of course, did not end the history of Caribbean raiding, but they did precipitate a conclusion to a brief and eventful era featuring one large-scale assault after another.

THE REMARKABLE SERIES OF raids between 1665 and 1670 illustrates that native groups and individuals played a crucial, sometimes decisive, role when buccaneers advanced deep into Central America to pillage sparsely protected towns. Part of the indigenous population was ready to provide intruders with guidance and at least some supplies. In the course of these five years, however, it became clear that most raiding gangs were too large to operate smoothly in inland regions. It was therefore nearly impossible to remain undetected by colonial authorities as well as peacefully acquire enough provisions to sustain themselves. Furthermore, the defense of the empire also relied on native support. Indigenous allies or auxiliaries turned out to be essential to any Spanish claim of territorial control in large parts of the Caribbean Rim. Evidence suggests that freebooters had little concern for Spanish militiamen or *pardos* of African descent, but native bowmen emerged as feared forces that could repel hostile intrusions.

In the following decade, raiding was at a low. Hundreds of buccaneers found employment in the logwood trade, which, at least for a few years, generated handsome returns. Others became involved in smuggling in the Lesser Antilles as well as in Spanish colonies, where the peace treaty had opened ports to English vessels in need of support, thus creating new opportunities to sell contraband ashore. At the same time, small-scale raiders faced increasing resistance. In December 1671 the Jamaican authorities even fitted out an expedition against what they termed pirates.[57] No notable offenders were apprehended, but the outlaw community in Port Royal was warned that further transgressions would not be tolerated. The situation in Tortuga where Governor Bertrand d'Ogeron tried to bring illicit activities under control was scarcely different.[58] In fact, many marauders who appeared to have abandoned their trade stayed in places and took up occupations from which it was not difficult to rejoin an armed gang if some promising venture beckoned. They knew that peace was precarious, and renewed conflicts in Europe would quickly sweep to the New World. It was only a matter of time before the next opportunity to ransack a major target arose.

Chapter 5

INTERCULTURAL ALLIANCES
ON THE MOSQUITO COAST

N APRIL 1671 A LEAKY VESSEL SAILED ALONG THE CARIBBEAN SHORE-
line of Costa Rica heading northwest. On board was a mixed crew of French
and Englishmen who had previously participated in the celebrated sack
of Panamá. In material terms, however, this raid was a disaster, and now
the thirsty and hungry men were desperate for an opportunity to restock their
supplies. After hostile natives thwarted their repeated attempts to acquire provisions ashore, the men aimed for Nicaragua's Mosquito Coast, a backwater far
beyond the colonial frontier where the Spaniards exercised no authority. The
gang dropped anchor near Cabo Gracias a Dios and were welcomed by indigenous people who spoke some English. A few Englishmen also lived among the
scattered native communities not too far from the shoreline. In the following
weeks, both parties bartered for whatever they desired from the other side. Locals, who became known as Mosquitos at that time, provided the visitors with
much-needed foodstuffs and in return may have received metal tools, textiles,
and trifles seized from the enemy.[1] Such trading ties were at the center of a remarkable alliance that had evolved over the preceding decades. Both the coastal
inhabitants and the buccaneers benefited in different ways from this cooperation, which, most importantly, transformed indigenous society. The process
was part of a long history of cross-cultural relations that are worth recounting
in some detail.

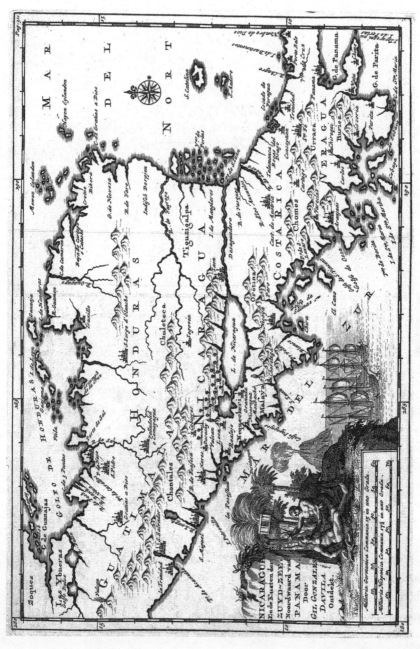

Honduras, Nicaragua, and Costa Rica. Pieter van der Aa,
"Nicaragua en de kusten der Zuyd-Zee, noordwaard van Panama," 1707.

COURTESY OF THE JOHN CARTER BROWN LIBRARY.

THE ENGLISH PRESENCE IN this region goes back to Christmas 1629, when Puritan colonists, mostly coming from Bermuda, took possession of a small uninhabited island, the Isla Santa Catalina, about 120 miles east off the coast, renamed it Providence Island, and began to clear the land for agricultural production. In the following years, more settlers joined the first pioneers. By 1637 about five hundred people were living on this isolated outpost of the English Empire, mostly indentured servants but also enslaved Africans as well as a few captured Pequot men and women from New England.[2] The colony was an early exercise in anti-Spanish imperialism, which received a considerable amount of material support from private investors in the motherland. In spite of great expectations, however, the plantations never generated any considerable returns. The tobacco crops were meager at best, and the vast distance to European markets made regular shipping connections almost impossible.

In order to search for additional commercial opportunities in the region, an expedition consisting of around fifty men sailed from Providence Island to the mainland coast. They were advised to forge amicable ties with native communities, gain their trust, and acquire through peaceful trade whatever seemed valuable to them. Although no surviving record tells the story of their arrival near Cabo Gracias a Dios in July 1633, the circumstances suggest that both sides were keen to establish an intercultural trade network. It is very likely that the newcomers brought some gifts with them, and the prospect of further material exchange led to a promising start. The Englishmen built an enclosure that served as a trading post and began to explore the area with an eye on potentially useful goods. Locals acquainted them with a wide variety of natural resources. As it turned out, however, finding sufficient commodities for shipment across the Atlantic proved challenging.[3] Like in so many colonial endeavors of the period, high hopes were soon disappointed.

In the following years, an alliance between the Puritans and the natives evolved. The dynamics that led to this development followed a pattern established by other overseas ventures of the time. When Europeans first encountered indigenous people in unknown territory, they always looked for local leaders with whom they intended to deal. At the time of the English arrival on the Mosquito Coast, however, native society was relatively egalitarian, and only during periods of conflict did headmen and shamans, known as *sukias*, exercise full authority over a population of male hunters and female cultivators.[4] The families lived in small communities dispersed across a large swath of land. Nevertheless, cross-cultural relations resulted in some coastal inhabitants gaining an elevated status in society. A notable example occurred in the latter half of 1634, when English traders took the son of a headman to London. The boy from the Mosquito Coast was reported to have stayed with the principal backer of the Providence Island Company, the Earl of Warwick, for about three years.[5] After his return home, the young man's knowledge of English and familiarity with European ways made him the center of attention with adventurers arriving on this stretch of coast. Furthermore, he lived with a sense of importance bestowed on him by his benefactors, and wonderful narratives of his experiences surely gained him prestige. He came to be known as Oldman, and over time he and his descendants increased their influence on a growing segment of the littoral.[6] Ties to non-Spanish outsiders—visitors and those who decided to stay—became a central element of the Mosquitos' power structure.

While the boy lived in England and gathered impressions of an unknown culture, two Puritans remained among the indigenous people as surety for his safe return. This risky move doubtlessly helped build trust and amicable relations between the two parties. Years later, in 1643, the freebooter William Jackson, who had arrived in the Caribbean as an officer of the Providence Island Company, appeared off Cabo Gracias a Dios and noted that the "Indians in their Canoas came aboard of our Vice Admirall, to visit their ould acquaintance, Capt[ain] Axe, & Lewis Morris, ye Master, who had formerly lived amongst them, these Cape Indians are our Friends, & divers of them Speake & understand our Language, by reason of ye great correspondence they held wth ye Islanders of providence."[7] It seems that the stay of the Englishmen had a lasting impact on the indigenous population.

Despite all attempts to expand activities in Central America, the Puritans' trade with native communities remained below expectations, and the tobacco planters grew increasingly desperate. Tensions and disputes among the officers in charge of the colony further weakened the entire undertaking. From an early stage, several men acted independently from the company and looked elsewhere for economic opportunities.

Raiding soon became the colonists' most profitable pursuit. An abortive Spanish invasion of Providence Island in July 1635 gave the Puritans a justification to issue licenses to privateers.[8] In April 1636 the first raid was launched.

This episode is remarkable because eighty-five natives joined the crew at the Mosquito Cays, about fifty miles southeast of Cabo Gracias a Dios, to participate in the assault of Trujillo. The foray had to be abandoned, however, when many men fell ill and the mixed crew withdrew before reaching their target.[9] Subsequent incursions must have been more successful. Towards the end of 1637, a visitor to Honduras and Nicaragua remarked that Spanish merchants as well as colonial authorities feared these enemies, who were inflicting great losses to trade and navigation, particularly between Portobelo and Cartagena.[10] Natives turned out to be eager to participate in such ventures. When another English vessel called at the Mosquito Cays in May 1639 to take in green turtle, the commander allowed seven indigenous men to come on board who "wer soe earnes to goe that they would take noe denial."[11] Even if they could not realistically hope to return home with rich spoils, close contact with the freebooters promised access to at least some material benefits, such as iron tools, textiles, or trinkets, with which they could impress others, especially young women. It appears that the experience of an overseas voyage on a European sailing vessel gave these Mosquito men a distinct status in their relatively egalitarian communities.

THE YEAR 1636 MARKED not only the beginning of a series of raids that Englishmen and natives carried out together but also a significant shift in the Mosquito population. In October of that year, Dutch privateers called at Providence Island to sell two shiploads of slaves that they had seized from Portuguese prizes, but the colonists only purchased about two hundred of the five hundred Africans. Since the Dutch had no access to another nearby slave market to trade the remaining captives, they decided to set the human cargo ashore near Cabo Gracias a Dios before they ran out of provisions.[12] Even if their number was greatly reduced by thirst and starvation after their arrival, the survivors had a major impact on this stretch of coast. Within a short time, the Africans mixed with the native population. As a society already accustomed to assimilating people with diverse backgrounds, which may have included enslaved people who had fled from Spanish mines in the interior, the Mosquitos readily incorporated the newcomers.[13] Initially the Africans may have served as slaves, but this would have been a first step toward integration into local communities.

The enslaved Africans set ashore in 1636 almost certainly originated in Angola, where warfare led to the enslavement of thousands of people, mostly young men. These war captives were thus an ethnically homogenous and militarily trained cohort. The men brought with them a fighting spirit that merged over time with native survival strategies.[14]

As a consequence of this influx, a division emerged among the Mosquitos. In the northern coastal region, near Cabo Gracias a Dios, the dark-skinned offspring of unions with the newcomers formed a polity that combined native heritage with cultural elements from Africa. This part of the population became known as Zambos.[15] The southern portion of the littoral was inhabited by people purely of indigenous stock. They were later called Tawira. In the following years, these different groups sometimes banded together, while on other occasions they acted independently.[16]

THE IMPACT OF OUTSIDERS—marauders, overseas traders, and enslaved Africans—brought about various tangible transformations to the Mosquito Coast. Before the first Europeans arrived, the indigenous population had seasonal waterfront dwellings for fishing and turtling and agricultural villages some distance inland. During the second half of the seventeenth century, however, several Mosquito groups established permanent settlements near the shoreline, particularly in the northern parts of the littoral, at Cabo Gracias a Dios and Sandy Bay, where visiting vessels typically dropped anchor. Many of these villages were not directly on the open sea but on the landward side of the numerous brackish lagoons. In the vicinity of this contact zone, the emphasis of economic pursuit shifted toward the seaboard, although, at least in some coastal stretches, the natural setting seemed to favor inland locations.[17] Frequent visits by foreigners likely diverted native endeavors away from traditional subsistence activities to the acquisition of trade items.

Indigenous groups quickly learned that ties to seafarers from abroad brought about beneficial trade relations. The inhabitants of coastal settlements gained access to iron tools and other goods that were hard to get even for Native Americans in *reducciones* and villages closer to the centers of Spanish authority. Some of these items may have been traded away, but the sparse population of this area, at least in the early contact period, does not seem to have established any far-reaching exchange networks.[18] It was therefore almost impossible for indigenous people living in the unconquered wilderness with no source of wealth to acquire such useful implements. However, cutting tools made of iron in particular were vastly superior to traditional stone tools and advanced material culture among many native groups.

For Mosquito men, a dugout canoe was probably their largest and most prized possession. It was the preferred means of transport, not only along the Caribbean shoreline but also on the various rivers that connected the coast with the hinterland. Canoes moved goods and enabled native people to fish and catch turtle or manatee in shallow waters. Most male inhabitants of the region were practiced seamen as well as boatbuilders. Canoe making required expert craftsmanship and was a communal activity undertaken by young men who had to prove their skills in the wild. Before metal tools became available, native groups all over the Americas used carefully controlled fires to hollow out a log of hardwood trees felled with stone implements. The fires were extinguished at intervals to scrape out the charred wood with shells or flints. This arduous process usually took more than a week or two, even under the most favorable circumstances.[19] With the help of iron axes, hatchets, and adzes, however, the indigenous population was able to produce dugout canoes with greater speed and precision.

Given the practical value of these iron cutting tools, coastal communities sometimes went to extraordinary lengths to acquire such trade goods. According to Alexandre-Olivier Exquemelin, who was on the vessel that arrived at Cabo Gracias a Dios in April 1671, visitors from overseas were offered Mosquito women in exchange for one knife or ax. These women were supposed to take care of the men as long as they stayed on the littoral.[20] Such arrangements were not unique. During the early modern period, various native groups aimed to establish beneficial relations with strangers by presenting women to visiting seafarers and traders. In general, females did not choose these roles. They were social obligations based on long-standing traditions. The practice of sexual hospitality likely goes back to the pre-Columbian period and gained a new meaning with the arrival of the Europeans.[21] Because of these traditions, Mosquitos could give buccaneers temporary homes in multifamily households and incorporate possible children into their own lines. Such unions not only brought about kinship ties to outsiders who possessed new and unusual crafts and skills, but they also enhanced the social status of the families that managed to get direct access to this source of prestige and wealth.[22]

THROUGHOUT THE seventeenth century, non-Europeans generally valued firearms above any other trade good in the Atlantic World. Matchlocks were notoriously unreliable, but the more dependable flintlocks that became available in the middle of the century were soon shipped in large numbers across the seas, and indigenous people all over the Americas were keen to acquire these new weapons. Muskets served both in violent conflicts and in the hunt. For the latter purpose, firearms had clear advantages. A ball was less likely to be deflected by vegetation than an arrow, which also lost velocity and became less accurate at longer ranges.[23] Balls, on the other hand, had more potential to kill game right away so that hunters did not have to pursue injured animals at the edge of the savannas, where Mosquito men traditionally hunted. Thus muskets were a significant asset to native groups in environments such as the Mosquito Coast and its hinterland.

The impact of firearms in skirmishes or warfare beyond the colonial frontier is not so clear. Violent conflicts in the unconquered parts of Central America, as elsewhere in the New World, typically consisted of ambushes and small-scale raids. Since even a trained hand required considerable time to reload muskets, they were of limited utility for mobile assailants. Moreover, surprise attacks often took place in twilight or at night, when dampness might prevent guns from shooting at all. Under these conditions the use of muskets was further restricted, and misfires could endanger the marksmen. The circumstances suggest that Mosquito bands employed firearms as first-stage weapons. They initiated an assault by shooting one or two volleys at their target and then rushed their enemies to exploit the ensuing panic to their advantage.[24] During face-to-face engagement, attackers wielded traditional weapons such as darts, war clubs, or lances. Machetes, if available, were also used in close encounters.

To better understand the meaning of guns for indigenous populations living outside the sphere of Spanish influence in the early contact period, it is important to realize that the firearm was an innovation quite unlike any device native craftsmanship had ever produced. While muskets were unreliable, they nevertheless made an extraordinary thunder, spewed forth something like lightning, and launched invisible projectiles. In the event of a hit, the effect on a solid target was often devastating. The prestige of owning such an intimidating novelty, regardless of its utility, cannot be overestimated. Not only did the musket itself impress, but the intercourse or alliance with Europeans it embodied also may have inspired some measure of respect and fear.[25] Coastal inhabitants such as Mosquitos certainly took advantage of the effect that firearm ownership probably had on the morale of groups farther removed from dealings with the visitors from overseas.

It is not known when Mosquito communities first witnessed the use of guns. Some may have encountered armed Spaniards, although it also seems possible that Dutch seafarers demonstrated their muskets to an astonished group of natives. The Puritan settlers, in any case, were reluctant to supply indigenous people with firearms.[26] There can be little doubt that raiding gangs and contraband traders from Jamaica later brought many guns into this region. As in other parts of the Americas, muskets initially served as prestige items and, as time progressed, became the weapon of choice. An increasing number of Mosquitos gained access to firearms, and throughout the remainder of the century they were greatly sought after. A Franciscan missionary, who visited several villages in eastern Honduras in 1698, noted with disdain that, if native men could not barter a slave for a musket, they would offer their wives to English visitors in exchange for guns.[27] In light of Exquemelin's statement about the acquisition of knives and axes, this does not appear to be grossly exaggerated.

Evidence suggests that Mosquito groups were able to dominate their indigenous neighbors in the hinterland, and many Sumu and Pech settlements fell victim to hostile raids. Such incursions likely represented an extension of conflicts that had occurred before the arrival of the English, but the influx of Africans brought about new military strength, and the advent of firearms may have amplified this effect. Little is known about the small-scale attacks of the Mosquitos in the latter half of the seventeenth century. Armed bands paddled up the rivers in their canoes, where they abducted members of rival groups. Numerous men were enslaved or killed. Captured women, who did most of the work raising crops, gathering wild plants, and making clothing and pottery, were kept as wives, with the children brought up as their own.[28] Thus coastal communities increased their size, and muskets helped them hunt the necessary game to feed their growing families.

While inland raids strengthened the Mosquito population basis, ties to Europeans continued to be an important source of wealth and prestige. Since the earliest contacts with the Puritans from Providence, natives adopted English cultural traits in various forms. Men took English names, and people all along the coast were eager to wear clothing obtained from visitors. It appears that trinkets from overseas were also held in high esteem among indigenous groups. With these adaptations or appropriations of foreign ways, certain natives signified their association with a distant realm and power.[29]

The most robust ties to the outside world were forged by individuals who joined Europeans in maritime ventures. Some young men found employment as sailors on vessels in coastal traffic. In the 1660s a Dutch privateer and contraband trader named Willem Albertszoon Blauvelt, the son of a former Providence Island Company pilot, lived among the native population not too far from Cabo Gracias a Dios.[30] He probably acted as an intercultural broker who helped visitors gain access to indigenous communities. Blauvelt had a barque with a crew of English, Dutch, and Mosquito sailors that he used for trading voyages as well as occasional raids on Spanish shipping in the region. Toward the end of 1663, for example, Blauvelt, along with his fellow Dutchman David Maarten, seized three merchant vessels near the mouth of the Río San Juan.[31] Some of the spoils may have been sold to Jamaican traders, but the remainder was surely distributed among coastal inhabitants. Thus Blauvelt secured the support of the locals who provided supplies and, if necessary, protection.

English, Dutch, and French freebooters were keen to have Mosquitos among their crews when they assaulted targets all over the Caribbean and beyond. At sea the natives were remarkably adept at spearing turtles and fish. One man was said to feed an entire ship's company of one hundred.[32] Even if this anecdote is exaggerated, there can be little doubt that these indigenous individuals supplied Europeans with valuable, if not vital, provisions for their forays into hostile realms. William Dampier, who spent years among buccaneers, witnessed on several occasions how these natives exhibited great skills acquiring foodstuffs and that they turned out to be reliable companions during long and arduous overseas voyages.[33] Mosquitos were also indispensable scouts for gangs operating at the fringes of the then-known world. They were masters in steering canoes and pirogues through rough waters, and they were highly regarded as strong paddlers. It is possible that an indigenous man even served as a quartermaster on one of the privateering vessels in Henry Morgan's fleet in 1669.[34] In the course of these ventures, the Mosquitos acquired useful knowledge not only about seafaring and raiding but also about other cultures. This development probably contributed to the early stages of specialization and stratification of coastal communities.

Toward the end of the seventeenth century, long-distance raids were increasingly carried out by Mosquito bands, sometimes accompanied by one or a few Europeans, sometimes without such support. The incursions were facilitated by advances in technology. Over time the natives learned to build larger seagoing pirogues that could carry about twenty men, provisions, firearms, and ammunition.[35] Some of these fast-moving watercraft had sails and keels that were difficult to manufacture in the region and could have been acquired through trade with visitors from overseas. Englishmen were also reported to have taught Zambos how to construct European-style boats made of planks.[36] These new craft were particularly useful if the spoils included slaves or bulky goods that needed to be transported across the open sea.

The Mosquito raids blended indigenous cultural elements with patterns established by Jamaican freebooters in the preceding decades. At the outset Tawiras traveled north to meet with Zambo leaders and coordinate individual or joint incursions. Ceremonies led by *sukias* then prophesied the success of specific plans and suggested strategies to overcome challenges. The execution of these raids followed the example set by buccaneers. As the gangs approached the intended target in their canoes and pirogues, they forced local guides to lead them through the wilderness. Attacks usually took place before dawn, and after looting churches and houses, the robbers endeavored to extort ransom for hostages. Besides silver, they demanded hatchets, axes, machetes, and other utilitarian items.[37] Despite a steady supply from the marauders and Jamaican traders, iron tools were still very valuable, presumably in growing exchange networks.

Mosquito bands launched long-distance raids from two bases. One Zambo group hailed from the villages near Cabo Gracias a Dios and primarily targeted settlements in Honduras and Guatemala, which included Spanish *reducciones*. Another group of Tawiras focused their attacks on settlements in Costa Rica and Bocas del Toro in western Panamá. This faction was based in Twapi, about seventy miles south of Cabo Gracias a Dios on the Caribbean littoral.[38] Native men from this stretch of coast were used to paddling to Costa Rica during the season when hawksbill turtles nested on the beaches there, and it seems likely that this tradition was expanded to incorporate pillaging. According to eyewitness accounts, armed Mosquitos, along with a few Europeans, began to assault undefended cacao plantations after 1678. Around 1687 or 1688, as buccaneering waned and inland groups such as the Sumus commenced paying tribute to the Mosquitos, such incursions became frequent.[39] Led by courageous young men who, besides material wealth, desired social esteem, the bands did not shy away from daring forays that involved confrontations with Spaniards. Back at home these men, like those who had accompanied English raiders at an earlier stage, were ready to take prominent positions in their respective communities.

WITHIN A FEW DECADES profound changes occurred in the relations between freebooters, natives, and the outside world. When the colonial authorities in Jamaica began to pursue freelance raiders in 1686, the influx of outlaws on the Mosquito Coast increased.[40] A number of unrepenting marauders sought refuge from pursuers, others may have been stranded, and most of them surely enjoyed the company of local women. A sailor shipwrecked on the northern part of the shore wrote: "Some of the white Men have taken *Indian* Wives, and others have their Women which are their Slaves, who are kept as Wives, by which they have several Children; some of them have also Negroes and *Indian* Slaves, which hunt for them, and provide for their Families, for they have no Flesh but what they kill in the Woods, and live in the same Manner as the *Indians*."[41] All evidence suggests that this human flotsam, as with the Africans years before, quickly integrated into Mosquito communities. The men availed themselves of native skills such as hunting, fishing, and navigating the rivers in canoes while they acquired a working knowledge of the language. A few of them also played leading roles in raids.

Conflicts emerged when the arm of the law reached the Mosquito Coast. Toward the end of 1686, news arrived in Jamaica that the freebooter Joseph Bannister, who had been involved in a fierce shootout with an English naval vessel, was hiding out in an indigenous community. Governor Hender Molesworth dispatched a note to local headmen asking them to detain the notorious outlaw. Since the natives valued their ties to Jamaica more than any personal connections, they apprehended Bannister and handed him over to the officers waiting in a vessel off the coast.[42] The allegiance of the indigenous population shifted at this point from the freelance raiders to the Jamaican authorities. Mosquito leaders were aware that they could only endure as an autonomous polity as long as they remained on friendly terms with representatives of the English Empire. In the latter half of 1687, therefore, a few headmen visited Jamaica to strengthen relations and, according to an official account, request protection not only against Spanish claims but also against the French and the Dutch.[43] The government in London would have welcomed the opportunity to establish a foothold in mainland Central America.

B Y THE END OF the seventeenth century, the Mosquito Coast had evolved from a marginal retreat and source of supplies for freebooters to a vibrant zone of cross-cultural exchange and cooperation. In particular, the marauders' presence played a significant role in the transformation of indigenous society. The population grew, outside elements were successfully integrated, and a few headmen emerged as opportunistic leaders. Furthermore, native communities gained access to highly valued trade goods and learned to strengthen their position in a resource-poor backwater where the Spaniards exercised no authority. This was both a gradual process, taking place over generations, as well as a violent one that included raids on indigenous settlements in the unconquered hinterland and later turned increasingly against colonial targets on the Caribbean shore or near major rivers, sometimes hundreds of miles away. In various respects the Mosquitos followed the example of Jamaica, which pursued an aggressive forward defense coupled with the aim of material gain.[44] Thus raiding became fundamental to the natives' social and economic organization. Indigenous groups continued to assault Spanish holdings well into the late eighteenth century.

Chapter 6

***

SHIFTING ALLIANCES ON
PANAMÁ'S DARIÉN FRONTIER

S PANISH CONQUEST FOCUSED ON RESOURCE-RICH AND STRATEGIC parts of Central America, but the colonial frontier even in central Panamá, where the silver from Peru was transported across the isthmus, was not too far away. The threat that hostile groups living just outside the orbit of imperial control could launch uprisings or ally with intruders was imminent from the earliest stages of colonization. French raiders were active on the Caribbean coast by 1536, and some were supposed to have forged ties to Africans who had escaped slavery and formed autonomous maroon communities in the northeast of the province. The early freebooters realized that, thousands of miles away from their home port, it was necessary to find a source of supplies, and knowledge of local conditions was crucial to have any realistic chance to seize riches. When Francis Drake appeared in the region in 1572, he was approached by maroons who guided the Englishmen during a foray to the South Sea coast. Four years later another gang led by John Oxenham built on these connections and crossed the isthmus to raid shipping between Panamá and Peru. Following these incursions the Spaniards substantially strengthened the defenses of the ports as well as those along the treasure route, and between 1579 and 1582, after years of fighting, the maroon communities submitted to the colonial regime.[1]

At the time of the marauders' arrival, the indigenous population was in sharp decline. Entire groups in central Panamá vanished, and haphazard attempts to impose colonial rule in the eastern periphery of this province met with widespread resistance.[2] Raiding gangs that sailed along the San Blas archipelago, off the Caribbean coastline east of Portobelo, in the seventeenth century could often count on friendly relations with the native inhabitants known as Cunas. In 1638 and 1639, for example, Dutch and English freebooters searched for opportunities to seize Spanish merchant shipping in the region. Crew members established contacts with coastal communities and acquired foodstuffs from them.[3] However, there were also instances of indigenous people proving their loyalty to the colonial regime. Such a case occurred in March 1650, when several Cunas alerted the authorities after learning that a number of Dutchmen, who had previously looted vessels between Cartagena and Portobelo, had gone ashore near the mouth of the Río Chagres.[4] These two examples set the stage for cross-cultural exchange in Panamá for the next half century. While some natives supported non-Spanish visitors in order to acquire material or strategic advantages, others used the appearance of buccaneers to secure perks for themselves and improve their position in colonial society. As a result, a complex picture of the relations between indigenous people and freebooters emerges.

ALTHOUGH NATIVES PLAYED only a minor role in Morgan's large-scale invasion of Panamá toward the end of 1670, the significance of this particular incursion on the history of raiding cannot be overestimated. After the arduous march across the isthmus, twelve hundred marauders saw for the first time the legendary South Sea. Quite a few robbers wanted to pursue the vessels that had disappeared beyond the horizon with much of the city's portable wealth. Morgan, however, was not willing to advance any farther and decided to return to Jamaica.[5] It seems reasonable to assume that, in the following months, narratives of narrowly missed fortunes circulated widely among the non-Iberian inhabitants of the Caribbean. Many men who were ready to risk their lives for an opportunity to strike it rich at the expense of Spaniards just waited for the right circumstances to launch another daring venture.[6]

In the later half of 1676, buccaneers based in Saint-Domingue began to prepare for another assault on Panamá. This idea gained traction when a mestizo claiming to have been one of Morgan's guides offered to lead a group of freebooters across the isthmus.[7] Rumors of the plan were picked up by the newly appointed bishop of Panamá, Lucas Fernández de Piedrahita, when he was abducted by an Anglo-French marauding gang during a raid on Santa Marta in June 1677. The robbers took the bishop to Jamaica, where Governor Lord Vaughan, who tolerated small-scale raiding and only intervened when violent excesses endangered the profitable but illicit business, decided to send the prominent captive back home. After his arrival in Cartagena, Fernández de Piedrahita penned a letter to the Spanish military command, the Junta de Guerra, warning of another looming incursion.[8]

Responding to this alarming intelligence, the colonial administration put considerable effort not only into strengthening coastal defenses but also into bringing indigenous people in strategic locations under imperial control. Much attention was focused on securing the treasure route. In 1678 a group of 415 Gorgonas from the south of the Darién in eastern Panamá was relocated to the Río Chagres because colonial authorities intended to use them as frontiersmen against a possible hostile intrusion.[9] Cuna communities that had launched a large-scale rebellion in 1651 were also affected by this policy. Various contacts with visiting marauders in the San Blas archipelago in 1675 and 1676 aroused additional suspicion. Spanish officials eventually settled about three hundred natives in a new *reducción* called Terable on the Río Chepo.[10] However, this attempt to stabilize the frontier zone by moving indigenous groups away from coastal areas closer to the center of colonial power failed. It may even have caused further resentment among the population. Within a few months, a number of Cuna families, led by the brothers Blas and Francisco de Peralta, fled from Terable and returned to their traditional ways of living outside the Spanish sphere of influence.[11]

Like many peoples in Central America, the Cunas were not easily subdued. They settled in dispersed hamlets near the numerous rivers and creeks of the Darién, practicing slash-and-burn agriculture. The population was organized into small, tightly knit communities with very limited social hierarchies and little authoritative leadership. As with other groups dwelling on the margins of empire, the Cunas tried to negotiate their cultural autonomy under the weak Spanish presence in the region. Repeated attempts to integrate these communities into the empire suffered one setback after another. For decades a mestizo family named Carrisoli, led by Julián and after 1667 by his son Luis, was employed as agents to foster good relations with Cuna leaders and expand at least some imperial authority into native lands. However, they never managed to exert any meaningful influence over a substantial portion of the population.[12] Indigenous groups that did not want to submit to Spanish colonial rule and abandon their patterns of life sought the support of Dutch, French, and English freebooters.

Establishing ties to people from afar was not a novelty for the Cuna elite. Political-spiritual leaders, the *neles*, traditionally acquired knowledge of distant cultures to wrap themselves in a cloak of mystery and enhance their status in indigenous society. Some young *neles* or would-be *neles* traveled to the Andean highlands to be taught cosmography as well as sacred symbols, lore, ritual, and esoteric language.[13] Others stayed for an extended period of time with foreigners. One man, presumably Francisco de Peralta, was even taken on an English vessel to the Mosquito Coast and lived there for a few years before he returned with a marauding gang to his native Darién.[14] It is reasonable to assume that he was impressed by the way the Mosquitos, with the help of Europeans, developed their autonomous polity. He was probably in the process of becoming a powerful *nele*, but his life took another direction when he, evidently inspired by his experiences among the buccaneers, turned into something like a warlord whose fortunes were closely tied to English and French intruders. After having fled from Terable, where missionaries failed to curb the influence of the *neles*, the two de Peralta brothers sought refuge near the Caribbean coast. They became involved in interloping trade with non-Spaniards and also looted goods from a shipwrecked vessel. In the course of such activities, in August 1679 Francisco de Peralta and his accomplices killed three Spaniards. Fearing retaliation, the brothers sent a message to their relatives in Terable urging them to leave everything behind and join the fugitives in the wilderness, which some did.[15] A few weeks later, they learned of the arrival of a buccaneering gang. Encouraged by the sudden emergence of potential allies, the de Peralta brothers must have been keen to join up with the marauders.

The gang of just over a hundred Frenchmen was led by Jean Bernanos. The freebooters likely met Blas and Francisco de Peralta on a tiny island in the mouth of the Río Concepción. The parties agreed to join forces, and in December 1679, while some of the crew careened the weed-infested hull of their vessel, eighty-two of Bernanos's men, accompanied by more than two hundred natives, made their way to the intended target of Chepo, a small frontier town in the interior of the Darién.[16] To evade discovery, the indigenous guides chose a difficult trail through the jungle. The arduous march took much lon-

Cunas in Darién. Lionel Wafer, *A New Voyage and Description of the Isthmus of America* (London: John Knapton, 1699), 140.

ger than expected. Meanwhile, inhabitants of Terable, less than ten miles east of Chepo, learned of the approaching gang and alerted the colonial authorities of the looming threat. While ninety men—sixty of whom were natives, mulattos, and black slaves—prepared the defense of the town, the president of the Audiencia de Panamá dispatched fifty soldiers to Chepo. The reinforcements arrived shortly after the intruders had begun their assault. When the attackers spotted the Spaniards, they retreated but lost five men and seven confederate natives in skirmishes that ensued.[17]

In the meantime, a third de Peralta brother, Jacinto, incited upheaval farther southeast in the heartland of the Darién. Emboldened by the foray of the Frenchmen, his followers roamed through the jungle, pillaged scattered gold camps, and killed about a dozen Spaniards working in the wilderness. Most of these men had been drawn into remote valleys far beyond the colonial frontier by recent gold finds, stoking further resentment among Cuna groups. The natives' hatred was particularly directed toward increasing numbers of African slaves who were sent by their owners to toil in the rich mine of Santa Cruz de Cana in the interior mountains. Eventually, the Spanish authorities dispatched about 450 armed men—soldiers, militiamen, and indigenous auxiliaries from elsewhere in Panamá—to the Darién to quell the unrest and pacify the region. Fierce fights in February and March 1680 resulted in numerous deaths, mostly native.[18]

This conflict coincided with the arrival of more marauders on Panamá's northeastern seaboard. In February 1680 a group of about 250 Englishmen led by John Coxon assaulted Portobelo. Once again the buccaneers followed a pattern established during previous incursions. They hid their vessels in the San Blas archipelago, paddled along the shoreline in a fleet of canoes, and landed out of sight of the port's defenses. Although a boy discovered the approaching force and alerted local authorities, the militia was unable to protect the town.[19] After Portobelo had been thoroughly looted, Coxon's gang joined other freebooters who had just arrived from Jamaica and contemplated the opportunities for further plundering in the region. Encouraged by this successful raid, Coxon together with Richard Sawkins, Bartholomew Sharpe, Peter Harris, and Edmund Cooke decided to repeat Morgan's earlier feat and cross the isthmus to seize targets on the South Sea coast.

I N FEBRUARY AND MARCH 1680, a buccaneering force consisting of seven small vessels sailed along Panamá's northern seaboard. The crews avoided the treasure route, presumably because they expected to meet with strong Spanish defenses, and contemplated other possible ways to cross the isthmus in the Darién. They sought the support of Cuna communities that had previously been hospitable to English and French seafarers. The men looked for a white flag as a sign that the natives were ready to receive visitors from overseas, but for days they searched in vain. After reaching the mouth of the Río Concepción, they advanced to the site of a nearby hamlet, which they found deserted. Following the sack of Portobelo, Spanish forces had attacked both locations, killing at least twenty inhabitants while the remainder sought refuge in the mountains. Only at Golden Island, near the southeastern end of the San Blas archipelago, did the newcomers finally meet with indigenous people—some of whom had fled from conflicts elsewhere in the Darién—who would assist them.[20]

In early April 1680, the gang of 337 freebooters landed at Rancho Viejo on the mainland coast. They reached an agreement with Cuna leaders willing to serve as guides across the isthmus to the South Sea coast. A native named Andrés de Ibarra along with his son Antonio and a man known as Golden Cap would accompany the foreigners through the wilderness. Golden Cap—Sombrero de Oro in Spanish—obtained his name from a kind of crown that he wore.[21] He evidently wanted to distinguish himself from other natives by displaying this insignia resembling a European crown, which he may have heard of from visiting seafarers. Exotic symbols indicative of power and sanctity were probably common among *neles*, but allying with heavily armed outsiders against colonial expansion was unprecedented. Doing so, however, gave aspiring members of high-status families the opportunity to expand their influence and establish themselves as chiefs in Cuna society.[22]

The buccaneers arriving in Panamá in April 1680 understood gift exchange as an important way to foster amicable relations with the natives they came into contact with. The crews brought items with them that they thought could be used either as gifts, as rewards for supporters, or as trade goods. Like other indigenous people, Cuna leaders desired "beads, nedles, knives, or any trifling bauble, but they cheifely covett Axes & Hatchetts."[23] Iron tools were particularly sought after since they were hard to obtain from the Spaniards. Colonial authorities generally attempted to restrict the distribution of axes and hatchets to loyal subjects in *reducciones*. Consequently, outside these settlements such implements were very expensive.[24] Marauders, on the other hand, freely distributed all sorts of prized goods among people who assisted them during their forays into difficult terrain. Axes and hatchets were not only useful in the dense jungles of Central America but were also featured in ceremonies. One visitor noted that Cuna men displayed their iron tools during a wedding, for example.[25] Possession of such imported devices conveyed status in indigenous society.

After several natives led by Andrés de Ibarra had agreed to accompany the buccaneers to the South Sea, the gang hid their vessels, left some guards on the rugged Caribbean coast, and began the march south across the isthmus. The ten-day passage was quite an ordeal. Driven by "the sacred hunger of Gold," the visitors, along with seven guides, made their way through the rainforest, over a sandy bar, and up a narrow rocky path.[26] They then had to cross a mountain chain and walk through a long valley before reaching the headwaters of the Río Chucunaque. Although Cuna communities provided the Englishmen with fourteen canoes, these were not enough to carry all the marauders and their guides downriver, so many were compelled to march with their native companions along an overland route. Some men were reluctant to be separated because they feared an ambush.[27] Still, they had no alternative but to trust the leadership of the locals. As in other parts of Central America, freebooters relied on indigenous support during their forays into uncharted territory.

There can be little doubt that Cuna groups sought alliances with the buccaneers to strengthen their autonomy and avenge injustices that they had endured at the hands of the colonial regime. It appears that Andrés de Ibarra even envisioned a large-scale assault on the Spaniards for which he proposed to mobilize a force of fifty thousand men, but this figure far exceeded the entire population of the Darién at that time.[28] This anecdote nevertheless demonstrates that the presence of the freebooters emboldened indigenous people to take up arms against the colonizers. And indeed, after the marauders had crossed the mountain chain, dozens of native fighters joined them. Cuna leaders convinced the Englishmen to abandon their plan to raid gold camps near the South Sea coast and instead pillage the isolated Spanish outpost El Real de Santa María, which was a center for gold collection from various camps in the region.[29] Here they expected substantial quantities of treasures to be stored.

The Isthmus of Darién. Lionel Wafer, *A New Voyage and Description of the Isthmus of America* (London: John Knapton, 1699), preface.

The buccaneers probably did not know that Santa María also served as the base of operations for the military campaign against the rebelling de Peralta brothers and their followers. When the combined raiding force arrived, 225 armed men were in the compound: 40 Spanish soldiers, 80 allied natives from Penonomé in central Panamá, 30 Gorgonas, and the remainder black and mulatto militiamen. As soon as the assault began, the indigenous auxiliaries fled into the woods, where many of them were massacred by Cuna fighters. At least twenty-two Spaniards lost their lives when the attackers overran the palisade, and most surviving soldiers were wounded in the onslaught. A few marauders later brought the captured Spaniards—among them their commander—to the Caribbean shore, where they were released.[30] The material aspect of this raid turned out to be rather disappointing. Only small amounts of gold were retrieved.

The fact that Cuna headmen used buccaneers for their own strategic purposes is further illustrated by the story of Lionel Wafer. In May 1681 a party of about twenty marauders made its way back from the South Sea to the Caribbean coast. On the march across the isthmus in the Darién, a quantity of gunpowder was accidentally ignited, injuring the ship surgeon, Wafer who, along with four others, was left behind at the mercy of what he later termed "Savage Indians."[31] Cuna people took these men into a village where Wafer recovered from his wounds. During his four-month stay he gained some insight into indigenous society and culture. By his own account, Wafer provided a native woman with medical aid after *neles* were unable to help. Her husband, who became friendly with Wafer, was most likely Jacinto de Peralta. Hiding from Spanish forces after the failed uprising, he must have been keen to form an alliance with the English marauders.[32] De Peralta evidently hoped that Wafer could help him achieve this goal. Furthermore, the Cuna leader may have assumed that his guest, as a surgeon from abroad, possessed a form of supernatural power that he himself did not have. De Peralta, who had discovered and recognized the stranger's potential, endeavored to keep himself associated with Wafer and sought access to his skill.[33] Thus the latter probably received special treatment of which he was unaware because of his limited understanding of native culture. This episode ended, however, as Wafer's desire to return to colonial society grew. Under a pretense he went back to the Caribbean coast, where a French vessel picked him up.

I T WAS NOT WITHOUT RISK for the indigenous population to deal with the freebooters and support them during their marches across the isthmus. Whenever the Spanish authorities learned of any alliances with foreigners, they retaliated swiftly. Toward the end of May 1680, for example, the governor and military commander of Cartagena dispatched three naval vessels to the Darién coast. Upon arriving at Golden Island, the sailors pretended to be French *flibustiers* and lured some unsuspecting natives on board. These unfortunate individuals were tortured until they revealed when and where they expected to meet with a marauding crew. Moreover, one man confessed that he knew the location of a hidden English vessel. The Spanish forces not only seized this craft but also destroyed a number of coastal dwellings, the surrounding fields, and all canoes they found along the shore and riverbanks.[34]

Shortly after the buccaneers had crossed the isthmus, the colonial administration began to put serious effort into bringing the entire population in the Darién under control. Its first initiative in late 1680 was to direct missionaries to scattered Cuna communities.[35] At the same time, intermediaries established contacts between native leaders and Spanish officials. In February 1681 Bishop Fernández de Piedrahita visited the region to pacify the inhabitants and conclude a peace agreement.[36] However, the authorities did not manage to win over any indigenous group on a permanent basis. It even appears that relations between Cunas and visitors from overseas intensified. A few months later, a vessel from Jamaica was supposed to carry Golden Cap to the Mosquito Coast to forge a larger alliance against the Spaniards.[37] Nothing ever came of this plan, but this episode illustrates that native populations had become an integral part of strategic considerations far beyond Panamá.

Aware that peace was far from secure, Fernández de Piedrahita returned to the Darién in February 1683. On both trips he took a considerable number of axes, hatchets, and other iron tools with him. These devices were presented to Cuna leaders as an incentive to revert their allegiance to the Spaniards.[38] It is evident that at this stage certain headmen obtained greater quantities of prized trade goods than they and their immediate kin could use. Some of this surplus was probably bartered away and may have fostered trade and specialization, but most surely ended up being redistributed among other men to reward loyalty, build reciprocal obligations, and hold a core of supporters. Thus the acquisition of foreign trade goods contributed to the differentiation and stratification of the indigenous population. These visits advanced the shift in the Cuna power structure toward chiefs whose legitimacy derived in large part from their ability to satisfy the material demands of their respective communities.

I F THE SPANISH AUTHORITIES hoped that valuable gifts would prevent further indigenous support for intruders, they were soon disappointed. In June 1684 another group of buccaneers led by Peter Harris followed the path of the marauders that had preceded them and crossed the isthmus. They landed on the Darién coast, made contact with Cuna leaders, and agreed to form an alliance. A combined force of ninety-eight Englishmen and about three hundred natives sealed their bond in a ceremony and then marched on El Real de Santa María, where they looted and destroyed the small garrison for a second time within just a few years. Shortly thereafter, the men seized a Spanish coastguard vessel stationed in the mouth of the Río Tuira, which connected the Río Chucunaque with the South Sea, thus blocking this crucial passage. With this prize the freebooters began to raid shipping off America's western seaboard.[39] In November of that year, 107 men under William Knight arrived on the Caribbean shore, hired some native guides, and crossed the isthmus. A subsequent band of 280 mostly French buccaneers led by Jean Lescuyer and François Grogniet made their way to the South Sea coast in February 1685. They were followed in the same month by a contingent of 180 Englishmen under Francis Townley, and in March by a combined group of 264 Frenchmen that included the crews of Jean Rose, Mathurin Desmarais, and captain known as Le Picard.[40] All these gangs relied on indigenous assistance to reach their destination. Cross-cultural cooperation was key to a speedy and safe passage to the South Sea.

The natives were hardly prepared to deal with such a massive influx of people from overseas. Providing these men with sufficient foodstuffs probably put a considerable strain on Cuna communities along the trans-isthmian route. The benefits, however, were tangible. On several occasions freebooters purchased supplies and canoes from native groups.[41] Early in 1685 there were not enough canoes available to carry all the marauders from the headwaters of the Río Chucunaque to the open sea. Some men chose an alternative overland passage, whereas others joined with the locals to build a number of dugout canoes.[42] This involved working together in the wilderness to select and fell a few large trees, cutting them into logs, carving out the insides, and shaping the pointed ends. While each side provided some expert craftmanship for this venture, there can be little doubt that the knowledge of the natives was crucial to the successful outcome of this collaborative endeavor. As on the Mosquito Coast, mixed groups used iron axes and hatchets for mutual gain.

The material and strategic advantages brought about by the arrival of various outlaw gangs were not the sole benefits for Cuna groups. According to a report that reached Jamaica at that time, the crew members who guarded a buccaneering vessel left on the Darién coast established fruitful relationships with the inhabitants of the region. The account mentions that two "Indians of quality" boarded a French ship "in order to Learne Eng[lish] and French."[43] Material exchange often went hand in hand with cultural exchange, and certain natives evidently recognized the appearance of foreigners as a welcome opportunity to acquire skills that could be useful in further dealings with the outside world.

After the destruction of El Real de Santa María and the seizure of the coast-guard vessel in July 1684, it took the Spanish authorities quite some time to organize any effective defenses against the new surge of intruders. The colonial administration knew that they needed to gain the support of various Cuna groups if they wanted to block the trans-isthmian route. As a first initiative to achieve this goal, the Crown agreed to remove a permanent source of conflict by ordering that all gold mines and camps in the Darién be closed.[44] Furthermore, officials from Cartagena forged renewed ties to native communities. In June and July 1685, six or seven chiefs were invited to come to Boca de Tarena, just north of where the Río Atrato flows into the Golfo de Urabá, and received gifts, mainly consisting of axes and machetes. The Spaniards promised even more rewards if the Cunas took up arms against all English and French robbers. It did not take long until one indigenous group slaughtered eleven marauders. The chief responsible for this assault obtained two or three axes, five machetes, a bell, and four ounces of corals.[45] A few weeks later, the *maestre de campo* of the province, Luis Carrisoli, instigated a number of native guides to lead forty-six Englishmen into an ambush. All but two were massacred.[46] Word of the difficult situation faced by freebooters in the South Sea quickly spread to Jamaica. The governor noted that their "returne home by Land is cutt off by ye revolting of the Indians."[47] In order to further integrate these communities into their sphere of influence, the Spanish authorities also established a trading post in Boca de Tarena. Here the indigenous population was allowed to purchase additional merchandise, including the desired tools.[48] At least some chiefs came to realize that they could profit more from ties to the imperial power than from the sporadic visits of itinerant buccaneers. They must have been aware that, as long as they kept the colonizers out of their homelands, the Spaniards offered the better long-term strategic options, whereas the raiders typically left after only a brief spell in the region. Above all, of course, ambitious natives understood that trade goods helped them secure a leading position in Cuna society.

The Spaniards managed to win the upper hand against the intruders at a time when most of these fortune seekers hailed from France. Early in 1687 a Spanish agent at the Golfo de Urabá was reported to have induced locals to kill about twenty Frenchmen who were exploring the area for an alternative passage to the South Sea. A few months later, a native force led by Carrisoli repulsed another group of some fifty men near the Caribbean shoreline and slaughtered eight or nine of them.[49] It appears that a few men realized they would have difficulties finding their way back to colonial society and thus decided to stay with the Cunas. A shipwreck washed even more French marauders ashore on this stretch of coast. In the following years, many retired *flibustiers* were supposed to be living in the Darién. They married native women and began to eke out an existence in this unstable frontier region.[50] Similar to the Mosquitos, Cunas readily integrated outsiders into their communities.

ALTHOUGH THE PERIOD when itinerant freebooters allied with Cuna groups was very brief, usually spanning a week or two, their relations had a lasting impact on indigenous society. They provided native people with access to highly valued goods and helped them achieve strategic goals. Cuna leaders, *neles* as well as chiefs, skillfully used these visitors to enhance their position in society and, in a larger context, negotiate their groups' political and cultural autonomy in a contested frontier zone. On occasion they even advanced their own agenda by pitting one intruding party against the other. This development was facilitated by a lack of Spanish military presence in the region. The arrival of Scottish settlers, who struggled to establish a colony on the Caribbean coast just southeast of Golden Island in 1698, provided the next opportunity for chiefs to expand their influence. The fact that Cuna communities gained strength during those turbulent years is substantiated by a number of incursions at the beginning of the eighteenth century, which threatened Spanish access to the highland of Antioquia.[51] The setting in the strategically significant and gold-rich Darién was fundamentally different from the Mosquito Coast, and yet the indigenous populations in both regions found ways to successfully defy imperial interference in their affairs. In each case, non-Spanish marauders played a key role in these efforts.

Chapter 7

※

THE SOUTH SEA INCURSIONS

THE MARAUDERS WHO REACHED THE SOUTH SEA IN APRIL 1680 were by no means the first ones active in this part of the globe. The treasure fleets transporting silver from Peru to Panamá as well as the heavily laden Manila galleons that brought the riches of Southeast Asia to Acapulco had aroused the greed of many raiding gangs. The first English intruder into this part of the globe was John Oxenham, who entered the South Sea via the Isthmus of Panamá in 1576. Oxenham's foray initially went well, but after capturing a few large prizes he was chased down by Spanish forces. His career ended rather unspectacularly at the gallows in Lima.[1] Such a fate did not deter other Englishmen from seeking their fortune in this region. Two years later Francis Drake, a former associate of Oxenham, followed by way of the Strait of Magellan to raid shipping in the South Sea. He sailed back to Portsmouth with considerable loot.[2] Another Elizabethan freebooter, Thomas Cavendish, took a Manila galleon in 1587. The spoils caused a sensation among his backers in England. However, when Cavendish returned to the South Sea in 1591 to emulate his earlier triumph, he was killed by the Spaniards.[3] Although these incursions, in terms of material gain, failed more often than they succeeded, the South Sea became a treasure trove in English popular imagination.

Beginning in 1598 the acceleration of hostilities between the Dutch and the Spanish Crown led to a second wave of raiding in the South Sea. In that year

Oliver van Noort and Jacob Nahu seized vessels off the coast of Chile but returned to Europe empty handed. Joris van Spilbergen followed in 1615, and although he destroyed a Spanish fleet off Cañete in Peru, he likewise failed to acquire substantial spoils.[4] Once the West-Indische Compagnie had been established in 1621, the South Sea became a destination for large-scale privateering expeditions directed against the Spanish colonial empire. Realizing that they would need local support after their long voyages around the southernmost parts of America, the Dutch sought to forge alliances with the indigenous people of the region. Jacques L'Hermite and Hugo Schapenham sailed with eleven ships to the South Sea in 1623 but missed a treasure fleet. Instead, they blocked the port of Callao, the gateway to Lima, to extort a ransom, and, after seizing a number of prizes, they sacked Guayaquil the following year. They had little contact with natives, however, and the plunder was insignificant. An ambitious foray to Valdivia in 1643 under Hendrick Brouwer also failed, in large part due to a lack of support from the indigenous population.[5] Despite an enormous amount of investment, none of these ventures led to any material or strategic gains.

The marauders who prowled the South Sea beginning in 1680 probably had scant knowledge of the Dutch experiences in this part of the globe, but unlike their predecessors they did not have to fear Spanish forces. A fleet designed to protect the trading routes, the Armada del Mar del Sur, had fallen into disrepair years prior, and, due to a lack of funding, the vessels were not replaced.[6] The critical confrontations, however, took place not at sea but on the western littoral of Central and South America, where the freebooters endeavored to acquire gold, silver, and supplies. Here they encountered numerous indigenous people of diverse backgrounds and capacities. As it turned out, these natives played a crucial, if not decisive, role in the fortunes of roving gangs.

THE BUCCANEERS AIMED to seize treasure shipments, but, as in previous ventures in the Caribbean, procuring supplies often presented a more immediate concern. Problems obtaining the necessities for raiding voyages occurred at the earliest stages of their forays. While marching across the Isthmus of Panamá, these men could only take small amounts of provisions with them. Starting with dugout canoes acquired from Cuna communities, the freebooters then seized larger Spanish vessels that they could use for long-distance incursions. Although most prizes had foodstuffs on board, sizable marauding gangs frequently needed more than was available. On some shores crews that usually included one or two Mosquitos could catch turtles, fish, hunt game, or collect fruits, but natural resources were limited and hard to obtain. As early as May 1680, Richard Sawkins's crew ran perilously short of provisions. In order to replenish their supplies, the men assaulted Remedios, a town on a river near Panamá's South Sea coast where native pearl divers lived. However, the attack was badly mishandled, and in the course of a skirmish Sawkins was killed.[7]

After this misfortune Bartholomew Sharpe became the new commander of the gang that was brought together by the desire to raid targets all along the South American seaboard. Over the next few months, Sharpe took a more cautious approach in his dealings with coastal inhabitants. His men made contact with various indigenous communities, bartering goods looted from two seized Spanish vessels for provisions. In June and July 1680, the marauders stayed more than five weeks on the Isla Gorgona to evade possible pursuers and refit their prizes. The inhospitable jungle had little to offer for visitors unfamiliar with the environment, but some natives supplied the hungry men with oysters, turtles, rabbits, snakes, and monkeys, which, according to a crew member, "accounted excellent good food."[8] Like other indigenous people, these locals were eager to acquire hatchets, knives, trinkets, and silver coins in exchange for victuals. In another instance, on the mainland coast of Panamá, when a native leader was reluctant to deal with a party of Englishmen, one of them was reported to have given "a Sky Coloured Pettycoate" to the leader's wife who then talked her husband into providing the requested assistance.[9]

Sharpe and his company realized that engaging with coastal populations was challenging. As soon as the freebooters left Panamá and sailed down the shoreline, they had few opportunities to establish beneficial relations with native communities. Furthermore, their knowledge about local conditions was very limited. The men were probably aware that the Spaniards exercised little authority outside the major port towns. Along the long and largely unprotected shore lived many diverse groups whose actions and beliefs were informed by their unique experiences.[10] When marauders arrived on the western littoral of Central and South America in the 1680s, a number of indigenous leaders had to almost immediately decide whether to support them or to show their loyalty to the colonial regime. As it turned out, most sided with the Spaniards.

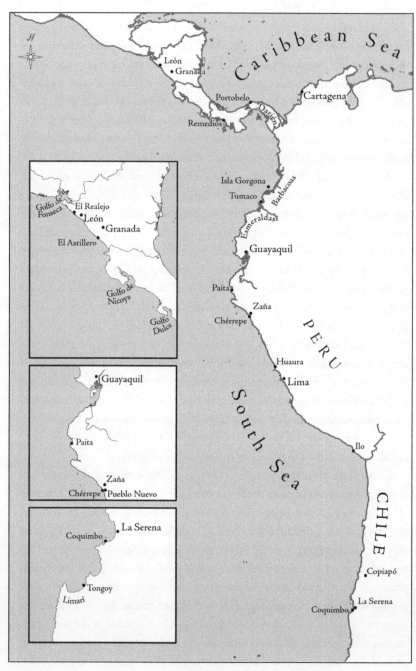

The South Sea coast.
BEAU AHRENS

The problems that occurred when marauders were active on the west coast of the Americas are perhaps best illustrated by the fate of Edward Doleman, who commanded a small barque seized in Panamá's coastal waters. Toward the end of May 1680, these men became separated from Sharpe's vessel.[11] For days they searched for their companions, but all efforts to rejoin the main company were in vain. The eight men onboard eventually gave up and decided to try their luck by looting scattered gold camps near Tumaco in Barbacoas. The dense jungle, shielded by mangrove swamps, was inhabited by Chachis as well as other natives from the Andean highlands. They made a living by providing foodstuffs, serving as carriers or canoemen, and building huts for miners and their slaves.[12] Based on their experiences with the Cuna in the Darién, the free-booters likely presumed that indigenous people hated all gold miners and their African slaves. Thus the gang captured a few natives, whom they treated well and released to demonstrate their good intentions and to try to reach a larger group of potential allies. But the plan failed. As Doleman and his consorts be-gan to march inland, they walked straight into a Spanish ambush. Seven men were killed on the spot, and only one survived.[13] The raiders had evidently mis-judged the situation. The coastal inhabitants were not willing to risk their lives by supporting selfish intruders.

Despite the haphazard attempts to establish good relations with the indig-enous population, violent encounters between marauders and native groups were not exceptional and only became more common as time progressed. Another incident occurred in October 1680, when Sharpe and his company landed near Ilo in southern Peru. They seized a sugar mill and advanced with sixty men toward the small town, which served as a market for people living in the hinterland. Aymara and Quechua speakers had settled here to partici-pate in economic opportunities, and the locals were determined to defend their livelihoods. One indigenous man was killed in a skirmish, but stiff resistance brought the assault to a standstill. This was the first time Sharpe's gang was confronted with massive native opposition. The attackers then sent a messen-ger to the town to extort a ransom. Realizing that they could not get any valu-ables there, the freebooters demanded eighty head of cattle for leaving the mill unharmed. Instead of receiving the awaited payoff, however, two days later a Spanish cavalry unit appeared to repulse the intruders. Angered by this un-expected turn of events, the men immediately set the mill on fire and left.[14]

This experience probably made the robbers more suspicious and hostile toward other coastal inhabitants they encountered.

In the following weeks, a series of assaults on settlements along the shoreline of the Atacama Desert continued. The marauders next sailed to Coquimbo, a small seaport at the southernmost portion of a flat sandy cuspate bay. From here they planned to advance a few miles inland to La Serena, where Sharpe likely assumed that gold from the nearby mountains was collected.[15] When the men dropped anchor off the port, they discovered a militia unit awaiting them. News of the approaching enemies had reached La Serena about a week before their actual arrival, giving the inhabitants enough time to make off for safety with their valuables and slaves.[16] The militia, nevertheless, was not strong enough to repel the attackers. After they had gone ashore and seized control of the town, the freebooters ransacked the houses but found little of use remaining. Again, they attempted to extort ransom for leaving the town unharmed. The locals, however, were unwilling to submit to the demands so easily. During the night a native man—evidently in the service of the Spaniards—swam to the stern of the vessel and attempted to ignite it, but the watch discovered the smoke and managed to defuse the dangerous situation. Following this incident the incensed raiders took revenge by burning down most of La Serena.[17] They then retreated to their vessel and set sail for the open sea.

The freebooters not only possessed scant intelligence about potential targets, but their knowledge about the geography of the entire region was also vague. During their voyages through the coastal waters of the South Sea, ships' crews relied on traditional maritime skills of dead reckoning, sounding, and celestial navigation. Carrying out successful raids, however, required accurate information about local conditions along the shore. The charts available to the non-Spanish seafarers, if they had any, were often unreliable. Thus, to navigate the vessel to promising destinations, Sharpe took the commanders and pilots—including natives—from captured Spanish prizes with him. He released these individuals only once the vessels reached northern Chile, where the gang reversed course and sailed northward.[18]

When marauders landed on an unknown coast, they frequently captured indigenous people and inquired about local conditions or, depending on the circumstances, forced them to serve as guides. In May 1681, for example, Sharpe's gang arrived at Isla Chira, deep in the Golfo de Nicoya in Costa Rica, where they sought a safe spot for repairing and provisioning their vessel. During a foray ashore they "tooke 3 Indian Men and 8 Indian Women" and pressed them for intelligence about the Spaniards in the region.[19] However, obtaining the desired information often turned out to be difficult, if not impossible. A few months later, as the men sailed along the southernmost coast of Chile, they spotted "an Indian Canoe with 3 men in her, but She being neare ye Shoare, one got a way, one they killed and tooke the other, & brought him on board, but could not understand him."[20] Besides the fact that this incident again illustrates the ruthless nature of the raiding gangs, it also shows how attempts to interact with natives sometimes were futile. Furthermore, freebooters constantly faced the danger that locals would either mislead or tell them whatever they wanted to hear. The marauders had good reasons to be cautious with the intelligence gathered from indigenous individuals.

AT THE TIME THE BUCCANEERS arrived in the South Sea in April 1680, Spanish authorities were hardly prepared to protect coastal regions against foreign assaults. Officials, supported by local merchants, endeavored to organize defensive measures, but the fortifications of most harbors had deteriorated and a lack of military presence along with insufficient supplies of firearms only fueled the precariousness of the situation. In Panamá the Spaniards relied on *pardo* militias to confront hostile intruders.[21] Elsewhere along the shoreline, however, such forces were confined to the few major ports where significant numbers of people of African descent lived. The colonial administration realized that the indigenous population, in various capacities and roles, was key to the defense of vulnerable stretches of the coast. Therefore, the authorities began to exert direct influence on native groups living in this part of the empire. For example, when freebooters reached the Golfo de Nicoya in May 1681, they encountered several locals. A crew member noted: "Butt these Indians [tha]t came to us told us [tha]t the Spaniards had told them if any Shipps came in [tha]t had any thing of redd in their collers, [tha]t thay should have a caire & not come on borde of them nor lett us see them telling them [tha]t wee would kill them, but as itt happen'd we went in with all white collers, w[hi]ch was the Spanish order [tha]t thay should Assist all these, for thay were their friends and would doe them no harme."[22] Until an effective policy against intruders could be put in place, they could do little else than plead with the native population not to support any foreigners.

As more raiding gangs entered the South Sea in the following years, the colonial authorities implemented new policies to protect Central America's western seaboard. One of the measures was to improve intelligence and communication in this part of the empire. In order to detect intruders near major ports, officials advised communities in coastal areas to establish a string of lookouts along the open sea. Villagers were conscripted to serve as sentinels. If they sighted a suspicious vessel, they were to give flag signals—or fires at night—and warn the nearest town or military post.[23] This system, however, not only imposed a further strain on native populations but also remained a haphazard attempt to prepare for hostile assaults. It certainly was not a deterrent.

Measures to cut off raiders from their sources of supplies were probably more effective. Beginning in 1684, on sighting suspicious vessels, inhabitants of coastal settlements were instructed to withdraw stores of food inland, destroy crops under cultivation, and burn all watercraft to prevent them from falling into enemy hands. This scorched-earth policy worked in some instances. When a group of marauders under Edward Davis landed near El Realejo in Nicaragua in July 1684, the locals torched their two boats and fled.[24] Two months later the same gang arrived on an island off the coast of Peru to acquire foodstuffs and fresh water. Following an order from the viceroy, the native fishermen burned a small barque on the beach before they were captured.[25] Another party of Englishmen reached a hamlet near Acapulco toward the end of December 1685. After having discovered the intruders, the inhabitants set ablaze two huts containing corn and sought refuge in the wilderness.[26] These examples show that many indigenous people adhered to the policy of the colonial regime and destroyed their property rather than pursue potential trading opportunities or even anti-Spanish alliances with heavily armed strangers. They had good reasons for doing so.

In July 1684 a roving gang led by Edward Davis and John Eaton sailed into the Golfo de Fonseca in Honduras in order to careen the hulls of their vessels. They first stopped at Meanguera, the island nearest the entrance of the deep bay, planning to hire locals to help them with the hard work. However, besides a friar only a handful of men were available. The marauders then set out for nearby Amapala in search of able-bodied men, but the indigenous population avoided contact with the strangers and disappeared in the woods. Only the native cacique and the scribe cautiously approached the visitors. After a while the villagers were coaxed out of hiding and assembled in the church.

Here the freebooters intended to explain their intention, but panic ensued, and the men killed the scribe and possibly some others by shooting into the crowd. Although it is not clear whether this incident was really caused by a misunderstanding, as later claimed by the perpetrators, it demonstrates that these men had no respect for human life and did not hesitate to resort to lethal force.[27] They lived in a social environment where the use of violence was a widely accepted means to achieve short-term goals. In the long term, however, such incidents alienated the robbers from the very people their fortunes relied on.

This was not an isolated incident. Shortly after Davis and Eaton had left the Golfo de Fonseca, Peter Harris led a gang of marauders to the Golfo Dulce in Costa Rica to replenish their provisions and careen their four recently seized prizes. Several crew members went ashore but failed to make contact with local natives, who ran away. The raiders then torched the houses and returned to their vessels.[28] One week later the men arrived in the Golfo de Nicoya with the same design. However, sentinels discovered the strangers as they proceeded into the deep bay. In the small port of Despensa, the alcalde of the province received an advance warning and conscripted all able men for the defense of the colony. When Harris sent a dozen heavily armed men in five canoes ashore to hunt goats and game, a handful of Spanish musketeers and about thirty indigenous bowmen ambushed them, killing eight or nine of the gang.[29] Surprised by this hostile reception, the survivors quickly retreated to their vessel, leaving both hungry and angry.

Over the next few months, conflicts with Native Americans became more common. This had an impact on efforts to seize lucrative targets. Several crews, for example, hoped to strike it rich by sacking Guayaquil, the most important seaport between Panamá and Peru. In November 1684 a combined force of three outlaw gangs led by Davis, Harris, and Charles Swan sailed their vessels to the mouth of the Río Guayas that led to Guayaquil. The men first landed at Paita, a small port predominantly inhabited by indigenous fishermen. The marauders took the adjacent fortification and ransacked all houses but found almost nothing of value. Since the locals did not provide any ransom, the Englishmen burned down most of the town.[30] In the next few days they progressed slowly through marshes and mangroves toward Guayaquil. The intruders endeavored to remain undetected until the final assault on their target. As the men approached the town, however, a forced guide escaped. Presuming that he would alert the Spaniards, the commanders decided to abandon

Freebooters mistreating a captive. Alexandre-Olivier Exquemelin,
Historie der boecaniers, of vrybuyters van America
(Amsterdam: Nicolaas ten Hoorn, 1700), pt. 1, 28.

their plans and try their luck elsewhere.[31] In this instance the inimical and self-serving treatment of indigenous people resulted in the failure of a large-scale assault.

In the following weeks, the freebooters sailed the length of the coast of Barbacoas and Esmeraldas. When the men arrived near Tumaco, Swan sent several canoes into the river estuary closest to the town to gather intelligence about Spanish defenses. This party came back with a native captive who was forced to act as their guide. The gang then paddled with over sixty men to Tumaco, where they arrived in the middle of the night and quickly seized control of the town. Having rounded up all inhabitants, mostly Chachi families, the marauders pressed hard to find out the exact location of nearby gold camps, but the captives refused to surrender the desired information. Not willing to give up so easily, they tortured an indigenous man, who also remained silent. This so incensed the Englishmen that they hanged this unfortunate individual.[32] After a few hours they left the town empty-handed and made their way back to their vessel waiting off the coast. A lack of native cooperation proved to be the decisive factor that prevented Swan's men from raiding a major gold-producing region.

During this period, relations between freebooters and the indigenous population deteriorated steadily. This situation was exacerbated by a series of violent assaults beginning in March 1686, when Davis and his cohort appeared on the northern coastline of Peru. The men first seized the native fishing village Chérrepe and detained all inhabitants to prevent them from alerting the authorities. Guided by a captured indigenous man and a mulatto, the marauders advanced about fifteen miles inland to pillage the town of Zaña, finding a substantial amount of silver. Further forays failed, however, because a boy had escaped from Chérrepe and raised alarm in Pueblo Nuevo. The next day the militia began to harass the intruders. The men quickly returned to the coast, looting and destroying a number of native dwellings on their way.[33] The gang then sailed north to sack Paita, which had been partly burned down in a previous raid. This region did not provide any attractive targets for robbers. But a few days before the men arrived on this stretch of coast, they had seized a Spanish trading vessel. From the cargo they took many bales of cloth, which they broke open and sold cheaply in Paita. Cross-cultural relations soon turned sour, however, when crew members abused local women.[34] Shortly thereafter the rogue band set sail for another port where the inhabitants probably received similar treatment. Davis's gang left a trail of destruction, and countless indigenous people were among the casualties.

This outburst of violence further alienated the intruders from the coastal population. The provincial of the Franciscans in Huaura, about a hundred miles north of Lima, visited a native village in April 1686 that had recently been sacked by freebooters. He heard stories of atrocities and reported that many locals had fled from their homes and would return only once all raiders had left the region.[35] Word of these assaults must have spread quickly among the people living along this shoreline and farther inland. Within a few months, inhabitants abandoned coastal settlements in Peru and the very north of Chile. According to an official report, numerous dwellings were deserted, trade came almost to a standstill, and Panamá was cut off from its usual sources of supplies.[36] By that time the marauding gangs had acquired a fearful reputation, in large part due to accounts of violent excesses, although Spanish propaganda also may have played a role.

While the assertion that most of the coastal areas were depopulated after these incursions is certainly exaggerated, there can be little doubt that ruthless behavior made it more difficult for subsequent raiders to establish beneficial relations with indigenous communities. This is illustrated by the experiences of William Knight and his crew in the north of Chile in May 1686, only a few weeks after Davis left the region. Knight's men first landed on the coast of Limarí, about twenty-five miles south of Coquimbo, hoping to contact locals willing to lead them to gold camps in the mountains. But they managed only to capture a mulatto, who later escaped from the freebooters. They then set course for nearby Tongoy, where the men faced a hostile reception and became embroiled in a skirmish. Eventually, the would-be robbers steered north and marched to the native village of Copiapó aiming to enlist allies for a foray to the gold fields.[37] All these attempts to launch a raid with indigenous assistance on a promising target proved unsuccessful. After about two weeks, the disappointed gang ran out of patience and sailed away.

THE MARAUDERS WHO sought their fortunes farther north met with similar issues. In July 1685 a force of 470 Englishmen led by Swan, Davis, and Townley arrived on the South Sea coast of Nicaragua. They anchored their vessels near the harbor of El Realejo, a major shipbuilding center hidden behind a long island, and went ashore in thirty-one canoes.[38] Instead of attacking the fortified town, the men decided to bypass the port and pillage León in the hinterland. As the seat of civic and ecclesiastical authority, the provincial capital also served as the region's commercial hub. Wealthy merchants maintained residences in León to capitalize on the patronage and corruption of local officials. The freebooters, therefore, hoped to find great spoils when they rushed about twenty miles inland to sack the town. A few miles prior to reaching their target, the gang encountered a small cavalry contingent. Following a brief skirmish, however, the Spaniards retreated and focused on the defense of the capital, which had about 2,500 inhabitants. Back in León the cavalry was supplemented by sixty to seventy indigenous horsemen.[39] The authorities mobilized all possible forces against the intruders. Nevertheless, the heavily armed Englishmen could not be stopped. In a fierce engagement they drove off the defenders, mostly consisting of *pardos*, and quickly overwhelmed León. After looting all the houses, they set some larger buildings on fire because the demanded ransom was not paid. The raiders then marched back to the coast to sack El Realejo, which they found completely abandoned. The men took what was left behind and burned down this town as well.[40]

As in so many other examples, even natives not directly affected by a devastating assault suffered from its far-reaching consequences. Under colonial rule all indigenous people not only had to deliver agricultural products as tribute and provide compulsory labor, they were also responsible for the maintenance of public institutions and infrastructure. After a major raid, Spaniards used the *repartimiento* system to get native communities to assist with rebuilding bridges, fortifications, and destroyed towns, as was the case with the native inhabitants of Sutiaba, just west of León. The locals had to construct twenty-four houses and all public buildings, including the convent, the episcopal palace, the seminary, the cathedral, and a hospital. Furthermore, they were obliged to deliver additional construction materials such as stones, bricks, tiles, lime, and considerable amounts of lumber. It must have taken years before all demands were met.[41] This incursion must have posed significant economic strains on innocent people.

The rebuilding of León had just begun when another raiding gang appeared and caused more mayhem. This time it was François Grogniet who arrived with 120 men at El Realejo in November 1685. As a result of the recent English pillage, the defenses were unmanned and the remnants of the town were deserted. Grogniet's destitute company then advanced to sack León, but before they reached their target the marauders learned from three captured sentinels that nothing was left to be looted. This prompted the Frenchmen to return to the coast. Here they pillaged a sugar estate and several cattle ranches as well as a native hamlet, where they eventually managed to secure some corn and beef.[42] A few months later, in April 1686, the same gang returned to the area and seized Granada. The triumph was short lived, however, once the attackers discovered that all foodstuffs had been removed from the town. The men next marched to two nearby indigenous villages, Jinotepe and Diriamba, which lay completely defenseless because the male inhabitants had been conscripted to defend Granada. After the robbers burned down both settlements, they ransacked a few ranches, where they butchered horses, mules, and cattle.[43] Acquiring sufficient provisions was a constant problem for all freebooters who sailed along the west coast of the Americas, and conditions only deteriorated as colonial authorities began to cut off the intruders from local supplies.

Indigenous communities near the South Sea that had been devastated by raids could not count on support from the colonial regime. The authorities, on the other hand, realized that it was not in their interest to antagonize the very people that the defense of the coastal areas relied on. Therefore, under certain conditions, actions were taken to provide limited assistance to victims of pillages. After their villages were burned to the ground by Grogniet's gang, the inhabitants of Jinotepe and Diriamba, for example, petitioned to the president of the Audiencia de Guatemala, pointing out that they had not only served as sentinels but also helped defend Granada, even though their efforts were in vain. The homeless families stated that they were forced to live in the woods for months. They pleaded to be exempted from the annual tribute of one-third of their earnings. Considering these special circumstances, it was decided that they did not have to pay tribute for one year.[44] This, of course, was only a small relief for the people who lost everything to foreign aggressions.

R AIDS IN THE SOUTH SEA were increasingly hindered as the Spaniards extended additional authority over certain stretches of the coast. Sentinels gave early warnings of possible attacks, and the policy to cut off intruders from any source of supplies ashore led to mounting problems for the freebooters. However, for many communities this came at a cost. A number of native villages were destroyed by ruthless robbers, and colonial authorities forced inhabitants of coastal settlements in exposed locations to leave their homes and move inland. This policy particularly affected small islands, which were often the preferred destinations of marauders to resupply and clean their vessels. In March 1684 a gang led by Swan arrived at the Isla Mocha, about twenty miles off central Chile. Here local Mapuche families welcomed the visitors and provided them with sheep, fowl, potatoes, and corn in exchange for two swords and trinkets. The natives paid a high price for this hospitality. Six months later the entire population consisting of seven hundred indigenous people, along with two Jesuits, was deported by order of the governor and settled in a *reducción* on a riverbank farther north on the mainland coast.[45] The removal of natives from their islands became an integral part of the campaign against the intruders. After repeated visits by raiding gangs in 1684 and 1685, the three indigenous communities on Conchagua and Meanguera in the Golfo de Fonseca were also resettled to locations that the colonial authorities considered safer. When Davis's crew arrived in Amapala in September 1685 to careen their vessel, they encountered only a handful native people, and within a year the entire region was deserted and the villages completely destroyed.[46]

As time passed, the colonial authorities gradually gained the upper hand against the intruders. Perhaps their most spectacular success was the well-prepared assault on Swan's crew on the west coast of México in February 1686. After a long and largely futile voyage, the gang ran short on supplies and went ashore at different points, but they soon discovered that all the cattle had been driven inland. A group of eighty men landed at the mouth of the Río Baluarte and, with the help of a native guide, made their way to Rosario, which they found deserted. At least some corn remained to be taken.[47] They learned from captured natives that Sentispac, located in a fertile agricultural area, would be a worthwhile target. The men then sailed north and marched to the town, which was also abandoned. After disagreements about how to proceed, the company split up. While some men led by Swan remained in Sentispac to acquire more foodstuffs, another party left to carry the spoils with thirty-one horses and mules back to the coast. Local officials, meanwhile, followed the events from a distance while mobilizing all available forces and setting up an ambush. About one mile outside the town, 220 men—60 Spaniards, 60 mulattos, and around 100 indigenous bowmen—surprised the intruders from both sides and killed all 48 or 49 Englishmen along with 9 slaves who had been seized months earlier. When Swan's contingent discovered the massacre they became so infuri-ated that they shot dead their three captives, including the native guide, and hurriedly returned to their vessels.[48]

The second wave of buccaneers faced many challenges and raiders increas-ingly turned to brute violence. Another example occurred in April 1687, when a combined gang of French and English freebooters led by Grogniet, Le Picard, and George Dew attacked Guayaquil. Since several men had participated in the aborted assault two and a half years before, they avoided indigenous dwell-ings and cautiously advanced through the wilderness toward their target. Led by a fugitive mulatto slave and a native river pilot whose guidance turned out to be crucial, the marauders overran the defenses and entered the town. After hours of house-to-house fighting, all resistance ceased. The sack of Guayaquil followed earlier patterns of pillage and hostage taking. The robbers wreaked havoc before they withdrew with a number of captives to a nearby island. In order to press for the delivery of ransom, four hostages were murdered in cold blood.[49] The perpetrators got away with substantial spoils.

The looting of Guayaquil was the last notable success for freebooters active in the South Sea. Although the surge of intruders coming from the Caribbean in 1685 and 1686 strengthened the marauding forces considerably, most of these newcomers soon realized that it was increasingly difficult, if not impossible, to acquire the desired booty. High hopes usually turned into disappointment and frustration. As a consequence, entire gangs decided to retreat to the more fa-miliar waters of the Atlantic Basin. A motley crew of thirty-eight disillusioned English and Frenchmen, for example, purchased six canoes from natives and paddled up the Río Chucunaque. Guided by Cunas, the group, which included a number of African slaves to carry spoils and provisions, then crossed the isth-mus in the Darién. Seven were captured by the Spaniards, but most of them managed to reach Jamaica and Tortuga.[50] On their return journey, exhausted and depleted in numbers, these men relied even more than they had in previ-ous years on indigenous support.

The crucial passage was across the Isthmus of Panamá. When the freeboo-ters realized that Cuna groups, with the support of colonial authorities, had blocked the way through the jungle of the Darién, they needed some time to react to this new development. In a rather desperate attempt to drive a wedge between the natives and the colonizers, Grogniet's gang released a number of indigenous captives on Panamá's south coast and told them that they would be killed if they were to ever be seen with Spaniards again.[51] Of course, this was an empty threat, but it once again illustrates that the Frenchmen understood the pivotal role of the natives in their ventures.

After a long raiding voyage along the west coast of America, a gang of 320 French marauders followed suit and returned to the Caribbean. They decided to circumvent the Isthmus of Panamá, seeking an alternative route through Nicaragua. In January 1688 the men landed at El Astillero and marched about forty miles to Granada. They then sacked the town, which had already lost most of its inhabitants in the aftermath of the three previous raids.[52] Assuming that the Spaniards controlled the passage down the Río San Juan, the company continued farther northward to Nueva Segovia. The freebooters advanced more than 160 miles along an old road passing through several indigenous villages that they found deserted. They stole some foodstuffs, horses, mules, and donkeys to carry their belongings along with the injured overland to their distant destination. After pillaging Nueva Segovia, they encountered an entrenched militia unit, but the intruders could not be stopped. The men then embarked on a number of catamaran-like rafts, known as *pipery*, to paddle down the Río Coco.[53] However, seven Frenchmen accidentally drowned and part of their spoils sank in the river. While the main cohort headed for the Mosquito Coast, about seventy-five men parted ways to march north to Olancho, a cattle-herding area in eastern Honduras, which they plundered and devastated. In order to acquire provisions and valuables, the raiders mistreated hostages, including women, seized along the way.[54] Indigenous people were also among the many victims. Eventually, both parties made it to the coast, where the groups dispersed.

The freebooters who remained active in the South Sea became increasingly entangled in armed confrontations. In various instances these encounters involved native people. In July or August 1688, another French gang reached a lagoon north of Sinaloa on México's west coast. Lacking accurate maps, they needed some time to determine their actual location. When forty men went ashore at the mouth of Río Yagüez, presumably to pillage the countryside for provisions, a skirmish with Yaqui men ensued. After the initial shootout, the Frenchmen assumed that the indigenous people had taken flight, but within a short time even more natives appeared and assaulted the intruders. Realizing that they would not be able to advance any farther, the French decided to retreat to their ship. They marched one day and night, close to starvation and with Yaqui fighters on their heels, but eventually all men—a few so weak that they had to be carried—managed to reach their canoes and escape unharmed.[55]

Beginning in the mid-1680s, the buccaneers who roamed the South Sea were dispersed. As a result of several divisions of the crews, most gangs became so small that they were hardly strong enough to seize silver fleets or larger merchant ships, let alone fortified harbors. Driven by need rather than choice, they looted native villages and small vessels employed in coastal trade.[56] In the end the forays into the South Sea turned out to be more about survival than treasure.

By the late 1680s, hundreds of marauders had died, either at the hands of their enemies or through accidents and diseases that took a heavy toll on the men who, under difficult circumstances, ventured to the fringes of the then-known world. After disappointing raids, many remaining freebooters seized the first opportunity to leave the South Sea and return to familiar pastures. Some of them sought new targets either off the west coast of Africa or in the Indian Ocean. In January 1685 and March 1686, two vessels commanded by John Eaton and Charles Swan sailed westward and made the arduous voyage across the vast and empty expanse of the South Sea to the so-called Spice Islands.[57] They then continued to the Indian Ocean. There the surviving crew members met other former buccaneers who had crossed the Atlantic and took course around Africa to the Indian Ocean. Piracy had become a global phenomenon. Scores of outlaws gathered in Madagascar, where, in 1691, a new raiding base with close commercial ties to New York and other colonial ports emerged.[58] Muslim pilgrim fleets would be the prime target for years to come.

Other not-so-daring freebooters made their way back to colonial society and may have found employment in the contraband and smuggling trades that appear to have flourished in the closing years of the seventeenth century.[59] There can be little doubt that some joined the illegal slave trade, where the profit margins were presumably higher than in the company trade, and the former marauders' knowledge of local conditions in the Caribbean must have been particularly valuable.[60] Others turned their attention to wrecking. The discovery of huge treasures—gold, silver, emeralds—in a sunken Spanish galleon, the *Nuestra Señora de la Concepción*, in January 1687 drew numerous men from Bermuda, Barbados, Jamaica, and elsewhere into salvage operations, which often relied on indigenous divers.[61] However, similar to raiding, these speculative ventures were also associated with considerable risks, and only a few lucky ones struck it rich. Many returned from such expeditions empty handed or even lost their lives. The dream of wealth and prosperity often proved to be elusive.

Toward the end of the century, Spanish forces apprehended and tried increasing numbers of freebooters. Many were severely punished. Between July 1681 and February 1682, for example, ten Frenchmen and one Englishman faced judgment on charges of piracy in Cartagena. The court found all eleven guilty, sentencing the four officers to death and the remaining seven to hard labor in the notorious mercury mines of Huancavelica in Peru.[62] Those condemned to forced labor in the Spanish colonies likely worked under atrocious conditions leading to a very high mortality rate. Some toiled as galley slaves, while others were used—along with indigenous people—to rebuild and strengthen the fortifications of port towns. A few prisoners were even paraded in chains through native villages as living trophies to serve as a reminder of imperial power and a warning to would-be malefactors.[63] The costly and often inefficient effort to combat hostile intruders placed a heavy burden on the population, particularly indigenous communities. In times of crisis, such demonstrations were important exercises in royal authority designed to build or restore trust, boost morale, and convey a sense of security.

In English colonies, arrests and convictions involving unlicensed raiders were far less frequent, although in the peace treaty of 1670 it was agreed to curtail all hostilities against Spanish possessions. Between 1672 and 1674, during the Third Dutch War, officials in Jamaica feared a massive assault by the enemy, and therefore all able men, regardless of previous brushes with the law, were needed to defend the island. In fact, the few imprisoned robbers condemned and sentenced to death in the 1670s were almost exclusively Dutch or Scots. It took years before that changed. In February 1682 three men formerly belonging to Bartholomew Sharpe's gang were captured in Jamaica. They were tried, found guilty of piracy, and subsequently hanged.[64] Such cases, however, represent exceptional circumstances. English colonial administrations seem to have resorted to piracy trials primarily to show imperial authorities in London that they were serious in their efforts to suppress maritime predations at a time when their economies—or at least certain business sectors—still profited from the spoils that other outlaws brought to Port Royal and other, more peripheral, harbors.

Several astute buccaneers left their trade for good before it was too late. Laurens Prins and Henry Morgan were the most prominent freebooters to settle down in Jamaica and purchase plantations from their loot. They were not alone. Historians have estimated that between one-fifth and one-quarter of the planter community toward the end of century were former residents, mostly merchants, of Port Royal who had ties to illegal activities.[65] It appears that French *flibustiers* were drawn to plantation life more often than their English and Dutch counterparts. About half of them were reported to have used their shares to purchase land in Saint-Domingue.[66] The trajectory of their lives represent a larger trend in imperial history, signifying a shift from raiding and illicit trade to agricultural production as the prime source of income. Others made their way back to Europe, where a few retired marauders presented themselves as adventurers and told their stories to the public. Their narratives eventually became an important element of popular culture.

Conclusion

———— ⚐ ————

BUCCANEERS HAVE BEEN ACCLAIMED FOR THEIR DARING, PRAISED
for their accomplishments, condemned for their greed, despised for
their brutality, and vilified for their depravity. They have been presented as early proponents of democracy, some have been recognized as skilled geographers, and a few have recorded their encounters with
indigenous groups virtually unknown outside their respective colonies. The
last achievement, unfortunately, has received little scholarly attention. Studies of international conflicts in the seventeenth-century Caribbean rarely include native populations. However, freebooters active in this region and along
the South Sea coast probably encountered more indigenous people than Spaniards. With few exceptions, every known raid involved Native Americans in
one way or another. Marauders, above all, relied on support from local communities living in coastal areas of the Spanish Empire. As it turned out, most
successful buccaneering expeditions were at least facilitated, if not entirely de-
pendent on, indigenous assistance.

The exact nature of the relations between these unequal parties is difficult to recover from the historical record. The evidence is limited in scope and
contents, and there can be little doubt that the overwhelming majority of encounters in Central America and beyond went unrecorded. Even when sources
have survived, important details of these contacts are lost forever. Despite these

limitations, a complex picture of the interactions between native groups and non-Spanish intruders emerges.

TOWARD THE MIDDLE OF the seventeenth century, certain coastal stretches of the Caribbean Rim where the Spaniards exercised little or no authority became areas of cross-cultural trade, communication, adaptation, and transformation. Natives and freebooters each possessed knowledge, technology, and resources that the other desired. An analysis of known encounters in Central America reveals a great deal of material exchange. Metal tools, particularly hatchets and axes, as well as other trade goods that included firearms, were bartered for whatever the intruders sought or required. Along with this came considerable cultural adaptation and accommodation. While opportunistic raiders needed to learn how to operate in tropical and subtropical environments, native elites were keen to acquire certain skills, or they simply wanted to benefit from ties to visitors perceived to be powerful. The interactions between these two parties were multifaceted and included motivations that the Europeans sometimes did not understand. Among the many relations, various degrees of cooperation and exchange can be identified.

A long-term alliance between marauders and the indigenous population emerged on the Mosquito Coast. Dispersed communities sought contact with English visitors, and over time cross-cultural relations intensified. Overseas connections helped small groups to grow to a powerful confederation outside the sphere of Spanish influence.[1] Even though the rise of this polity was facilitated by the lack of Spanish presence in the Caribbean regions of Honduras, Nicaragua, and Costa Rica, it is nevertheless remarkable how locals adapted to foreign influence and, in an evolutionary way, advanced their development. As with the buccaneers, for the indigenous people, raiding became a central feature of their social and economic organization.

In the course of the seventeenth century, native leaders in certain coastal areas learned through their interactions with the newcomers that they could exploit European hostilities to preserve at least some political and cultural independence. Perhaps the best example for temporary alliances occurred in the Darién, where scattered Cuna communities defied colonization. A comparison with the emergence of the Mosquito polity shows that both groups successfully integrated outside elements into a traditional social and cultural framework. Leading ranks used ties to marauders to elevate their status in society and establish new power structures. Nevertheless, the different strategic settings led to divergent developments. While the Mosquitos lived in an unpromising backwater far beyond the colonial frontier, the Darién was penetrated by missionaries and frontiersmen, along with their slaves, who exploited gold deposits. The rugged terrain in combination with a lack of support from the motherland, however, made conquest all but impossible. This enabled Cuna leaders to skillfully negotiate their autonomy under the sparse presence of the colonial regime. The arrival of non-Spanish visitors added a new dimension to these complex relations. They provided at least some groups with an alternative option to form temporary alliances with Europeans who not only recognized the strategic significance of the region but also valued trading relations with indigenous populations.

Leading ranks in both Mosquito and Cuna communities capitalized on their connections to newcomers from overseas to accumulate wealth and influence. The power structures that evolved in either part of Central America, however, were rather different. On the Mosquito Coast, men from semipermanent hamlets used ties to English visitors to elevate their status in society and establish themselves as headmen with limited authority who, most importantly, were unified in their assaults on Spanish targets. In the Darién, by contrast, where the distribution of metal tools was controlled by local leaders, the power structure shifted toward chiefdoms with a degree of social hierarchy and stratification. In both cases these new polities proved to be resilient in their efforts to resist colonization and ensured native autonomy well into the nineteenth century.

WHILE LOCALS ON the Mosquito Coast and in the Darién must have been prepared to encounter non-Spaniards, for most natives outside these regions the sudden arrival of heavily armed strangers who were not representatives of the colonial regime must have come as a complete surprise. Indigenous leaders—sometimes ordinary people—had to instantly decide how to deal with these intruders. Many opted to offer their support. It is questionable whether they were fully aware of the nature of European conflicts or the true intention of the raiders, but they often became active participants in paramilitary operations against Spanish holdings.

Indigenous people who accompanied marauding gangs on land raids are usually referred to as guides. During long passages through the jungle and difficult mountainous terrain, it was necessary to employ locals who could navigate the wilderness. Freebooters also relied on guides when they approached colonial towns overland, particularly at night or through swampy areas. Their tasks, however, often went beyond such guidance. Natives among these gangs typically had to carry heavy equipment or paddle the robbers to their destination. They were also crucial for dealing with the natural environment, making use of its resources and ensuring the intruders' survival under hostile, often unforgiving, conditions. Moreover, indigenous individuals who joined raiding parties acted as intercultural brokers. They were valued for their ability to build trust and help cultivate amicable relations when a group of buccaneers encountered other native people. Intermediaries played significant, if not decisive, roles in the incursions of the marauders.

On their way either along sparsely defended coasts or through remote terrain, invaders frequently relied on provisions obtained from local communities. Canoes and pirogues built by coastal inhabitants were indispensable in many incursions. There can be little doubt that most marauders preferred to forge friendly ties to indigenous people they encountered. In order to engage in peaceful and mutually beneficial exchange, however, the raiders needed to offer goods that were rarely available after a lengthy and unsuccessful voyage. Under such circumstances, destitute gangs regularly robbed whatever they desired or needed from native populations. As the freebooters faced growing resistance from local defenders and were progressively cut off from sources of supplies, violent confrontations became more common. The senseless, wanton destruction of indigenous settlements along the South Sea coast in the mid-1680s marks a low point in cross-cultural relations and contributed to the decline of raiding.

For many communities the relentless assaults by marauders shook the very foundation of colonial rule. Numerous Native Americans discovered that the Spaniards failed to protect them against increasingly ruthless attackers. Hundreds of innocent people were killed in onslaughts, hungry outlaws robbed the meager foodstuffs of coastal settlements, and sexual violence against indigenous women was rampant. At the same time, the overwhelmed authorities conscripted native men to serve in several capacities of the defenses that had been set up all along the sparsely populated shorelines of the colonial empire.

Others were forced to rebuild the infrastructure after devastating raids. The strain on indigenous groups in coastal regions was enormous.

The assaults of freebooters exposed fundamental weaknesses in the defense of Spain's far-flung empire. Imperial authority outside the major colonial towns was weak, suffering from imperial overstretch, and far too few Spaniards were living in the New World to be able to protect potential targets against hostile attacks. When they were called to arms, rarely were enough firearms available. Against this background, native groups could be exceedingly dangerous when they chose to support or form alliances with intruders. Officials as well as settlers exploited and mistreated native people at their peril. The threat of indigenous insurrection was real, and although foreign raiders repeatedly misjudged this potential, late Habsburg colonial rule was far more tenuous than some historians have assumed.[2]

In order to counter foreign intrusions, the few Spanish forces expanded their numbers with militias consisting of men of African descent, known as *pardos*, who have been the subject of considerable research in recent years. However, these troops were typically armed with lances and rarely contributed to the successful defense of any given colony.[3] With the surge in raiding in the latter half of the seventeenth century, new forces were needed to confront and halt foreign intruders. In various provinces officials began to establish informal units of indigenous fighters. It appears that native auxiliaries initially emerged in regions where loyal groups, the *indios amigos*, were employed against rival populations. When raiders from overseas became the primary threat, indigenous bowmen and horsemen under the leadership of Spanish officers did their best to defend their respective colonies. Sometimes they had to travel long distances to secure certain targets against invading forces. Toward the end of the century, the authorities relied in large part on native support to repel attackers, and some groups were integrated in the militias.

The history of seventeenth-century raiding demonstrates how indigenous peoples in Central America were increasingly drawn into European conflicts, which were carried out at the margins of the emerging colonial empires. While it seems that many natives were keen to forge ties to itinerant marauders at an early stage of buccaneering, over time more people realized that short-term alliances did not serve their long-term goals and, when possible, stayed away from hostile incursions or made themselves available to the Spaniards as auxiliaries. In the course of this process, the colonial regime expanded its authority into areas threatened by intruders. This development, in a larger context, coincided with a shift in power toward the end of the century. At about the same time when Spanish American elites—particularly in strategic regions of the empire—rather than the Crown took control of the campaign against the freebooters, English and French central authorities augmented their power, often at the expense of corrupt and inefficient colonial officials.[4] This factor, among others, contributed to the decline of raiding in the New World.

In the final analysis, it is important to realize that interactions between buccaneers and indigenous populations only had a direct impact on certain groups, most of whom were living in coastal regions. Even there the period of contact was usually minimal. After a brief stay, most intruders left for good. The assaults, however, had indirect but long-lasting implications far beyond the immediate conflict zones. Large parts of colonial society were affected. Native refugees or deportees found new homes in areas that had not been devastated by hostile attacks. Others migrated for defense purposes or to rebuild destroyed infrastructure. Citizens of Spanish descent left ravaged towns, while indigenous families moved into these urban areas to seek employment as wage laborers. This process brought natives and nonnatives into frequent and intense contact, causing them to lose their cultural and ethnic identities. Cross-cultural exchange increased, but colonial society also became more stratified. In a broader perspective, the seventeenth-century raids contributed to a shift from a mosaic of diverse communities to a complex social fabric. The histories of indigenous groups and marauding gangs, as it turned out, were more closely intertwined than scholars have led us to believe.

Note on Sources

———————— ⚐ ————————

Studies of the seventeenth-century raiders often rely on an uncritical reading of published sources. These accounts, however, provide limited insight into the encounters that influenced, if not shaped the lives of thousands of Native Americans dwelling at the periphery of the Spanish Empire at a time when hostile marauders assaulted targets all over the Caribbean and along the South Sea coast. A more comprehensive approach that focuses on cross-cultural relations requires not only a broad knowledge but also a critical evaluation of the surviving sources.

Above all, historians have made extensive use of Alexandre-Olivier Exquemelin's account of the buccaneers published in Dutch in 1678. The author was a French barber-surgeon who had come to Tortuga in July 1666 as an indentured servant but later joined a gang of freebooters.[1] Unfortunately, little is known for certain about Exquemelin's activities during the following two and a half years. His chapters on L'Olonnais's various incursions and Morgan's assault on Portobelo in 1668 are probably based on hearsay.[2] During the years he spent in the Caribbean, he must have talked with hundreds of men, who provided him with comprehensive information. Descriptions in his book suggest that Exquemelin joined Morgan to seize Maracaibo and Gibraltar in 1669, and in 1670 he was part of the multinational force that sacked Panamá in a foray that left most participants with little in their pockets. Shortly thereafter he made his way back to Europe to seek a new career.

Exquemelin's book is mostly accurate in the events where the author was present, but rather unreliable in other parts. Caution is the historian's best friend. This also applies to the subsequent French edition. Although internal evidence suggests that Exquemelin must have completed work on this version in 1682, the two volumes were only published in early 1686.[3] New passages and chapters provide additional information on a number of raids that had not been covered in the original edition.

In England, interest in the exploits of the freebooters received a boost following the arrival of a number of South Sea raiders led by Bartholomew Sharpe in March 1682. The men not only had stolen silver and emeralds in their chests, they also brought a mythical *derrotero* along with one African slave and two indigenous captives with them.[4] After two competing English versions of Exquemelin's account had been published in May 1684 under the title *Bucaniers of America*, the second edition by William Crooke that came out only a few months later was augmented by a description of Sharpe's South Sea foray, sometimes attributed to William Dyck. This was followed by a thin book published by Philip Ayres recounting the same voyage. Indigenous people only played a marginal role in these accounts. In February 1685 a transcript of Basil Ringrose's journal of his voyage with Sharpe was sold by Crooke as the second volume of Exquemelin's book.[5] This remarkable narrative illustrates in great detail the march across the Isthmus of Panamá in April 1680, with references to the Cuna communities and the subsequent raiding expedition to Cape Horn and back to the Caribbean as well as intermittent encounters with native groups.

Perhaps more important to posterity is William Dampier's account of his voyages with logwood cutters and freebooters between June 1675 and May 1688. He kept a journal, of which a large part survives as transcript in his own hand in the British Library. Dampier was a man of enormous curiosity. In his journal he described many raids he participated in, but he also devoted much attention to the environment where these incursions took place. When Dampier revised his manuscript for publication, the latter feature was strengthened. New passages on natural and cultural aspects were added, and interspersed observations about the indigenous population were augmented. He inserted a great deal of information on the appearance and character of remote peoples, including their social organization, forms of governance, hunting and fishing practices, and other communal activities. Many passages in his book are elaborate descriptions of small details that the author must have noticed in the wilderness. As a result, Dampier's *New Voyage Round the World*, published in February 1697, marks a shift from narratives of buccaneering raids to natural history and ethnography.[6]

Dampier was not the only freebooter to present himself as adventurer upon return to England. In 1690 Lionel Wafer, who had spent four months in the Darién in 1681, appeared in London and began to work on a book about his experiences. Unlike Dampier's account, Wafer's book is not based on extensive notes taken during his time in Central America. It appears that he largely relied on memory when writing about his stay with the Cunas. He presented himself as an expert with a comprehensive understanding of indigenous culture, even though he certainly did not acquire more than a few superficial impressions of the people who had picked him up in the jungle and kept him as a possible asset to forge ties to non-Spanish forces. Although the book does provide much ethnographic detail, it should be noted that Wafer, like other authors of the time, judged all these cultural features through the eyes of an observer primarily interested in colonization.[7]

Another account of a cruising voyage along America's South Sea coast was published by Jérôme Raveneau, better known under the fake noble's title *chevalier de Lussan*, which he took at sea.[8] During several forays ashore and a dramatic crossing of Nicaragua on the way back to the Caribbean he must have encountered numerous natives, but these people are barely mentioned in his journal. Raveneau began to prepare his manuscript for publication immediately after his return home. Only a few passages were substantially revised and supplemented with new information, mostly about Spanish defenses. When Raveneau's book was published in July 1689, war had already broken out between France and Spain, which absorbed the attention of the entire country.

The literary ambitions of the freebooters can be critically evaluated by comparing and contrasting their accounts with records that survive in Spanish archives. The main depository for all colonial papers is the Archivo General de Indias in Sevilla. The archive is a treasure trove of information, and the volume of transatlantic communication is massive. Among the most interesting sources for historians of seventeenth-century raiding are the original letters from royal officials, which are grouped together under their province's respective *audiencias*, or high court districts. Attached to some reports are declarations of captives or abducted victims of raids who had been forced to spend time with the marauders and later fell into the clutches of colonial authorities. Many of these unfortunate individuals were Native Americans who were then suspected of having supported the enemies. Their stories, usually told under torture or the threat of torture, provide valuable information about the voyages and attacks of the freebooters. Another category of sources that contain useful descriptions of raids are the *juicios de residencia* among the Escribanía de Cámara records. These booklets were generated to audit the conduct of colonial officials, and cases that included hostile assaults in particular were thoroughly investigated. Along with the *pleitos de gobernación*, or inquests on various matters, these official documents afford good insights into the involvement of native populations in the conflicts with foreign intruders. The often fruitless efforts of the Spanish authorities to fight these enemies are chronicled in Indiferente General records. Countless stories are still waiting to be discovered in this huge archive.

Comprehensive collections of records from the colonial period that were not sent across the Atlantic to the Spanish authorities exist in various archives in Latin America. Most notably, the Archivo General de la Nación in México holds an extensive collection of manuscripts that provides essential information about colonial affairs during the period when hostile marauding gangs were active off the coast. Scattered references to freebooters can be found among the Inquisición records, the Provincias Internas records, the Marina records, and in other classes as well.

The Archivo General de Centro América in Guatemala also has colonial records from Guatemala, Honduras, and Nicaragua that were not sent to Spain. Unfortunately, countless manuscripts have been destroyed or are badly damaged. Only fragments of many documents survive, while others are hardly legible due to poor storage over time. Among the various record classes that contain crucial information for historians of the seventeenth-century conflicts are the A1, Superior Gobierno, and, to a lesser degree, the A3, Real Hacienda, manuscripts for the respective provinces. Information about events in or off Honduras and Nicaragua however can also be found in the Guatemala section. The most useful records include specific investigations and numerous judicial writs as well as other legal papers. Nevertheless, a lack of finding aids poses another major challenge for researchers.

Conditions in the Archivo Nacional de Costa Rica in San José are much better than in Guatemala. Among the most interesting seventeenth-century records are some manuscripts of the Guatemala section dealing with the 1666 assault and a few Complementario Colonial manuscripts. The majority of the latter documents are copies of letters that can also be found in the Archivo General de Indias.

The most important repository of records dealing with the raids of the seventeenth-century freebooters outside the Spanish-speaking world is the National Archives in London. The Colonial Office papers contain the entire correspondence of Jamaica's governors and other officials as well as those of other Caribbean colonies. The enclosed reports of the commanders of privateering voyages are rather thin and sometimes purposely misleading but provide a general outline of events. The Colonial Office papers also include occasional letters from private individuals to the authorities. Assaults on Spanish targets are frequently mentioned in the correspondence, even though references to the indigenous population are rare. However, these records form the backbone to every investigation of the inter-imperial conflicts in the period under consideration.

The manuscripts department of the British Library has a copy of William Dampier's original journal as well as other journals and notes from marauders active in the South Sea in the 1680s. Most of these papers were acquired by Sir Hans Sloane, whose collection later formed the foundation of the British Library. Some documents contain fascinating descriptions of encounters with native groups. The comprehensive records relating to Jamaica and other Caribbean colonies in the Additional Manuscripts collection provide further information about the raids of the notorious freebooters.

Various private collections acquired by American research libraries contain information about seventeenth-century raiders and their interactions with local populations. One such collection is the William Blathwayt papers. The correspondence and working papers of the secretary of the Committee on Trade and Plantations are spread over three research libraries. The most important manuscripts survive in the Rockefeller Library of the Colonial Williamsburg Foundation in Virginia. Another part of the collection can be accessed in the Huntington Library in San Marino, California, and the remainder is in the Beinecke Rare Book and Manuscript Library of Yale University in New Haven, Connecticut. While references to native populations are rare, a wealth of information on international conflicts involving English colonies exists.

The Archives nationales in Paris holds the voluminous Marine records containing all kinds of information for historians. French freebooters such as Jean de Grammont or Jérôme Raveneau and his officers were keen to be recognized as legitimate privateers, and thus they filed lengthy reports or even journals with the authorities back in France. Among the various other records researchers can find are descriptions of waterways, coasts, and port towns in what would have been barely known parts of the New World. The records are cataloged so that users can easily navigate their way through these manuscripts.

Most French colonial records survive in the Archives nationales d'Outremer in Aix-en-Provence. The Correspondance à l'arrivé of the Série Colonies from Saint-Domingue, Martinique, and Guadeloupe is well organized, but the volume of these manuscripts is rather thin compared with the Spanish and the English colonial correspondence. Besides these essential records, there is also the Collection Moreau de Saint-Méry, which largely consists of transcripts of colonial papers that the lawyer and writer had gathered when he worked on his monumental description of Saint-Domingue, published in 1789. Many of these documents contain information not available elsewhere.

The Bibliothèque nationale de France in Paris is another major repository that houses comprehensive manuscripts with information about the incursions of the seventeenth-century raiders. These remarkably well-preserved papers can be found in the Fonds français, the Mélanges de Colbert, and the Nouvelles acquisitions françaises.

Commanders of French vessels were required to file reports with the local office of the Amirauté upon return from an overseas voyage. These records, among others, are in the regional archives of the major Atlantic ports, such as the Archives départementales de la Charante-Maritime in La Rochelle or the Archives départementales de Loire-Atlantique in Nantes. Numerous interesting reports are digitized, but a lack of good search aides makes these voluminous manuscripts difficult to use for historians seeking information about specific New World regions.

Sources relating to the Dutch overseas empire can be found in the Nationaal Archief in Den Haag. However, most records of the West-Indische Compagnie from Curaçao as well as other Caribbean colonies from the period under consideration have been sold for scrap paper in the early nineteenth century. Only few manuscripts survive. Among the other classes, the relatively thin records of the Sociëteit van Suriname are extant in their entirety. A group of South Sea raiders who tried to sail via the Indian Ocean back to England was captured by the Dutch authorities near Mindanao in Indonesia in September

1687. The governor of Ternate confiscated two logs that were then translated into Dutch and sent to Batavia.[9] These records were later brought to the Netherlands and remain among the manuscripts of the Verenigde Oost-Indische Compagnie. Like so many other treasures in the archives, this source reveals its true value only in conjunction with other sources.

Notes

ABBREVIATIONS

AGCA	Archivo General de Centro América, Guatemala
AGI	Archivo General de Indias, Sevilla
AGN	Archivo General de la Nación, México
AN	Archives nationales, Paris
ANCR	Archivo Nacional de Costa Rica, San Juan
ANOM	Archives nationales d'Outre-mer, Aix-en-Provence
BL	British Library, London
BnF	Bibliothèque nationale de France, Paris
HL	Huntington Library, San Marino, California
NA	Nationaal Archief, Den Haag
TNA	The National Archives, London

INTRODUCTION

1. William Dampier, *A New Voyage Round the World* (London: James Knapton, 1697), 128–29. Based on a faulty interpretation of Dampier's narrative, this raid has been misdated as having happened in 1654. For an outline of events, see AGI, Guatemala 25, ramo 1, no. 15, Francisco de Bustamente to Fernando Francisco de Escobedo, 19 May 1676; AGI, Guatemala 39, ramo 44, no. 201, Juan Francisco Sáenz Vázquez to Crown, 25 December 1676. Nicolas Sanson d'Abbeville's 1656 "Les Isles Antilles" map mislocated the mouth of the Río Coco, which, following this depiction, would have made it impossible to advance to Nueva Segovia.

2. AGI, Guatemala 39, ramo 43, no. 199, Juan López de la Flor to Crown, 14 January 1670; AGI, Indiferente General 2542, no. 5, Sebastián Álvarez y Alfonso to Crown, 13 March 1670; AGI, Guatemala 22, ramo 5, no. 49, petition of Francisco de los Ríos, 23 November 1670. While canoes are generally smaller and pointed at both ends, pirogues tend to be larger with a pointed end and a flat one. The flat end allows

for standing while fishing or poling in shallow waters. Raids are surprise attacks into enemy territory without the intention of holding ground.

3. AGI, Guatemala 25, ramo 1, no. 15, Fernando Alonso de Salvatierra to Fernando Francisco de Escobedo, 26 May 1676. The lack of Spanish presence in the region becomes clear from AGI, Guatemala 280, no. 7, fols. 44–49, Diego de Aguilera to Fernando Francisco de Escobedo, 7 March 1673. See also Jaime Incer Barquero, *Geografía dinámica de Nicaragua* (Managua: Editorial Hispamer, 1998), 229–30.

4. Jaime Incer Barquero, *Toponimias indígenas de Nicaragua* (San José: Libro Libre, 1985), 263–68; Linda A. Newson, *Indian Survival in Colonial Nicaragua* (Norman: University of Oklahoma Press, 1987), 34–37.

5. AGI, Guatemala 74, no. 18, Fernando Francisco de Escobedo to Crown, 15 April 1676; AGI, Guatemala 39, ramo 44, no. 201, Juan Francisco Sáenz Vázquez to Crown, 25 December 1676; AGI, Guatemala 74, no. 49, Bartolomé de Escoto to Crown, 18 March 1681; Pedro de Ovalle, *Razon del estado en que se hallan las Reducciones de Indios infieles* (Guatemala: Joseph Pineda Ibarra, 1674).

6. Jilma Romero Arrechavala, *La región segoviana: Evolución histórica de Nueva Segovia, Madriz y Estelí* (Managua: Grupo Editorial Acento, 2006), 77–84. Why the raiders chose this target is unclear. Newer mines farther north in Honduras may have been mistaken for a major gold-mining area, but the marauders' Mosquito allies may have deliberately misled the men for strategic purposes. In the latter half of the seventeenth century, Nueva Segovia primarily produced pine pitch for the shipyard at El Realejo on the South Sea coast.

7. Throughout this book, the term "mulatto" is taken directly from Spanish sources, describing the offspring of a European and a person of African descent. For the seventeenth-century usage, see, for example, Jack D. Forbes, *Africans and Native Americans: The Language of Race and the Evolution of Red-Black Peoples* (Urbana: University of Illinois Press, 1993), 168–77.

8. AGI, Guatemala 25, ramo 1, no. 15, Fernando Alonso de Salvatierra to Fernando Francisco de Escobedo, 26 May 1676.

9. For recent examples, see, above all, Peter Earle, *The Sack of Panamá* (London: Norman and Hobhouse, 1981), 187–99; Carlos Saiz Cidoncha, *Historia de la piratería en América española* (Madrid: San Martín, 1985), 211–84; Gérard Jaeger, *Pirates, flibustiers et corsaires: histoire et légendes d'une société d'exception* (Avignon: Aubanel, 1987), 75–94; Rafael Abella, *Los piratas del Nuevo Mundo* (Barcelona: Planeta, 1989), 79–106; Jenifer Marx, *Pirates and Privateers of the Caribbean* (Malabar, Fla.: Krieger, 1992), 127–69; Manuel Lucena Salmoral, *Piratas, bucaneros, filibusteros y corsarios en América: Perros, mendigos y otros malditos del mar* (Madrid: Mapfre, 1992), 151–98; Gilles Lapouge, *Les pirates: forbans, flibustiers, boucaniers et autres gueux de mer* (Paris: Hachette Illustrated, 2001), 55–68; Robert Bohn, *Die Piraten* (München: C. H. Beck, 2003), 38–49; Anna Spinelli, *Tra l'inferno e il mare: Breve storia economica e sociale della pirateria* (Ravenna: Fernandel, 2003), 138–51; Helena Ruiz Gil and Francisco Mo-

rales Padrón, *Piratería en el Caribe* (Sevilla: Renacimiento, 2005), 69–101; Jean-Pierre Moreau, *Pirates: flibuste et piraterie dans la Caraïbe et les mers du Sud, 1522–1725* (Paris: Tallandier, 2006), 82–98; Stephen Snelders, *Het grijnzend doodhoofd: Nederlandse piraten in de Gouden Eeuw* (Amsterdam: Aksant, 2006), 57–60; Jon Latimer, *The Buccaneers of the Caribbean: How Piracy Forged an Empire* (Cambridge, Mass.: Harvard University Press, 2009), 132–81; Jean-Jacques Seymour, *Les chemins des proies: une histoire de la flibuste* (Matoury: Isis Rouge Editions, 2010), 90–114; Alessandro López Pérez and Mónica Pavía Pérez, *Malhechores de la mar: Corsarios, piratas, negreros, ragueros y contrabandistas* (La Habana: Ediciones Boloña, 2015), 145–48.

10. Linda A. Newson, *The Cost of Conquest: Indian Decline in Honduras under Spanish Rule* (Boulder, Col.: Westview, 1986), 286–96; W. George Lovell and Christopher H. Lutz, *Demography and Empire: A Guide to the Population History of Spanish Central America, 1500–1821* (Boulder, Col.: Westview, 1995), 123–25.

11. Alfredo Castillero Calvo, *Conquista, evangelización, y resistencia: Triunfo o fracaso de la política indigenista?* (Panamá: Editorial Mariano Arosemena, 1995), 37–53; Eric Roulet, *L'évangélisation des Indiens du Mexique: impact et réalité de la conquête spirituelle au XVIe siècle* (Rennes: Presses universitaires de Rennes, 2008), 59–107; Juan Carlos Solórzano Fonseca, *Los indígenas en la frontera de la colonización: Costa Rica, 1502–1930* (San José: Editorial Universidad Estatal a Distancia, 2013), 95–116.

12. Patrick S. Werner, *Los reales de minas de la Nicaragua colonial y la ciudad perdida de Nueva Segovia* (Managua: Instituto Nicaragüense de Cultura, 1996), 42–58.

13. For an overview of the "New Conquest History" with further references, see, above all, Matthew Restall and Felipe Fernández-Armesto, *The Conquistadors: A Very Short History* (Oxford: Oxford University Press, 2012), 28–36; Vitus Huber, *Die Konquistadoren: Cortés, Pizarro und die Eroberung Amerikas* (München: C. H. Beck, 2019), 45–51.

14. Throughout the early modern period, the term "adventurer" was defined as someone who was willing to take risks outside established society for personal gain. See John A. Simpson and Edmund S. Weiner, *The Oxford English Dictionary* (Oxford: Oxford University Press, 1989), 1:187.

15. Barbara Potthast, *Die Mosquitoküste im Spannungsfeld britischer und spanischer Politik, 1502–1821* (Köln: Böhlau Verlag, 1988), 18–29; Robert A. Naylor, *Penny Ante Imperialism: The Mosquito Shore and the Bay of Honduras, 1600–1914* (Cranbury, N.J.: Fairleigh Dickinson University Press, 1989), 19–45.

16. The frontier is defined as the extreme limit of land where a colonial power exercised at least some authority. For conditions in Central America, see, for example, Bernd Schröter, "La frontera en hispanoamérica colonial: Un estudio historiográfico comparativo," *Colonial Latin American Historical Review* 10 (2001): 351–85.

17. Manuel Trigo Chacón, "La navegación por la mer océana y el Tratado de Tordesillas," *Revista de Historia Naval* 27 (2009): 7–21. One league is three nautical miles.

18. Paul Butel, *Les Caraïbes au temps des flibustiers* (Paris: Aubier Montaigne, 1982), 37–71; Peter R. Galvin, *Patterns of Pillage: A Geography of Caribbean-based Piracy in Spanish America, 1536–1718* (New York: Peter Lang, 1999), 33–47.

19. TNA, High Court of Admiralty 49/59, fol. 92, commission for George Brimacain, 18 September 1662. This was presumably a standardized text at that stage. A copy of a French version survives in BnF, Mélanges de Colbert 31, fols. 634–35, commission for William Griffin, 18 September 1668. Griffin was an Irishman who preyed on the English. For a French example directed against Spanish and Dutch holdings, see TNA, Colonial Office 1/38, fol. 120, commission for John Bennet, 3 April 1675. The term "corsair" emerged in the medieval Mediterranean and was later widely used in all Romance languages. For the meaning of the terminology, see, above all, N. A. M. Rodger, "The Law and Language of Private Naval Warfare," *Mariner's Mirror* 100 (2014): 5–16; John Coakley, "'The Piracies of Some Little Privateers': Language, Law, and Maritime Violence in the Seventeenth-Century Caribbean," *Britain and the World* 13 (2020): 9–26.

20. Angela Pérez Mejía, "Fronteras de la legalidad: Bucaneros en el siglo XVII," *Historia y Sociedad* 8 (2002): 179–98; Lauren Benton, "Legal Spaces of Empire: Piracy and the Origins of Ocean Regionalism," *Comparative Studies in Society and History* 47 (2005): 706–13.

21. This description derives from various sources, particularly AN, Marine 3JJ 282, no. 10, memorandum of Philippe Bequel and Moïse Vauquelin, ca. 1670; AGI, México 560, ramo 1, no. 1, declaration of Samuel Johns, 5 June 1684. See also Emma Martinell Gifre, *La comunicación entre Españoles e Indios: Palabras y gestos* (Madrid: Mapfre, 1992), 123–41; Céline Carayon, *Eloquence Embodied: Nonverbal Communication among French and Indigenous Peoples in the Americas* (Chapel Hill: University of North Carolina Press, 2019), 94–104. Studies of gift exchange involving Native Americans in the seventeenth century include Gilles Havard, *La grande paix de Montréal de 1701: les voies de la diplomatie franco-amérindienne* (Montréal: Recherches amérindiennes au Québec, 1992), 13–25; David Murray, *Indian Giving: Economies of Power in Indian-White Exchanges* (Amherst: University of Massachusetts Press, 2000), 15–47; Arnaud Balvay, *L'épée et la plume: Amérindiens et soldats des troupes de la marine au Louisiane et au Pays d'en haut, 1683–1763* (Québec: Presses de l'Université Laval, 2006), 136–47; Joseph M. Hall Jr., *Zamuno's Gifts: Indian-European Exchange in the Colonial Southeast* (Philadelphia: University of Pennsylvania Press, 2009), 55–94.

22. Neal Salisbury, "The Indians' Old World: Native Americans and the Coming of Europeans," *William and Mary Quarterly* 53 (1996): 449–54; Laurier Turgeon, *Une histoire de la Nouvelle-France: Français et Amérindiens au XVIe siècle* (Paris: Belin, 2019), 114–20.

23. Christopher L. Miller and George R. Hamell, "A New Perspective on Indian-White Contact: Cultural Symbols and Colonial Trade," *Journal of American History* 73 (1984): 311–28.

24. Antônio Geraldo da Cunha, *Dicionário histórico das palavras portuguesas de origem tupi* (São Paulo: Melhoramenros, 1989), 212–13.

25. Jean de Léry, *Histoire d'un voyage fait en la terre du Bresil* (La Rochelle: Antoine Chuppin, 1578), 152–54; Guillaume Coppier, *Histoire et voyage des Indes occidentales* (Lyon: Huguetan, 1645), 65.

26. Jean de Laon, *Relation du voyage des François fait au cap de Nord en Amérique* (Paris: Edme Pepingué, 1654), 156–57.

27. Edmund Hickeringill, *Jamaica Viewed* (London: John Williams, 1661), 33–34. For the French use of these terms, see, for example, Georges Guillet, *Les arts de l'homme d'épée, ou le dictionnaire du gentilhomme* (Paris: Gervais Clouzer, 1678), 167. At the turn of the century, *boucanne* was a common term for smoked meat. See Gautier de Tronchoy, *Journal de la campagne des isles de l'Amérique* (Paris: Troyes, 1709), 175. The term *flibustier* probably derives from the Dutch word *vrijbuiter* for "freebooter."

28. Alexandre-Olivier Exquemelin, *Histoire des avanturiers qui se sont signalez dans les Indes* (Paris: Jacques Le Febvre, 1686), 1:151–52; William Dampier, *Voyages and Descriptions* (London: James Knapton, 1699), 94–95.

29. Most English-speaking historians working in this field have been influenced by Richard White, *The Middle Ground: Indians, Empires, and Republics in the Great Lakes Region, 1650–1815* (Cambridge: Cambridge University Press, 1991). Other studies and approaches include Denys Delâge, *Le pays renversé: Amérindiens et Européens en Amérique du nord-est* (Montréal: Boréal, 1985), 104–52; Urs Bitterli, *Alte Welt, neue Welt: Formen des europäisch-überseeischen Kulturkontakts vom 15. bis zum 18. Jahrhundert* (München: DTV, 1986), 101–15; Gilles Havard, *Empire et métissages: Indiens et Français dans le Pays d'en haut, 1660–1775* (Sillery, Que.: Septentrion, 2003), 515–61; Cynthia J. van Zandt, *Brothers among Nations: The Pursuit of Intercultural Alliances in Early America, 1580–1660* (Oxford: Oxford University Press, 2008), 86–136. For an example of native groups that, in the course of conflicts with colonizers, turned to the sea, see Andrew Lipman, *The Saltwater Frontier: Indians and the Contest for the American Coast* (New Haven, Conn.: Yale University Press, 2015), 125–64.

30. Antoine Biet, *Voyage de la France equinoxiale en l'isle de Cayenne* (Paris: François Clouzier, 1664), 334; Alexandre-Olivier Exquemelin, *De Americaensche Zee-Roovers* (Amsterdam: Jan ten Hoorn, 1678), 27.

31. Charles de Rochefort, *Histoire naturelle et morale des iles Antilles de l'Amérique* (Rotterdam: Arnold Leers, 1658), 450–53; Raymond Breton, *Dictionnaire Caraïbe-Français* (Auxerre: Gilles Bouquet, 1665), 331; Jean-Baptiste du Tertre, *Histoire générale des Antilles habitée par les François* (Paris: Thomas Jolly, 1667), 2:397–99.

32. Brian Dyde, *A History of Antigua: The Unsuspected Isle* (London: Macmillan Caribbean, 2000), 20–29. The French word *pirogue* derived from the Spanish term *piragua*, which in turn came from a Carib language. *Pirogue* entered English by the mid-seventeenth century.

33. Philip P. Boucher, *Cannibal Encounters: Europeans and the Island Caribs, 1492–*

1763 (Baltimore: Johns Hopkins University Press, 1992), 39–53; Roberto Cassá, *Los indios de las Antillas* (Madrid: Mapfre, 1992), 259–81.

34. Gérard Lafleur, *Les Caraïbes des Petites Antilles* (Paris: Karthala, 1992), 77–84; Hilary McD. Beckles, "Kalinago (Carib) Resistance to European Colonisation of the Caribbean," *Caribbean Quarterly* 38 (1992): 6–11.

35. A notable exception is Guyana, where rival claims by Spain, the Netherlands, and France provided native groups with an opportunity to profit from European conflicts. See Neil L. Whitehead, *Lords of the Tiger Spirit: A History of the Caribs in Colonial Venezuela and Guyana, 1498–1820* (Dordrecht: Foris, 1988), 91–103; Simone Dreyfus, "Les réseaux politiques indigènes en Guyane occidentale et leurs transformations aux XVIIᵉ et XVIIIᵉ siècles," *L'Homme* 122–24 (1992): 78–85.

36. María del Pilar Bernal Ruiz, *La toma del puerto de Guayaquil en 1687* (Sevilla: Escuela de Estudios Hispano-Americanos, 1979), 73–86.

CHAPTER I. THE RISE OF THE BUCCANEERS

1. Timothy R. Walton, *The Spanish Treasure Fleets* (Sarasota, Fla.: Pineapple Press, 1994), 37–77; Carlos Canales and Miguel del Rey, *El oro de América: Galeones, flotas y piratas* (Madrid: Editorial Edaf, 2016), 97–105. For the institutional development, see José Cervera Pery, *La Casa de Contratación y el Consejo de Indias: Las razones de un superministerio* (Madrid: Ministeriode Defensa, 1997), 23–63. Beginning in 1680, vessels were also allowed to call at Cádiz.

2. Michel Le Bris, *D'or, de rêves et de sang: l'épopée de la flibuste, 1494–1588* (Paris: Hachette, 2001), 23–28; Leopoldo Daniel López Zea, *Piratas del Caribe y Mar del Sur en el siglo XVI* (México: Universidad Nacional Autónoma de México, 2003), 25–30. For this early treasure shipment, see, above all, Matthew Restall, *When Montezuma Met Cortés* (New York: Ecco, 2018), 127–28; Vitus Huber, *Beute und Conquista: Die politische Ökonomie der Eroberung Neuspaniens* (Frankfurt a.M.: Campus Verlag, 2018), 282–85. One of Cortés's officers in charge of the treasure, Alonso de Ávila, was also seized and held captive in La Rochelle until 1525, when he was ransomed by the Spaniards.

3. Kris E. Lane, *Pillaging the Empire: Piracy in the Americas, 1500–1750* (New York: M. E. Sharpe, 1998), 20–21; Luis Britto García, *Señores del Caribe: Indígenas, conquistadores y piratas en el mar colonial* (Caracas: Fundación Traditiones Caraqueñas, 2001), 32–36. For the topography of the early raiding voyages, see Rodrigo Alejandro de la O Torres, "La presencia de corsarios franceses en el Golfo-Caribe entre 1536 y 1566," *Historia* 6 (2016): 36–55.

4. Paul E. Hoffman, *The Spanish Crown and the Defense of the Caribbean, 1535–1585: Precedent, Patrimonialism, and Royal Parsimony* (Baton Rouge: Louisiana State University Press, 1980), 213–36.

5. Martha de Jármy Chapa, *Un eslabón perdido en la historia: Piratería en el Caribe, siglos XVI y XVII* (México: Universidad Nacional Autónoma de México, 1983), 55–

76; Peter R. Galvin, *Patterns of Pillage: A Geography of Caribbean-based Piracy in Spanish America, 1536–1718* (New York: Peter Lang, 1999), 33–47; Helena Ruiz Gil and Francisco Morales Padrón, *Piratería en el Caribe* (Sevilla: Renamiciento, 2005), 27–91.

6. Carl E. Swanson, "Privateering in Early America," *International Journal of Maritime History* 1 (1989): 265–67; Jean Merrien, *Histoire des corsaires* (Saint-Malo: Editions l'Ancre de marine, 1992), 9–16; Marjolein 't Hart, "Kaapvaart en staatsmacht: Dilemma's van de geprivatiseerde oorlogvoering op zee," *De Seventiende Eeuw* 13 (1997): 425–37; Alain Berbouche, *Pirates, flibustiers et corsaires: le droit et les réalités de la guerre de Course* (Saint-Malo: Pascal Galodé, 2010), 37–53.

7. Gary M. Anderson and Adam Gifford Jr., "Privateering and the Private Production of Naval Power," *Cato Journal* 11 (1991): 99–110; Óscar Cruz Barney, "En torno al concepto, marco jurídico y vigencia del corso español en Indias," *Revista de Historia Naval* 14 (1996): 35–43; Joke E. Korteweg, *Kaperbloed en koopmansgeest: Legale zeeroof door de eeuwen heen* (Amsterdam: Balans Uitgeverij, 2006), 50–83; Bryan Mabee, "Pirates, Privateers, and the Political Economy of Pirate Violence," *Global Change, Peace & Security* 21 (2009): 144–51; Óscar Cruz Barney, "Sobre el régimen jurídico del corso marítimo en Francia: La *Ordennance de la Marine* de 1681," *Revista de Historia Naval* 27 (2009): 101–27.

8. Lauren Benton, "Towards a New Legal History of Piracy: Maritime Legalities and the Myth of Universal Jurisdiction," *International Journal of Maritime History* 23 (2011): 225–33.

9. Anthony Pagden, *Lords of all the World: Ideologies of Empire in Spain, Britain, and France, c. 1500–1800* (New Haven, Conn.: Yale University Press, 1995), 91–102; Manuel Lucena Salmoral, *Rivalidad colonial y equilibrio europeo, siglos XVII–XVIII* (Madrid: Editorial Síntesis, 1999), 45–74.

10. Armel de Wismes, *Pirates et corsaires* (Paris: Editions France-Empire, 1999), 83–93; Patrick Villiers, *Les corsaires du Littoral: Dunkerque, Calais, Boulogne de Philippe II à Louis XIV* (Lille: Presses universitaires de Septentrion, 2000), 20–38; Pierre Rectoran, *Corsaires basques et bayonnais du XVe au XIXe siècle: pirates, flibustiers, boucaniers* (Pau: Cairn, 2004), 251–62; Michel Lécureur, *Corsaires et pirates de Normandie* (Paris: Magellan et Cie, 2011), 57–91.

11. Barbara Fuchs, "Faithless Empires: Pirates, Renegadoes, and the English Nation," *English Literary History* 67 (2000): 45.

12. The literature on the English incursions is vast. For recent examples, see Harry Kelsey, *Sir Francis Drake: The Queen's Pirate* (New Haven, Conn.: Yale University Press, 1998), 11–89; David Loades, *England's Maritime Empire: Seapower, Commerce, and Policy, 1490–1690* (Harlow: Longman, 2000), 79–103; James McDermott, *Martin Frobisher: Elizabethan Privateer* (New Haven, Conn.: Yale University Press, 2001), 294–331; Stephen Coote, *Drake: The Life and Legend of an Elizabethan Hero* (New York: Simon & Schuster, 2003), 125–90; Harry Kelsey, *Sir John Hawkins: Queen Elizabeth's Slave Trader* (New Haven, Conn.: Yale University Press, 2003), 21–93; Susan Ronald, *The Pirate Queen: Queen Elizabeth I, Her Pirate Adventurers, and the Dawn of*

Empire (New York: Harper, 2007), 38–125; Peter C. Mancall, *Hakluyt's Promise: An Elizabethan's Obsession for an English America* (New Haven, Conn.: Yale University Press, 2007), 72–101; Hugh Bicheno, *Elizabeth's Sea Dogs: How the English Became the Scourge of the Seas* (London: Conway, 2012), 103–35. For the sailors' origins, see Cheryl A. Fury, *Tides in the Affairs of Men: The Social History of Elizabethan Seamen, 1580–1603* (Westport, Conn.: Greenwood Press, 2002), 1–34.

13. Jurrien van Goor, *De Nederlandse koloniën: Geschiedenis van de Nederlandse expansie, 1600–1675* (Den Haag: SDU Uitgeverij, 1993), 37–45; Henk den Heijer, *De geschiedenis van de WIC* (Zutphen: Walburg Pers, 1994), 55–65.

14. Virginia W. Lunsford, *Piracy and Privateering in the Golden Age Netherlands* (New York: Palgrave Macmillan, 2005), 9–34.

15. The extent of Spain's decline has long been a matter of controversy among historians. For a balanced perspective with further references, see, above all, Alain Hugon, *Philippe IV: le siècle de Vélasquez* (Paris: Payot, 2014), 157–212.

16. Francisco M. Mota, *Piratas y corsarios en las costas de Cuba* (La Habana: Gente Nueva, 1997), 91–98; Ronald Prud'homme van Reine, *Admiraal Zilvervloot: Biografie van Piet Hein* (Amsterdam: De Arbeiderspers, 2003), 105–38; César García del Pino, *El corso en Cuba, siglo XVII: Causas y consecuencias* (La Habana: Editorial Unión, 2007), 85–89; Graddy Boven, *Piet Hein: De held van Matanzas* (Soesterberg: Aspekt, 2010), 86–114.

17. Carla Rahn Phillips, *Six Galleons for the King of Spain: Imperial Defense in the Early Seventeenth Century* (Baltimore: Johns Hopkins University Press, 1986), 181–89; Fernando Serrano Mangas, *Armadas y flotas de la plata, 1620–1648* (Madrid: Banco de España, 1989), 256–58.

18. Frank Peña Pérez, *Antonio Osorio: Monopolio, contrabando y despoblación* (Santiago: Universidad Católica Madre y Maestra, 1980), 93–111; Arturo Morales Carrión, *Puerto Rico y el lucha por la hegemonía en el Caribe: Colonialismo y contrabando* (San Juan: Universidad de Puerto Rico, 1995), 59–74; Carlos Esteban Deive, *Tangomangos: Contrabando y piratería en Santo Domingo, 1522–1606* (Santo Domingo: Fundación Cultural Dominicana, 1996), 93–181.

19. Juan José Ponce Vázquez, *Islanders and Empire: Smuggling and Political Defiance in Hispaniola, 1580–1690* (Cambridge: Cambridge University Press, 2020), 106–33.

20. Michel-Christian Camus, "Aux origines de la colonisation française de Saint-Domingue," *Revue de la Société haïtienne d'histoire et de géographie* 45 (1987): 62–67; Jean-Pierre Moreau, *Pirates: flibuste et piraterie dans la Caraïbe et les mers du Sud, 1522–1725* (Paris: Tallandier, 2006), 51–65.

21. Trevor Burnard, "'This Countrie Continues Sicklie': White Mortality in Jamaica, 1655–1780," *Social History of Medicine* 12 (1999): 43–72; Matthew Mulcahy, *Hurricanes and Society in the British Greater Caribbean, 1624–1783* (Baltimore: Johns Hopkins University Press, 2006), 10–20.

22. Jean-Pierre Moreau, *Les Petites Antilles de Christophe Colomb à Richelieu, 1492–1635* (Paris: Karthala, 1992), 185–211; Frank Moya Pons, *History of the Caribbean: Plan-*

tations, Trade, and War in the Atlantic World (Princeton, N.J.: Princeton University Press, 2007), 44–55; Consuelo Naranjo Orovio, *Historia mínima de las Antillas hispanas y británicas* (México: Colegio de México, 2014), 56–62.

23. Michel Carmona, *La France de Richelieu* (Paris: Fayard, 1984), 177–93; Simon Groenveld and Huib L.Ph. Leeuwenberg, *De bruid in de schuit: De consolidatie van de Republiek, 1609–1650* (Zutphen: Walburg Pers, 1985), 58–64; Geoffrey V. Scammell, *The First Imperial Age: European Overseas Expansion, c. 1400–1715* (Cambridge: Routledge, 1989), 30–44; Pierre Castagnos, *Richelieu face à la mer* (Rennes: Editions Ouest-France, 1989), 72–77; Claudia Schnurmann, *Atlantische Welten: Engländer und Niederländer im amerikanisch-atlantischen Raum, 1648–1713* (Köln: Böhlau Verlag, 1998), 161–99; Maarten Prak, *Gouden Eeuw: Het raadsel van de Republiek* (Nijmegen: Sun, 2002), 125–36; Christian Bouyer, *Au temps des isles: les Antilles françaises de Louis XIII à Napoléon III* (Paris: Tallandier, 2005), 28–36; Wim Klooster, *The Dutch Moment: War, Trade, and Settlement in the Seventeenth-Century Atlantic World* (Ithaca, N.Y.: Cornell University Press, 2017), 34–46; Eric Roulet, *La Compagnie des îles de l'Amérique, 1635–1651: une entreprise coloniale au XVIIᵉ siècle* (Rennes: Presses universitaires de Rennes, 2017), 74–99.

24. Karen Ordahl Kupperman, *Providence Island, 1630–1641: The Other Puritan Colony* (Cambridge: Cambridge University Press, 1993), 93–110; Gérard Lafleur, "Saint-Eustache aux XVIIᵉ et XVIIIᵉ siècles," *Bulletin de la Société d'histoire de la Guadeloupe* 38 (2001): 28–33; Pablo Montero, *Imperios y piratas* (México: Editorial Porrúa, 2003), 211–28.

25. Jean-Pierre Moreau, *Un flibustier français dans la mer des Antilles en 1618–1620* (Paris: Clamart, 1987), 206–17.

26. Manuel Arturo Peña Batlle, *La Isla de la Tortuga: Plaza de armas, refugio y seminario de los enemigos de España en Indias* (Santo Domingo: Editorial Taller, 1988), 135–58; Michel-Christian Camus, "L'île de la Tortue et la flibuste," *Revue de la Société haïtienne d'histoire et de géographie* 48 (1992): 2–3.

27. Michel-Christian Camus, *L'île de la Tortue au cœur de la flibuste caraïbe* (Paris: L'Harmattan, 1997), 33–61; Casey Schmitt, "Pirates, Planting, and the Rights of Mankind in Seventeenth-Century Tortuga," *Latin Americanist* 61 (2017): 84–94. In the following years French colonization increasingly focused on the uninhabited north and west coasts of Hispaniola.

28. Rafael Cartay Angulo, *Ideología, desarrollo e interferencias del comercio caribeño durante el siglo XVII* (Caracas: Academie Nacional de la Historia, 1988), 167–91; Nuala Zahedieh, "'A Frugal, Prudential, and Hopeful Trade': Privateering in Jamaica, 1655–1689," *Journal of Imperial and Commonwealth History* 18 (1990): 157–62; Patrick Villiers and Jean-Pierre Duteil, *L'Europe, la mer et les colonies, XVIIᵉ-XVIIIᵉ siècle* (Paris: Hachette, 1997), 58–65; Milton Zambrano Pérez, "Piratas, piratería y comercio ilícito en el Caribe: La visión del otro, 1550–1650," *Historia Caribe* 12 (2007): 48–56; Erik Gøbel, *Vestindisk-guineisk Kompagni, 1671–1754: Studier og kilder til kompagniet og kolonierne* (Odense: Odense Universitetsforlag, 2015), 17–20. Danes first landed in

Saint Thomas in 1665 or 1666, but it was not until 1672 that the Vestindisk-guineisk Kompagni occupied the island, which quickly became a center of illicit trade.

29. Timothy Venning, *Cromwellian Foreign Policy* (London: Palgrave Macmillan, 1993), 71–90; David L. Smith, "The Western Design and the Spiritual Geopolitics of Cromwellian Foreign Policy," *Itinerario* 40 (2016): 279–83.

30. Carla Gardina Pestana, "English Character and the Fiasco of the Western Design," *Early American Studies* 3 (2005): 6–31; Nicole Greenspan, *Selling Cromwell's Wars: Media, Empire, and Godly Warfare, 1650–1658* (London: Taylor & Francis, 2012), 69–98; Carla Gardina Pestana, *The English Conquest of Jamaica: Oliver Cromwell's Bid for Empire* (Cambridge, Mass.: Harvard University Press, 2017), 65–138.

31. For the English struggles after the conquest see Carla Gardina Pestana, "State Formation from the Vantage of Early English Jamaica: The Neglect of Edward Doyley," *Journal of British Studies* 56 (2017): 493–99; Casey Schmitt, "Centering Spanish Jamaica: Regional Competition, Informal Trade, and the English Invasion, 1620–1662," *William and Mary Quarterly* 76 (2019): 719–24.

32. Trevor Burnard, "A Failed Settler Society: Marriage and Demographic Failure in Early Jamaica," *Journal of Social History* 28 (1994): 65–72; Trevor Burnard, "European Migration to Jamaica, 1655–1780," *William and Mary Quarterly* 53 (1996): 769–72.

33. Carla Gardina Pestana, "Early English Jamaica without Pirates," *William and Mary Quarterly* 71 (2014): 330–32.

34. Jon Latimer, *The Buccaneers of the Caribbean: How Piracy Forged an Empire* (Cambridge, Mass.: Harvard University Press, 2009), 132–43.

35. BL, Add. Ms. 11410, fol. 8, "An Accompt of the Inhabitants on the Island," 28 October 1662; TNA, Colonial Office 1/25, fol. 5, Charles Modyford to Earl of Arlington, 22 January 1670. Spanish intelligence estimated the number of raiders at two thousand. See AGI, Santo Domingo 136, ramo 2, no. 58, report of Cristóbal Arnaldo de Issasi, 6 November 1662.

36. Rafael Abella, *Los piratas del Nuevo Mundo* (Barcelona: Planeta, 1989), 68–76; Patrick Villiers, *Marine royale, corsaires et trafic dans l'Atlantique de Louis XIV à Louis XVI* (Dunkerque: Société Dunkerquoise, 1991), 182–85; Manuel Lucena Salmoral, *Piratas, bucaneros, filibusteros y corsarios en América: Perros, mendigos y otros malditos del mar* (Madrid: Mapfre, 1992), 150–56; Seán O'Callaghan, *To Hell or Barbados* (Dingle: Brandon, 2000), 171–87; Anna Spinelli, *Tra l'inferno e il mare: Breve storia economica e sociale della pirateria* (Ravenna: Fernandel, 2003), 139–43; Philippe Hrodĕj, "Les premiers colons de l'ancienne Haïti et leurs attaches en métropole à l'aube de premiers établissements, 1650–1700," *Les Cahiers de Framespa* 9 (2012).

37. Hilary McD. Beckles, "From Land to Sea: Runaway Barbados Slaves and Servants, 1630–1700," *Slavery and Abolition* 6 (1985): 82–83; Alain-Philippe Blérald, *Histoire économique de la Guadeloupe et de la Martinique* (Paris: Karthala, 1986): 24–29; Hilary McD. Beckles and Andrew Downes, "The Economic Transition to the Black Labor System in Barbados," *Journal of Interdisciplinary History* 18 (1987): 225–47.

38. Gérard Lafleur, "Les protestants aux Antilles françaises du Vent sous l'Ancien Régime," *Bulletin de la Société d'histoire de la Guadeloupe* 71–74 (1987), 37–51; Carla Gardina Pestana, *Protestant Empire: Religion and the Making of the British Atlantic World* (Philadelphia: University of Pennsylvania Press, 2009), 66–99.

39. Ricardo García Cárcel, *La leyenda negra: Historia y opinión* (Madrid: Alianza Editorial, 1992), 21–89; Gijs Versteegen, "Bewondering, verwondering en verachting: De beeldvorming omtrent Spanje en de Zwarte Legendes," *Theoretische Geschiedenis* 24 (1997): 270–72; E. Shaskan Bumas, "The Cannibal Butcher Shop: Protestant Uses of las Casas's *Brevísima relación* in Europe and the American Colonies," *Early American Literature* 35 (2000): 107–36; Benjamin Schmidt, *Innocence Abroad: The Dutch Imagination and the New World, 1570–1670* (Cambridge: Cambridge University Press, 2001), 90–99; José Antonio Vaca de Osma, *El Imperio y la leyenda negra* (Madrid: Ediciones Rialp, 2004), 147–81.

40. Nuala Zahedieh, "Trade, Plunder, and Economic Development in Early English Jamaica, 1655–1689," *Economic History Review* 39 (1986): 215–22; Alan D. Myers, "Ethnic Distinctions and Wealth among Colonial Jamaican Merchants, 1685–1716," *Social Science History* 22 (1998): 50–54. For a different development with a similar result in Saint-Domingue, see Karsten Voss, *Sklaven als Ware und Kapital: Die Plantagenökonomie von Saint-Domingue als Entwicklungsprojekt, 1697–1715* (München: C. H. Beck, 2015), 157–97.

41. Michael Pawson and David Buisseret, *Port Royal, Jamaica* (Kingston: University of the West Indies Press, 2000), 38–44, 135; Mark G. Hanna, *Pirate Nests and the Rise of the British Empire, 1570–1740* (Chapel Hill: University of North Carolina Press, 2015), 125–26.

42. AGI, Indiferente General 1600, no. 181, articles of agreement of Henry Morgan, 8 January 1669. Only few documents providing information about the exact arrangements among the participants of privateering expeditions survive. This copy belonged to George Reeves whose vessel was seized by the Spaniards off Campeche in August 1670.

CHAPTER 2. MAYAS BESIEGED

1. Nancy Farriss, *Maya Society under Colonial Rule: The Collective Enterprise of Survival* (Princeton, N.J.: Princeton University Press, 1984), 29–103; Isabel Fernández Tejedo, *La comunidad indígena maya de Yucatán, siglos XVI y XVII* (México: Instituto Nacional de Antropología y Historia, 1990), 91–127; Robert W. Patch, *Maya and Spaniard in Yucatan, 1648–1812* (Stanford, Cal.: Stanford University Press, 1993), 21–38; Pedro Bracamonte y Sosa and Gabriela Solís Robleda, *Espacios Mayas de autonomía: El pacto colonial en Yucatán* (Mérida: Universidad Autónoma de Yucatán, 1996), 66–76.

2. María Eugenia Romero, "La navegación maya," *Arqueología Mexicana* 33 (1998): 6–15; Heather McKillop, "Ancient Maya Canoe Navigation and its Implications for

Classic to Postclassic Maya Economy and Sea Trade," *Journal of Caribbean Archaeology* 9 (2010): 93–105.

3. Isaac García Venegas, *Puerto, ladrones de los mares y muralla: Una propuesta de interpretación de la villa de San Francisco de Campeche en el siglo XVII* (Campeche: Instituto de Cultura de Campeche, 2001), 60–93; Manuela Cristina García Bernal, *Campeche y el comercio atlántico yucateco, 1561–1625* (Campeche: Universidad Autónoma de Campeche, 2006), 20–51.

4. Luis A. Ramírez Aznar, *De piratas y corsarios: La piratería en la península de Yucatán* (Mérida: Universidad Autónoma de Yucatán, 2001), 55–69; Jorge Victoria Ojeda, *Piratas en Yucatán* (Mérida: Editorial Área Maya, 2007), 29–36.

5. AGI, México 184, no. 41, testimony of Gregorio Díaz Leandro, 5 September 1633; AGI, México 360, ramo 2, no. 8, Jerónimo de Quero to Crown, 16 August 1634. A detailed account of an unknown eyewitness who had participated in the fighting survives in AGN, Inquisición 1503, fols. 1–2. For the Dutch perspective, see Joannes de Laet, *Historie ofte iaerlijck verhael van de verrichtinghen der geoctroyeerde West-Indische Compagnie* (Leiden: Abraham Elsevier, 1644), 355–57. After the raid most ships sailed back to the Netherlands, but three vessels commanded by Cornelis Jol remained in the Caribbean and continued to assault Spanish targets. See Cornelis C. Goslinga, *The Dutch in the Caribbean and on the Wild Coast, 1580–1680* (Gainesville: University of Florida Press, 2017), 229–39.

6. Diego de los Reyes had been master of a turtling barque that was seized by Dutch freebooters off Cuba in April 1632. After a spell in the Netherlands, he returned to the Caribbean and spent years raiding Spanish vessels. For his remarkable career, see, above all, Jean-Pierre Moreau, *Pirates: flibuste et piraterie dans la Caraïbe et les mers du Sud, 1522–1725* (Paris: Tallandier, 2006), 67–72.

7. AGI, México 360, ramo 5, no. 17, declarations of Michael Faulkner and Pedro del Castillo, 25 and 30 June 1636.

8. John F. Chuchiak IV, "*Cuius Regio Eius Religio*: Yucatec Maya Nativistic Movements and the Religious Roots of Rebellion in Colonial Yucatán, 1547–1697," *Ketzalcalli* 1 (2004): 44–59.

9. AGI, México 360, ramo 5, no. 22, Diego Zapata de Cárdenas to Crown, 10 July 1638. The governor reported that the raiders turned the church door into firewood. This reference illustrates that certain Spanish officials were more concerned with the looting and desecration of local churches than with the plight of the native victims of foreign assaults.

10. Gemeentearchief Amsterdam, Notariële archieven 5075/1280, no. 128, declaration of Jean Seguinard, Pierre Gougeon, Frans Jacobsen, et al., 8 September 1639.

11. Grant D. Jones, *Maya Resistance to Spanish Rule: Time and History on a Colonial Frontier* (Albuquerque: University of New Mexico Press, 1989), 204–29.

12. AGN, Reales Cédulas (Originales) 2, exp. 23, fol. 40, real cédula, 1 October 1643. Royal decrees sometimes contain information sent to the Crown that does not survive elsewhere in the colonial correspondence.

13. AGI, Guatemala 16, ramo 3, no. 19, Diego de Avendaño to Crown, 7 July 1642; AGI, México 360, ramo 5, no. 33, Diego Zapata de Cárdenas to Crown, 7 February 1643; AGI, Guatemala 17, ramo 1, no. 4, Diego de Avendaño to Crown, 26 October 1647.

14. Archives départementales de la Charente-Maritime, La Rochelle, Amirauté B5656, fols. 149–59, declarations of Henri Pinneau, Benjamin Bernon de Lileau, Mathurin Martin, et al., 24 and 25 December 1641; AGI, Guatemala 44A, no. 39, Francisco Mejias y Tebas, Andrés Rodríguez Zuñiga, Miguel de Atorruca, et al. to Crown, 6 February 1643. In 1642 and 1650, Spanish forces deported the natives of Roatán to mainland Honduras and Guatemala. See AGI, Guatemala 39, ramo 23, no. 135, Juan de Luaza y Otalora to Crown, 5 September 1650. For the situation in early Dutch Curaçao, see Biblioteca Nacional, Madrid, Ms. 11146, fols. 207–12, Pedro Porter y Casanate, "Relacion de la isla Curacao, i de los Piratas de las Indias," 1642.

15. BL, Sloane Ms. 793, fols. 24–25, journal of William Jackson, 11 August 1644; AGI, México 35, no. 33, Pelayo Álvarez to Antonio de la Plaza Eguilaz, 23 August 1644. In early November 1644 Jackson arrived in Bermuda, where he sold "dyvers Indians & Nigroes," but their origin remains obscure. See Bermuda Archives, Hamilton, Bermuda Colonial Records 2, fol. 53, Bermuda council minutes, 18 and 20 January 1645.

16. AGCA, A1 (Honduras), leg. 382, exp. 3482, fol. 15, memorandum of Benito Gallardo, 1648; AGI, Guatemala 17, ramo 1, no. 13, Diego de Avendaño to Crown, 18 and 24 February 1649; Diego López de Cogolludo, *Historia de Yucathan* (Madrid: Juan García Infanzon, 1688), 714–17. Chunhuhub remained home for Bacalar's inhabitants for almost a century.

17. AGI, Patronato 273, ramo 7, fols. 233–35, Jerónimo de Alzate to Crown, 13 March 1654. The Spanish records do not seem to contain any previous references to this assault. In Tortuga were also enslaved Africans who had been seized from Portuguese vessels.

18. BL, Add. Ms. 13992, fols. 533–42, Juan Francisco de Montemayor Córdoba y Cuenca to Luis Melchor Ponce de León, 30 March 1654; AGI, Patronato 273, ramo 7, fol. 203, Juan Francisco de Montemayor Córdoba y Cuenca to Crown, 11 April 1654.

19. AGI, México 360, ramo 11, no. 58, Francisco de Bazán to Crown, 15 July 1658.

20. AGI, Guatemala 22, ramo 1, no. 11, confession of Nicolás Covoh, 9 October 1668. The fishermen were probably captured by an Anglo-French gang that was active in the region between May and October 1661. See AGI, México 1006, fols. 71–76, José Campero de Sorredevilla to Crown, 20 May 1662.

21. David F. Marley, *Pirates of the Americas* (Santa Barbara, Cal.: ABC-Clio, 2010), 1:275–81.

22. British Museum, London, Anthropology Library, Am 2006, Drg. 210, fols. 17–23, Antonio Maldonado de Aldana to Francisco Calderón y Romero, 11 March 1663; TNA, State Papers 94/45, fols. 43–44, Henry Rumbold to Henry Bennet, 4 May 1663; AGI, México 1006, fols. 294–96, José Campero y Sorredevilla to Juan Fran-

cisco de Leyva y de la Cerda, 10 June 1663; AN, Marine 3JJ 282, no. 1, memorandum of Claude-François du Lion, 22 November 1665. For modern accounts, see, for example, Martha de Jármy Chapa, *Un eslabón perdido en la historia: Piratería en el Caribe, siglos XVI y XVII* (México: Universidad Nacional Autónoma de México, 1983), 194–96; Carlos Saiz Cidoncha, *Historia de la piratería en América española* (Madrid: San Martín, 1985), 238–40.

23. AGI, México 1006, fols. 463–65, Juan Francisco de Esquivel to Crown, 27 November 1663; AGI, México 361, ramo 2, no. 21, Juan Francisco de Esquivel to Crown, 30 April 1664.

24. AGI, México 559, no. 89, Juan Francisco de Esquivel to Crown, 23 October 1663.

25. AGI, México 361, ramo 2, no. 23, Juan Francisco de Esquivel to Crown, 13 September 1664; BL, Add. Ms. 12430, fol. 31, journal of William Beeston, 23 November 1664.

26. Jorge Victoria Ojeda, *Mérida de Yucatán de las Indias: Piratería y estrategia defensiva* (Mérida: Departamento de Comunicación Social, 1995), 162–77; Alfredo Barrera Rubio and Miguel Leyba, "Las trincheras: Un sistema colonial de defensa de la costa norte de Yucatán," *Cuadernos de Arquitectura Virreinal* 14 (1996): 45–53; José Enrique Ortiz Lanz, *Piedras ante el mar: Las fortificaciones de Campeche* (México: Consejo Nacional para la Cultura y las Artes, 1998), 37–45; Takeshi Fushimi, "La militarización y la sociedad colonial de Yucatán del siglo XVII," *Anales de Estudios Latinoamericanos* 20 (2000): 126–33; Michel Antochiw, *Las primeras fortificaciones de la villa y puerto de San Francisco de Campeche, siglo XVII* (Campeche: Gobierno del Estado de Campeche, 2003), 49–102. For the native contribution, see Gabriela Solís Robleda, *Bajo el signo de la compulsión: El trabajo forzoso indígena en el sistema colonial yucateco, 1540–1730* (México: Miguel Ángel Porrúa, 2003), 126–28.

27. Jorge Victoria Ojeda, "Vigías en el Yucatán novohispano: Nota para un estudio complementario entre las torres costeras de España y las de América hispana," *Fronteras de la Historia* 14 (2009): 242–45; Mark Christensen and Matthew Restall, "Maya Militia: The Defense and Government of Colonial Ixil, Yucatán," *Colonial Latin American Review* 29 (2020): 76–78.

28. Manuela Cristina García Bernal, *Economía, política y sociedad en el Yucatán colonial* (Mérida: Universidad Autónoma de Yucatán, 2005), 143–94; Matthew Restall, *The Black Middle: Africans, Mayas, and Spaniards in Colonial Yucatan* (Stanford, Cal.: Stanford University Press, 2009), 158.

29. Laura Caso Barrera, *Caminos en la selva: Migración, comercio y resistencia* (México: El Colegio de México, 2002), 184–93.

30. AGI, México 361, ramo 5, no. 69, Andrés Margre, Bartolomé Ortiz de la Sonda, Gregorio Cárdenas, et al. to Rodrigo Flores de Aldana, 26 July 1668; AGI, México 307, no. 8, Luis de Cifuentes de Sotomayor to Crown, 28 July 1668.

31. AGI, México 361, ramo 2, no. 70, Rodrigo Flores de Aldana to Crown, 8 August 1668.

32. Jorge Victoria Ojeda, "La piratería y su relación con los indígenas de la península de Yucatán: Mito y practica social," *Mesoamérica* 14 (1993): 209–16. The possibility of alliances between buccaneers and Mayas is proposed by Georges Baudot, "Dissidences indiennes et complicités flibustières dans le Yucatán du XVIIe siècle," *Caravelle* 46 (1986): 21–33.

33. Arne Bialuschewski, "Slaves of the Buccaneers: Mayas in Captivity in the Second Half of the Seventeenth Century," *Ethnohistory* 64 (2017): 47–52.

34. Matthew Restall, *The Maya World: Yucatec Culture and Society, 1550–1850* (Stanford, Cal.: Stanford University Press, 1997), 142–43. This reference appears in a Maya petition filed in 1774 against four Spanish priests.

CHAPTER 3. THE GRANADA RAID

1. Nuala Zahedieh, "'A Frugal, Prudential, and Hopeful Trade': Privateering in Jamaica, 1655–1689," *Journal of Imperial and Commonwealth History* 18 (1990): 154.

2. Elizet Payne Iglesias, *El puerto de Truxillo: Un viaje hacia su melancólico abandono* (Tegucigalpa: Editorial Guaymuras, 2007), 37–39; José Manuel Cardona Amaya, *Invasiones de corsarios a la Honduras de Felipe IV, 1633–1643* (Tegucigalpa: Editorial Guardabarranco, 2020), 18–103. For the geography of the region, see Alain Musset, *L'Amérique centrale et les Antilles: une approche géographique* (Paris: Armand Colin, 1994), 27–34.

3. TNA, Colonial Office 1/20, fols. 38–39, examinations of John Morris, Jacob Fackman, and Henry Morgan, 20 September 1665. Morgan was presumably questioned because he had risen to the rank of commander in the course of the expedition. For Morgan's career, see, above all, Mark G. Hanna, *Pirate Nests and the Rise of the British Empire, 1570–1740* (Chapel Hill: University of North Carolina Press, 2015), 103–43. Operating under a Portuguese commission, this gang included seven or eight Frenchmen and a few Dutchmen.

4. AGI, México 40, no. 12, Tomás Muñoz and Juan de Paces y San Pedro to Antonio Sabastián de Toledo Molina y Salazar, 26 February 1665; AGI, Santo Domingo 104, ramo 4, no. 23, Rodrigo Flores de Aldana to Francisco Dávila Orejón Gastón, 7 April 1665.

5. AN, Marine 3JJ 282, no. 1, memorandum of Claude-François du Lion, 22 November 1665. The governor of Gualeloupe must have obtained comprehensive information from a participant of the raid, presumably David Maarten.

6. TNA, Colonial Office 1/20, fols. 38–39, examinations of John Morris, Jacob Fackman, and Henry Morgan, 20 September 1665; AN, Marine 3JJ 282, no. 1, memorandum of Claude-François du Lion, 22 November 1665.

7. BL, Sloane Ms. 793, fols. 24–25, journal of William Jackson, 11 August 1644; AGI, México 35, no. 33, Joseph Luis Tello de Vera to García Sarmiento de Sotomayor, 20 September 1644.

8. AGI, México 1006, fol. 552, Rodrigo Flores de Aldana to Crown, 7 April 1665;

AGI, Santo Domingo 104, ramo 4, no. 23, Rodrigo Flores de Aldana to Francisco Dávila Orejón Gastón, 7 April 1665; AGI, México 361, ramo 2, no. 32, Juan Francisco de Esquivel to Crown, 26 April 1665. Three of the four vessels were stranded during this operation, and the militiamen had to use boats to reach their destination. The only vessel that made the Tabasco coast as planned carried a mulatto militia unit. For the poor reputation of these forces, see Matthew Restall, *The Black Middle: Africans, Mayas, and Spaniards in Colonial Yucatan* (Stanford, Cal.: Stanford University Press, 2009), 140–41.

9. AGI, México 361, ramo 2, no. 37, Juan Francisco de Esquivel to Crown, 20 July 1666. The freebooters released most hostages but took four captives of African descent with them.

10. AGI, Santo Domingo 104, ramo 4, no. 23, Rodrigo Flores de Aldana to Francisco Dávila Orejón Gastón, 7 April 1665. The commanders, John Morris and David Maarten, set two captured Spaniards ashore with a letter to the governor of Campeche warning him not to harm the seven Englishmen who had been seized on their vessels in the mouth of the Río Grijalva the previous week.

11. TNA, Colonial Office 1/20, fols. 38–39, examinations of John Morris, Jacob Fackman, and Henry Morgan, 20 September 1665.

12. AGI, Guatemala 43, no. 49, Andrés de Arbieto y Ozaeta to Crown, 12 December 1653.

13. Thomas Gage, *The English-American, His Travail by Sea and Land: or, A New Survey of the West-Indies* (London: Richard Cotes, 1648), 185–88. Later editions were published in 1655 and 1677. Gage traveled through the country as a Dominican friar but later converted to Protestantism and became a prominent advocate of Cromwell's Western Design.

14. TNA, Colonial Office 1/20, fols. 38–39, examinations of John Morris, Jacob Fackman, and Henry Morgan, 20 September 1665.

15. Amphibious hit-and-run raids involving small watercraft were part of the conflicts in Ireland and in the west of Scotland at the turn of the seventeenth century. See, for example, Steve Murdoch, *The Terror of the Seas? Scottish Maritime Warfare, 1513–1713* (Leiden: Brill, 2010), 135–38; Alison Cathcart, "Maritime Dimension to Plantation of Ulster, 1550–1600," *Journal of the North Atlantic* 12 (2019): 103–06. However, it is doubtful that the buccaneers were conversant with this peripheral chapter of military history.

16. TNA, Colonial Office 1/20, fols. 38–39, examinations of John Morris, Jacob Fackman, and Henry Morgan, 20 September 1665.

17. AGCA, A1 (Guatemala), leg. 4681, exp. 40319, fols. 44–52, testimonies of Gonzalo Noguera and Juan Gonzáles de Sá, 5 and 6 September 1665. Gallardo was born on the Solentiname archipelago at the southeastern end of Lago de Nicaragua, not far from where the lake drains to the Caribbean via the Río San Juan. He received the sentence under José Portal y Artadia, who was interim governor of Nicaragua from 1659 to 1661. See Arne Bialuschewski, "Juan Gallardo: A Native American Buccaneer,"

Hispanic American Historical Review 100 (2020): 236–37. The fact that even official documents use the diminutive "Gallardillo" may indicate a disrespectful attitude toward this man. Gallardo would most likely have encountered the intruders as a forced laborer, either clearing a blocked passage of the Río San Juan or carrying heavy cargo around such an obstacle.

18. Jaime Incer, *Nicaragua: Viajes, rutas y encuentros, 1502–1838* (San José: Libro Libre, 1990), 331–32; Carlos Meléndez Chaverri, "Historia más antigua de la ciudad de Granada en Nicaragua y de su fase de desarrollo como puerto del Caribe, 1542–1685," *Revista del Archivo Nacional* 63 (1999): 125–29.

19. AGI, Guatemala 21, ramo 4, no. 51, Martín Carlos de Mencos to Crown, 12 July 1665; AN, Marine 3JJ 282, no. 1, memorandum of Claude-François du Lion, 22 November 1665.

20. AGCA, AI (Guatemala), leg. 4681, exp. 40319, fols. 44–49, testimony of Gonzalo Noguera, 5 September 1665. Spanish records generally do not contain details about torture, but, according to a Jamaican planter, freebooters bragged about the various forms of brutal torture they used to acquire information. See TNA, Colonial Office 1/25, fols. 2–4, John Style to Sir Henry Bennett, 4 January 1670. The methods included putting matches under fingernails and slowly strangling the victims. It appears that some wealthy citizens of Granada were viciously beaten.

21. AGCA, AI (Guatemala), leg. 4681, exp. 40319, fols. 49–52, testimony of Juan Gonzáles de Sá, 6 September 1665. The raiders estimated that a thousand native men marched to Granada, but this is certainly exaggerated, as the total population, including women and children, of all villages was below two thousand. For scattered background information, see Germán Romero Vargas, *Las estructuras sociales de Nicaragua en el siglo XVIII* (Managua: Editorial Vanguardia, 1988), 36–39; Javier García Bresó, *Monimbó: Una comunidad india de Nicaragua* (Managua: Editorial Multiformas, 1992), 60–61. An outline of reasons for indigenous unrest is in Severo Martínez Peláez, *Motines de indios* (Guatemala: Ediciones en Marcha, 1991), 33–77.

22. TNA, Colonial Office 1/20, fols. 38–39, examinations of John Morris, Jacob Fackman, and Henry Morgan, 20 September 1665 (quote); BnF, Mélanges de Colbert 142, fols. 59–60, Bertrand d'Ogeron to Jean-Baptiste Colbert, 1 November 1665.

23. TNA, Colonial Office 1/20, fols. 38–39, examinations of John Morris, Jacob Fackman, and Henry Morgan, 20 September 1665.

24. AGI, Guatemala 21, ramo 4, no. 51, Martín Carlos de Mencos to Crown, 12 July 1665; AGCA, AI (Guatemala), leg. 5363, exp. 45338, fol. 1, Martín Carlos de Mencos to Juan de Salinas y Cerda, 25 July 1665.

25. AGI, Guatemala 157, ramo 4, no. 4, Alfonso Payo de Rivera to Crown, 15 December 1668. The cost of building and maintaining the fortification was initially defrayed by the twenty-eight vacant *encomiendas* in the province, and when this turned out to be insufficient, a portion of the tribute paid by *encomenderos* was added, which effectively meant that native communities had to cover the expenses. In the following years, citizens of Granada complained that the natives employed by local authorities

for the defense of the region would not be available to work on raches, in sugar mills, and in the cacao production, which was crucial for the prosperity of the town. See AGI, Guatemala 280, no. 7, fols. 80–81, petition of Andrés de Senía, 20 March 1673.

26. AGCA, A1 (Guatemala), leg. 1553, exp. 10189, nos. 150 and 162, reales cédulas, 11 March and 25 October 1667. For the significance of tribute from the natives, see Héctor Pérez Brignoli, *Breve historia de Centroamérica* (Madrid: Alianza Editorial, 1990), 49.

27. AGI, Guatemala 157, ramo 4, no. 3, report of Juan Dinarte Palomino, 26 November 1668; AGI, Guatemala 280, no. 7, fols. 74–76, report of Francisco de Flete, 30 January 1673. It appears that the number of natives living in this region barely exceeded a hundred.

28. BL, Add. Ms. 12430, fol. 31, journal of William Beeston, 20 August 1665. See also Nuala Zahedieh, "Trade, Plunder, and Economic Development in Early English Jamaica, 1655–1689," *Economic History Review* 39 (1986): 215–20; Michael Pawson and David Buisseret, *Port Royal, Jamaica* (Kingston: University of the West Indies Press, 2000), 25–44. For the acquisition of strategic information during this foray, see Karl H. Offen, "English Designs on Central America: Geographic Knowledge and Imaginative Geographies in the Seventeenth Century," *Early American Studies* 18 (2020): 400–408.

CHAPTER 4. NATIVES AND INTRUDERS IN CENTRAL AMERICA

1. AGI, Santo Domingo 104, ramo 4, no. 29, declaration of Antón Reccio, 3 January 1666; Bodleian Library, University of Oxford, Ms. Clarendon 84, fols. 80–81, Sir Thomas Modyford to Edward Hyde, 5 June 1666. For Mansfield's career, see Jon Latimer, *The Buccaneers of the Caribbean: How Piracy Forged an Empire* (Cambridge, Mass.: Harvard University Press, 2009), 154–57; David F. Marley, *Pirates of the Americas* (Santa Barbara, Cal.: ABC-Clio, 2010), 1:228–32.

2. AGI, México 42, no. 4, declaration of Francisco Díaz, 3 August 1666; AGI, Guatemala 22, ramo 1, no. 11, Martín Carlos de Mencos to Crown, 3 September 1666.

3. Philip MacLeod, "Auge y estancamiento de la producción de cacao en Costa Rica, 1660–1695," *Anuario de Estudios Centroamericanos* 22 (1996): 83–88; Juan Carlos Solórzano Fonseca, "Indígenas insumisos, frailes y soldados: Talamanca y Guatuso, 1660–1721," *Anuario de Estudios Centroamericanos* 23 (1997): 151–55; Rina Cáceres, *Negros, mulatos, esclavos y libertos en la Costa Rica del siglo XVII* (México: Instituto Panamericano de Geografía e Historia, 2000), 100–101.

4. AGI, Guatemala 22, ramo 1, no. 11, Juan López de la Flor to Martín Carlos de Mencos, 2 May 1666. The barrio was the residence for native craftsmen and servants, so-called *laboríos*, who had left their villages and tried to improve their livelihoods by abandoning part of their cultural identity. For the *laboríos*, see Christopher H. Lutz, *Santiago de Guatemala, 1541–1773: City, Caste, and the Colonial Experience* (Norman: University of Oklahoma Press, 1994), 54–57.

5. ANCR, Sección Histórica, Guatemala 110, fols. 24–28, Alonso de Bonilla to Juan López de la Flor to Crown, 26 April 1666; ANCR, Sección Histórica, Guatemala 110, fols. 88–89, Juan López de la Flor to Crown, 5 June 1666. Mansfield's crew falsely reported in Jamaica that the inhabitants of several native villages had joined them during the march inland, presumably to give this venture some kind of legitimacy. See TNA, Colonial Office 1/20, fols. 43–44, Sir Thomas Modyford to Duke of Albemarle, 8 June 1666.

6. ANCR, Sección Histórica, Guatemala 110, fols. 59–62, declaration of Bartolomé de Ortega, 6 May 1666; ANCR, Sección Histórica, Guatemala 110, fols. 62–64, declaration of Pedro Fernández Galindo, 9 May 1666.

7. ANCR, Sección Histórica, Guatemala 110, fol. 144, petition of Pedro de Miranda Santillán, 29 July 1666.

8. ANCR, Sección Histórica, Guatemala 110, fols. 39–40, report of Juan López de la Flor, 12 May 1666. For interethnic relations, see Eugenia Ibarra Rojas, "Política y etnicidad en sociedades en transición en la zona sur de Costa Rica: Boruca y Talamanca," *Vínculos* 24 (1999): 121–51; Rodrigo Salazar Salvatierra, *El indígena costarricense: Una visión etnográfica* (Cartago: Editorial Tecnológica, 2002), 15–19; Francisco Corrales Ulloa, "Arqueología y etnohistoria de los grupos indígenas del sureste de Costa Rica," *Revista del Archivo Nacional* 70 (2006): 141–88.

9. Juan Carlos Solórzano Fonseca, *Los indígenas en la frontera de la colonización: Costa Rica, 1502–1930* (San José: Editorial Universidad Estatal a Distancia, 2013), 144–52.

10. AGI, Guatemala 22, ramo 1, no. 11, Juan López de la Flor to Martín Carlos de Mencos, 2 May 1666; ANCR, Sección Histórica, Guatemala 110, fol. 143, order of Martín Carlos de Mencos, 24 September 1666; AGI, Guatemala 280, no. 7, fols. 43–44, Juan López de la Flor to Fernando Francisco de Escobedo, 6 March 1673. Since an official report only four years earlier had estimated the total number of Votos families at two hundred, it seems reasonable to assume that many natives evaded the forced deportation.

11. ANCR, Sección Histórica, Guatemala 110, fols. 48–52, Juan López de la Flor to Benito Díaz, 1 June 1666; AGCA, A3 (Guatemala), leg. 2318, exp. 34254, fols. 73–74, real cédula, 14 October 1666; AGI, Guatemala 39, ramo 43, no. 199, Juan López de la Flor to Crown, 30 March 1669; AGCA, A1 (Guatemala), leg. 1520, exp. 10075, fol. 61, real cédula, 22 June 1672; AGI, Guatemala 39, ramo 44, no. 201, Juan Francisco Sáenz Vásquez to Crown, 25 December 1676.

12. ANOM, Colonies C⁹ᴬ 1, fols. 18–21, Bertrand d'Ogeron to Jean-Baptiste Colbert, 20 September 1666; BnF, Mélanges de Colbert 142, fols. 59–60, Bertrand d'Ogeron to Jean-Baptiste Colbert, 1 November 1666.

13. AGI, Guatemala 22, ramo 1, no. 11, testimonies of Jean de Lebaquoi and Pierre Dugren, 8 October 1668.

14. It appears that d'Aristegui commanded the vessels and L'Olonnais the land force. Like so many French seamen, François obtained his nickname from his birth-

place—in this case the Atlantic port town Les Sables d'Olonne. For his name, see AGI, Santo Domingo 196, ramo 2, no. 55, testimony of Diego Sánchez Cabeza, 7 January 1681. Most records give his name as François L'Olonnais or L'Olonnois. A comprehensive account of his raids is in Jacques Gasser, *Dictionnaire des flibustiers des Caraïbes* (Les Sables d'Olonne: Editions de Beaupré, 2017), 362–74.

15. AGI, Indiferente General 2540, no. 18, Antonio Sebastián de Toledo Molina y Salazar to Crown, 19 December 1666.

16. AGI, Santo Domingo 62, ramo 2, no. 18, report of Juan Sánchez Borrego, Ambrosio González de Acosta, Andrés Gallardín y Barrega, et al., 7 November 1666.

17. AGI, Guatemala 22, ramo 1, no. 11, declaration of Nicolás Rodríguez, 15 January 1667.

18. Lucas Guillermo Castillo Lara, *Las acciones militares del gobernador Ruy Fernández de Fuenmayor, 1637–1644* (Caracas: Academia Nacional de la Historia, 1978), 91–94. *Pardos* do not seem to have played a role in the defense of this colony, although many people of African descent were forced to work in the agricultural sector. It appears that, among other factors, a lack of firearms prevented the local authorities from relying on *pardos*. Some natives, unused to handling bows and arrows, learned this skill under Spanish supervision. For the incursions, see Cornelis C. Goslinga and Margaret Stefanko, *De Nederlanders in Venezuela* (Caracas: Asociación Holandesa de Venezuela, 1992), 11; Luis Britto García, *Demonios del mar: Piratas y corsarios en Venezuela, 1528–1727* (Caracas: Comisión Presidencial V Centenario de Venezuela, 1998), 412–31.

19. Museo Naval, Madrid, Colección Vargas Ponce 17, fols. 328–29, declaration of Gabriel Suárez Maldonado, 14 December 1666. The governor's son was subsequently awarded the *encomienda* of the native inhabitants of the village Santo Domingo in recognition of his father's services. For the fighting, see AGI, Santo Domingo 62, ramo 2, no. 18, report of Juan Sánchez Borrego, Ambrosio González de Acosta, Andrés Gallardín y Barrega, et al., 7 November 1666; AGI, Indiferente General 2540, no. 18, Antonio Sebastián de Toledo Molina y Salazar to Crown, 19 December 1666; AGI, Guatemala 22, ramo 1, no. 11, declaration of Nicolás Rodríguez, 15 January 1667.

20. AGI, Escribanía de Cámara 841B, pieza 4, fols. 315–20, declaration of Francisco de Arriola, 25 August 1666. This robbery led to an investigation because de Arriola, the owner of the ranch where the valuables were hidden, was accused of having seized the opportunity to embezzle 600 silver coins that belonged to the crown.

21. Archivo General de la Nación (Colombia), Bogotá, Sección Colonia 29, Historia Civil, leg. 16, doc. 28, fol. 892, Pedro Ramírez Floriano, Manuel Ruz de Aranguren, Lucas de Laguado, and Sebastián de Soto to Crown, 31 July 1666; Alexandre-Olivier Exquemelin, *De Americaensche Zee-Roovers* (Amsterdam: Jan ten Hoorn, 1678), 57–58.

22. AGI, Santo Domingo 62, ramo 2, no. 18, declaration of Pedro de Carvajal, 23 September 1666; AGI, Guatemala 22, ramo 1, no. 11, declaration of Nicolás Rodríguez, 15 January 1667.

23. AGI, Santo Domingo 62, ramo 2, no. 18, Juan Sánchez Borrego, Ambrosio

González de Acosta, Andrés Gallardín y Barrega, et al. to Crown, 7 November 1666. While L'Olonnais's gang was busy in Maracaibo, a Spanish ship arrived, but the raiders decided not to attack it because they wanted to avoid any losses.

24. ANOM, Colonies C^{9A} 1, fols. 33–34, Bertrand d'Ogeron to Jean-Baptiste Colbert, 20 April 1667; AGI, Santo Domingo 196, ramo 2, no. 55, testimony of Juan Fernández Ortiz, 15 May 1680.

25. AGI, Santo Domingo 273, no. 60, declaration of Pedro Velasco, 11 November 1666; AGI, Guatemala 22, ramo 1, no. 11, declarations of Jean de Lebaquoi and Pierre Dugren, 8 October 1668; AGI, Santo Domingo 196, ramo 2, no. 55, declaration of Juan Fernández Ortiz, 15 May 1680. The natives may have preferred enslaved people to other spoils, but it is also possible that they did not have a choice after the French crew members had claimed all material wealth for themselves. For the slave markets, see Liliane Crété, *La traite des nègres sous l'Ancien Régime: le nègre, le sucre et la toile* (Paris: Francia Perrin, 1989), 177–80; Philippe Hrod⊠j, "Et le sucre fut: l'apparition de l'or blanc dans la partie française de Saint-Domingue," *Actes du colloque techniques et colonies* 1 (2005): 203–07. In the late 1660s the hinterland of Gonaïves was known as a major hunting ground for buccaneers.

26. Exquemelin, *De Americaensche Zee-Roovers*, 60. This community probably consisted of native families that originated in Florida. For previous concerns that these people could become targets of assaults see AGI, Santo Domingo 273, no. 51, Francisco Dávila Orejón y Gastón to Crown, 15 June 1666. In retaliation for a series of buccaneers' raids on Batabanó, Spanish forces seized a number of English and French turtle fishermen in the Cayman Islands. See TNA, Colonial Office 1/25, fol. 178, deposition of Samuel Hutcheson, 16 June 1669; AGI, Indiferente General 2542, no. 4, declaration of Jean Pichon, 9 April 1670.

27. AGI, Guatemala 22, ramo 1, no. 11, declaration of Baltasar Álvarez, 23 January 1669. Many captives were later questioned by the Spanish authorities about their voyages with the raiders. These records provide valuable information that is not available elsewhere.

28. Alexandre-Olivier Exquemelin, *Histoire des avanturiers qui se sont signalez dans les Indes* (Paris: Jacques Le Febvre, 1686), 1:294–95. Río Xagua is present-day Río Papaloteca. There do not seem to be any surviving Spanish records of this assault, indicating that the victims were exclusively native communities.

29. AGI, Guatemala 22, ramo 3, no. 26, Sebastián Álvarez y Alfonso to Crown, 26 May 1668; AGI, Guatemala 39, ramo 43, no. 199, declarations of Juan de la Cruz and Jean de Villebon, 6 and 8 April 1669; AGI, Guatemala 26, ramo 3, no. 91, testimonies of Francisco Martínez de Higuillar, Domingo de la Hoya Riva Agüero, Bartolomé López de Baena, and León de Ferrera, 9 and 10 March 1680. For the native population see William V. Davidson, "Geografía de los indígenas toles (jicaques) de Honduras en el siglo XVIII," *Mesoamérica* 6 (1985): 58–66; Linda A. Newson, *The Cost of Conquest: Indian Decline in Honduras Under Spanish Rule* (Boulder, Col.: Westview, 1986), 35–38.

30. AGI, Guatemala 22, ramo 3, nos. 26–27, Sebastián Álvarez y Alfonso to Crown, 26 and 28 May 1668; AGI, Guatemala 26, ramo 3, no. 91, testimony of Francisco Martínez de Higuillar, 30 January 1680. Most inhabitants of San Pedro sought refuge in nearby native villages. When the town was rebuilt Sula was added to the name, referring to one of these villages, but the exact reasoning behind the new name remains obscure.

31. AGI, Guatemala 39, ramo 43, no. 199, declaration of Juan de la Cruz, 6 April 1669.

32. Evidence suggests that Maya craftsmen learned how to rework iron obtained from European visitors and other Mayas living under Spanish control. This practice had apparently become common at the time of L'Olonnais's stay. Other goods may have been traded away or were used as ritual offerings. See Elizabeth Graham, David M. Pendergast, and Grant Jones, "On the Fringes of Conquest: Maya-Spanish Contact in Colonial Belize," *Science* 246 (1989): 1258–59; Timothy W. Pugh, "Contagion and Alterity: Kowoj Maya Appropriations of European Objects," *American Anthropologist* 111 (2009): 378–83; Jaime J. Awe and Christoph Helmke, "The Sword and the Olive Jar: Material Evidence of Seventeenth-Century Maya-European Interaction in Central Belize," *Ethnohistory* 62 (2015): 341–53.

33. AGI, Guatemala 22, ramo 1, no. 11, declarations of Antonio Moreno, Alberto de Recondo, Jorge Quinette et al., 6 to 10 December 1668. For the conflicts between Maya groups in this region see Grant D. Jones, *The Conquest of the Last Maya Kingdom* (Stanford, Cal.: Stanford University Press, 1998), 3–28; Laura Caso Barrera, "Guerre et factionnalisme entre les Itzaes durant la periode coloniale," *Civilisations* 55 (2006): 52–69.

34. AGI, Guatemala 22, ramo 1, no. 11, declaration of Alonso de Contreras, 8 December 1668; AN, Marine 3JJ 282, no. 10, memorandum of Philippe Bequel and Moïse Vauquelin, ca. 1670; AGI, Escribanía de Cámara 1090B, pieza 16, fols. 9–17, declaration of Ignacio de Leiva, 5 March 1670. Most seventeenth-century maps depict a distorted image of the Yucatán Peninsula, which may have given the freebooters a skewed impression of the distance to Mérida.

35. AGI, Guatemala 22, ramo 1, no. 11, confession of Nicolás Covoh, 9 October 1668.

36. AGI, Guatemala 39, ramo 43, no. 199, Antonio de Temiño y Dávila to Crown, 19 September 1668; AGI, Escribanía de Cámara 1090B, pieza 16, fols. 50–53, confession of Pierre Le Treille, 5 February 1671; AGI, México 48, ramo 1, no. 39, declaration of Jan Lucas, 17 October 1673.

37. AGI, Guatemala 22, ramo 1, no. 11, declarations of Antonio Moreno, Alberto de Recondo, Jorge Quinette, et al., 6 to 10 December 1668; AGI, Guatemala 178, no. 88, Alfonso Payo de Rivera to Crown, 25 December 1668.

38. AGI, Guatemala 22, ramo 1, no. 11, declaration of Baltasar Álvarez, 23 January 1669; AGI, Escribanía de Cámara 1090B, pieza 16, fols. 9–17, declaration of Ignacio de

Leiva, 5 March 1670; AGI, México 48, ramo 1, no. 39, declaration of Jan Lucas, 17 October 1673.

39. AGI, Panamá 24, ramo 2, no. 18, Juan Pérez de Guzmán to Crown, 5 October 1669; AGI, Escribanía de Cámara 1092A, pieza 34, fols. 1–3, declaration of José de Antequera, 29 September 1672. After a long odyssee two men, a Frenchman and a Maya who had belonged to L'Olonnais's gang, surrendered to a Spanish sentinel in Costa Rica. See AGI, Guatemala 39, ramo 43, no. 199, declarations of Juan de la Cruz and Jean de Villebon, 6 and 8 April 1699. It is not known what happened to the remainder of this company. Some men probably found refuge in indigenous communities on the Mosquito Coast. However, an eyewitness reported that many more were killed by natives in Costa Rica. See AGI, Contaduría 1485B, fols. 197–98, declaration of Francisco Jaime, 10 May 1669.

40. AGI, Escribanía de Cámara 577A, no. 1, pieza 5, fols. 15–24, declaration of Jean Picard, 19 August 1668. For the significance of turtle for provisioning freebooters, see Karl H. Offen, "Subsidy from Nature: Green Sea Turtles in the Colonial Caribbean," *Journal of Latin American Geography* 19 (2020): 185–87; Lynn B. Harris, "Maritime Cultural Encounters and Consumerism of Turtles and Manatees: An Environmental History of the Caribbean," *International Journal of Maritime History* 32 (2020): 792–97.

41. AGI, Escribanía de Cámara 462A, pieza 1, fols. 414–19, declaration of Antonio de Sierra and Pasqual García, 22 July 1668; ANOM, Colonies C^{10B} 2, no. 46, relation of Jean Duglas, 7 January 1669; TNA, Colonial Office 1/25, fols. 2–4, John Style to Sir Henry Bennet, 4 January 1670.

42. For similar examples, see W. Jeffrey Bolster, *Black Jacks: African American Seamen in the Age of Sail* (Cambridge, Mass.: Harvard University Press, 1997), 68–101. It appears that Gallardo was not only of practical value for the outlaws, but his branded face was also a visual reminder of the illegitimacy and brutality of the Spanish colonial regime and therefore his presence may have helped justify the raids.

43. AGI, México 559, no. 144, declarations of Jan Jung and Johannes Beck, 29 December 1669; AGI, Santa Fé 43, ramo 7, no. 37, declarations of Luis Gerónimo and Juan Bautista, 11 July 1670.

44. TNA, Colonial Office 1/23, fols. 100–103, information of Henry Morgan, Edward Collier, John Morris, et al., 7 September 1668. For the native population in the región, see Álvaro Chaves Mendoza, Jorge Morales Gómez, and Horacio Calle Restrepo, *Los indios de Colombia* (Madrid: Mapfre, 1992), 119–26; Lola G. Luna, *Resguardos coloniales de Santa Marta y Cartagena y resistencia indígena* (Bogotá: Fondo de Promoción de la Cultura del Banco Popular, 1993), 54–61; Victor Zuluaga Gómez, *Pueblos indígenas de Colombia* (Pereira: Supercopias, 1998), 12–16. The secondary literature contains no hint of an uprising in or near Mompox, but Guahibos besieged in January and February 1668 the Jesuit mission of San Joaquín de Atanare, located on a tributary of the Orinoco, which may have been the source of this rumor. See Jane

M. Rausch, *A Tropical Plains Frontier: The Llanos of Colombia, 1531–1831* (Albuquerque: University of New Mexico Press, 1984), 70. An outline of hostile incursions is in Francisco Ospina Navia and Tatyana Torres del Río, *Historia breve de Santa Marta y la costa caribe colombiana: Taironas, conquistadores y piratas* (Bogotá: Editorial Carrera 7a, 2003), 105–22.

45. AGI, Santa Fé 43, ramo 7, no. 37, Pedro de Ulloa to Crown, 21 July 1670. For a similar case of another native man set ashore as a spy, see AGI, Indiferente General 2578, no. 1, declaration of Felipe Méndez, 9 January 1669. The written record only provides information about spies that were captured. It is therefore not known whether it was common practice to use indigenous people for spying.

46. AGI, Santa Fé 43, ramo 7, no. 37, Pedro de Ulloa to Crown, 21 July 1670; AGI, Panamá 93, no. 1191, Pedro de Ulloa to Crown, 16 December 1670. For the use of poisoned arrows, see Elsa M. Redmond, *Tribal and Chiefly Warfare in South America* (Ann Arbor: University of Michigan, 1994), 84–85. In the seventeenth century, enslaved and free men of African descent gradually replaced natives in navigating the Río Magdalena. See David Ernesto Peñas Galindo, *Los bogas de Mompox: Historia del zambaje* (Bogotá: Tercer Mundo, 1988), 47–53. It appears that the intruders dealt exclusively with the indigenous population, but the exact role played by the various natives is almost impossible to recover from the surviving sources.

47. AGI, Guatemala 22, ramo 1, no. 11, Sebastián Álvarez y Alfonso to Antonio Sebastián de Toledo Molina y Salazar, 9 September 1670.

48. TNA, Colonial Office 1/25, fols. 148–49, Sir Thomas Modyford to Earl of Arlington, 31 October 1670.

49. ANCR, Complementario Colonial 5289, Juan Pérez de Guadamuz to Juan López de la Flor, 28 August 1670; TNA, Colonial Office 1/25, fols. 148–49, Sir Thomas Modyford to Earl of Arlington, 31 October 1670. According to an eyewitness, Gallardo commanded a pirogue with twenty-four men.

50. Many citizens of Spanish descent found new homes on haciendas or even took up residence in nearby native villages. Such migrations began in the early seventeenth century as a consequence of declining economic opportunities in urban areas, but the raids of 1665 and 1670 undoubtedly accelerated this process. At the same time, Chorotega families moved to Granada, which led to more diverse but also ethnically segregated and stratified communities. See Linda A. Newson, *Indian Survival in Colonial Nicaragua* (Norman: University of Oklahoma Press, 1987), 130–31.

51. AGI, Guatemala 22, ramo 1, no. 11, Diego Jiménez de Luna to Nicolás de Luna, 6 October 1670; BL, Add. Ms. 12430, fol. 33, journal of William Beeston, 19 October 1670; AGI, Panamá 93, no. 1199, fols. 132–36, declaration of Juan Sánchez de Salas, 9 March 1671.

52. AGI, Guatemala 22, ramo 1, no. 11, Francisco de Valdés to Sebastián Álvarez y Alfonso, 30 August 1670.

53. AGI, Santa Fé 43, ramo 7, no. 40, declaration of Juan del Castillo, 14 December 1671; *Oprechte Haerlemsche Courant*, 19 February 1671. According to the bishop of Nic-

aragua, Native Americans rather than Spaniards were the prime victims of the pillage of 1670. See AGI, Guatemala 157, ramo 4, no. 48, Juan de Santo Matías to Crown, 14 March 1671.

54. Peter Earle, *The Sack of Panamá* (London: Norman and Hobhouse, 1981), 200–225.

55. AGI, Panamá 93, no. 1199, fols. 54–58, testimony of Juan de Lao, 14 February 1671. For the Spanish auxiliaries, see AGI, Guatemala 22, ramo 1, no. 11, Juan Pérez de Guzmán to Juan de Santo Matías, 11 February 1671; AGI, Panamá 93, no. 1172, Juan Pérez de Guzmán to Conde de Lemos, 8 April 1671; AGI, México 45, no. 55, Juan de Santo Matías to Antonio Sebastián de Toledo, 7 June 1671; AGI, Escribanía de Cámara 461B, pieza 10, fols. 715–22, testimony of Pedro Ocampo, 9 September 1671; AGI, Santa Fé 43, ramo 7, no. 40, declaration of Diego Machado, 14 December 1671; Exquemelin, *De Americaensche Zee-Roovers*, 126–32. The fires were ignited by locals before they retreated, but archaeological evidence seems to suggest that accounts of a widespread fire may have been exaggerated.

56. Sandra Petrovich, *Henry Morgan's Raid on Panama: Geopolitics and Colonial Ramifications, 1669–1674* (Lewiston, N.Y.: Edwin Mellen, 2001), 91–100; Michael Kempe, *Fluch der Weltmeere: Piraterie, Völkerrecht und internationale Beziehungen, 1500–1900* (Frankfurt a.M.: Campus Verlag, 2010), 140–45.

57. Peter Earle, *The Pirate Wars* (London: Methuen, 2003), 96–97; Jesse Cromwell, "Life on the Margins: (Ex)Buccaneers and Spanish Subjects on the Campeche Logwood Periphery, 1660–1716," *Itinerario* 33 (2009): 46–49.

58. Jacques Ducoin, *Bertrand d'Ogeron, 1613–1676: fondateur de la colonie de Saint-Domingue et gouverneur des flibustiers* (Brest: Le Télégramme, 2013), 143–48. Beginning in May 1670, French authorites were confronted with unrest in the colony, which broke out after two Dutch vessels had been confiscated by the governor's deputies in Petit-Goâve. The exact reasons for this development are a combination of factors that go beyond raiding. See ANOM, Colonies C⁹ᴬ 1, fols. 70–71, Bertrand d'Ogeron to Jean Renou, 8 June 1670; ANOM, Colonies F³ 164, fols. 223–25, complaint of Louis Gabaret, 19 August 1670; ANOM, Colonies C⁹ᴬ 1, fols. 83–86, Bertrand d'Ogeron to Jean-Baptiste Colbert, 4 March 1671.

CHAPTER 5. INTERCULTURAL ALLIANCES ON THE MOSQUITO COAST

1. Alexandre-Olivier Exquemelin, *De Americaensche Zee-Roovers* (Amsterdam: Jan ten Hoorn, 1678), 149–54. The term "Mosquito" originally served as a place name referring to the area around Cabo Gracias a Dios and later was also applied to the people living on this stretch of coast. The presence of Europeans has attracted quite some scholarly attention in the recent past. See, for example, Craig L. Dozier, *Nicaragua's Mosquito Shore: The Years of British and American Presence* (Tuscaloosa: University of Alabama Press, 1985), 9–29; Geneviève Lemercinier, *Les Miskitos au Nicaragua: notes chronologiques sur la population et l'histoire économico-politique de la Côte Atlantique*

(Louvain: Centre tricontinental, 1985), 6–7; Eleonore von Oertzen, "El colonialismo británico y el reino Misquito en los siglos XVII y XVIII," *Encuentro* 24 (1985): 8–11; Jorge Jenkins Molieri, *El desafío indígena en Nicaragua: El caso de los Miskitos* (Managua: Editorial Vanguardia, 1986), 25–26; Jean Preston, *Mosquito Indians and Anglo-Spanish Rivalry in Central America, 1630–1821* (Glasgow: University of Glasgow, 1988), 3–9; Barbara Potthast, *Die Mosquitoküste im Spannungsfeld britischer und spanischer Politik, 1502–1821* (Köln: Böhlau Verlag, 1988), 29–34; Daniel Noveck, "Class, Culture, and the Miskito Indians: A Historical Perspective," *Dialectical Anthropology* 13 (1988): 19–22; Gregorio Smutko, *Mosquitia: Historia y cultura de la Costa Atlántica* (Managua: La Ocarina, 1988), 65–73; Robert A. Naylor, *Penny Ante Imperialism: The Mosquito Shore and the Bay of Honduras, 1600–1914* (Cranbury, N.J.: Fairleigh Dickinson University Press, 1989), 19–38; Wolfgang Gabbert, "'Das Königreich Mosquitia': Eine ethnohistorische Untersuchung zur politischen Organisation der Miskito, 1670–1821," *Wiener Ethnologische Blätter* 35 (1990): 45–55; Bernard Nietschmann, "The Miskito Nation and the Geopolitics of Self-Determination," *Journal of Political Science* 19 (1991): 23–26; Claudia García, "Género, etnia y poder en la Costa de Mosquitos, siglos XVII y XVIII," *Mesoamérica* 21 (2000): 95–116; Nicholas Rogers, "Caribbean Borderland: Empire, Ethnicity, and the Exotic on the Mosquito Coast," *Eighteenth-Century Life* 26 (2002): 117–23.

2. Karen Ordahl Kupperman, *Providence Island, 1630–1641: The Other Puritan Colony* (Cambridge: Cambridge University Press, 1993), 149–80; Alison Games, "'The Sanctuarye of our Rebell Negroes': The Atlantic Context of Local Resistance on Providence Island, 1630–1641," *Slavery and Abolition* 19 (1998): 5–8; Linda M. Heywood and John K. Thornton, *Central Africans, Atlantic Creoles, and the Foundation of the Americas, 1585–1660* (Cambridge: Cambridge University Press, 2007), 30–33.

3. Karl H. Offen, "Puritan Bioprospecting in Central America and the West Indies," *Itinerario* 35 (2011): 28–31; Karl H. Offen, "English Designs on Central America: Geographic Knowledge and Imaginative Geographies in the Seventeenth Century," *Early American Studies* 18 (2020): 420–25.

4. Germán Romero Vargas, *Las sociedades del Atlántico de Nicaragua en los siglos XVII y XVIII* (Managua: Fondo de Promoción Cultural-Banic, 1995), 211–17.

5. Alden T. Vaughan, *Transatlantic Encounters: American Indians in Britain, 1500–1776* (Cambridge: Cambridge University Press, 2006), 101–02. The evidence about the boy's stay in England appears very thin.

6. It has been argued that the line of succession beginning with this family lasted until the nineteenth century, but there are serious doubts about this interpretation. See Michael D. Olien, "The Miskito Kings and the Line of Succession," *Journal of Anthropological Research* 39 (1983): 200–237; Philip A. Dennis and Michael D. Olien, "Kingship Among the Miskito," *American Ethnologist* 11 (1984): 718–37; Michael D. Olien, "General, Governor, and Admiral: Three Miskito Lines of Succession," *Ethnohistory* 45 (1998): 277–97.

7. BL, Sloane Ms. 793, fol. 19, journal of William Jackson, 8 September 1643.

8. TNA, Colonial Office 124/2, fols. 122–24, minutes of the Company of Adventurers, 12 February 1636. See also Jon Latimer, *The Buccaneers of the Caribbean: How Piracy Forged an Empire* (Cambridge, Mass.: Harvard University Press, 2009), 80–91; Mark G. Hanna, *Pirate Nests and the Rise of the British Empire, 1570–1740* (Chapel Hill: University of North Carolina Press, 2015), 69–92.

9. AGI, Guatemala 16, ramo 2, no. 13, declaration of Simón de Alemán, 12 May 1636.

10. Thomas Gage, *The English-American, His Travail by Sea and Land: or, A New Survey of the West-Indias* (London: Richard Cotes, 1648), 198–99.

11. BL, Sloane Ms. 758, fol. 149, journal of Nathaniel Butler, 2 and 3 June 1639.

12. AGI, Santa Fé 40, ramo 2, no. 40, declaration of William Rous, 1 November 1636; AGI, Guatemala 16, ramo 2, no. 13, confession of John Pinckard, 5 October 1637.

13. In the following years, shipwrecks may have increased the number of Africans on the Mosquito Coast. However, historians have been unable to clearly determine whether such disasters had an impact on the local population. In July 1640 Dutch privateers seized a Portuguese slave ship, the *Nossa Senhora de los Remédios y San Lorenzo*, and the entire human cargo was set ashore east of Trujillo. The escapees were later recaptured. See AGCA, AI (Guatemala), leg. 1559, exp. 10203, fols. 35–37, report of Lorenzo Andrés Gramajo, 2 January 1642; AGI, Guatemala 39, ramo 21, no. 133, Francisco Dávilla y Lugo to Crown, 26 February 1643. This prize was subsequently wrecked by its captors on Roatán, not on the Mosquito Coast. The *William and Sarah* was lost near Cabo Gracias a Dios in the latter half of 1641 but had only fifty-five refugees from Providence Island on board. See TNA, High Court of Admiralty 13/58, fol. 205, deposition of Thomas Fitch, 15 August 1642. It seems that different events were mixed up in oral tradition. For a later reference to the wrecking of a slave ship that was supposed to have occurred in 1652, see AGI, Guatemala 299, fols. 923–28, testimony of Manuel Martínez Robledo, 5 March 1707.

14. John K. Thornton, "The Zambos and the Transformation of the Moskito Kingdom, 1641–1740," *Hispanic American Historical Review* 97 (2017): 8–13.

15. Eugenia Ibarra, "La complementariedad cultural en el surgimiento de los grupos zambos del Cabo Gracias a Dios, en la Mosquitia, durante los siglos XVII y XVIII," *Revista de Estudios Sociales* 26 (2007): 109–14. In the eighteenth century, Spanish officials selected racial labels for the Mosquitos, using *Zambo* in times of conflict and *Indio* during periods of peace. See Samantha R. Billing, "Indios, Sambos, Mestizos, and the Social Construction of Racial Identity in Colonial Central America," *Ethnohistory* 68 (2021): 274–79.

16. Karl H. Offen, "The Sambo and Tawira Miskitu: The Colonial Origins and Geography of Intra-Miskitu Differentiation in Eastern Nicaragua and Honduras," *Ethnohistory* 49 (2002): 328–54; Claudia García, *Etnogénesis, hibridación y consolidación de la identidad del pueblo Miskitu* (Madrid: Consejo Superior de Investigaciones Científicas, 2007), 27–44. *Tawira* meant straight or heavy hair.

17. Linda A. Newson, *Indian Survival in Colonial Nicaragua* (Norman: University

of Oklahoma Press, 1987), 202; Karl H. Offen, "Ecologia cultural miskita en los años 1650–1850," *Wani* 30 (2002): 42–54.

18. Gloria Lara Pinto and George Hasemann, "Honduras antes del año 1500: Una visión regional de su evolución cultural tardía," *Revista de Arqueología Americana* 8 (1995): 29–32; Thomas W. Cuddy, *Political Identity and Archaeology in Northeast Honduras* (Boulder: University Press of Colorado, 2007), 138–40.

19. Andrew Lipman, *The Saltwater Frontier: Indians and the Contest for the American Coast* (New Haven, Conn.: Yale University Press, 2015), 66–70.

20. Exquemelin, *De Americaensche Zee-Roovers*, 149–50. Exquemelin probably obtained additional information in conversations with other seafarers who had lived among the indigenous population. This passage is omitted in the French edition of the book.

21. Such short-term unions existed in various indigenous societies, particularly in the Great Plains of North America, which are better studied. See, above all, Gilles Havard, *Histoire de coureurs de bois: Amérique du Nord, 1600–1840* (Paris: Les Indes savantes, 2016), 635–61.

22. Claudia García, "Relaciones sexual-afectivas entre los Miskitu de la Costa de Mosquitos, siglos XVII y XVIII," *Wani* 28 (2002): 19–20; Claudia García, "Hibridación, interacción social y adaptación cultural en la Costa de Mosquitos, siglos XVII y XVIII," *Anuario de Estudios Americanos* 59 (2002): 445–46.

23. Pierre-Louis Duchartre, *Armes de chasse: histoire et emploi* (Fribourg: Office du Livre, 1978), 103–24; Melvin L. Brown, *Firearms in Colonial America: The Impact on History and Technology, 1492–1792* (Washington, D.C.: Smithsonian Institution Press, 1980), 151–58.

24. AGI, Guatemala 183, no. 62, report of Pedro del Valle and Lorenzo de Guevara, 4 March 1681; AGI, Guatemala 297, fols. 237–45, report of Pedro de la Concepción and Raymundo Barrientos, 26 August 1699. See also Lawrence H. Keeley, *War Before Civilization: The Myth of the Peaceful Savage* (Oxford: Oxford University Press, 1996), 65–69; Eugenia Ibarra Rojas, *Del arco y la flecha a las armas de fuego: Los Indios Mosquitos y la historia centroamericana, 1633–1786* (San José: Editorial de la Universidad de Costa Rica, 2011), 54–56.

25. Brian J. Given, *A Most Pernicious Thing: Gun Trading and Native Warfare in the Early Contact Period* (Ottawa, Ont.: Carleton University Press, 1994), 52–53.

26. TNA, Colonial Office 124/1, fols. 62–66, instructions for Sussex Cammock, 30 July 1634.

27. AGI, Guatemala 297, fols. 58–69, report of Pedro de la Concepción, 13 January 1699. De la Concepción had been in Central America since 1693 and led the Nuestra Señora de los Dolores mission in the interior of Honduras. He obtained information about Mosquitos while he visited scattered communities on tributaries of the Río Coco to search for native families that had fled into the wilderness for fear of disease.

28. AGI, Guatemala 223, no. 7. fols. 53–59, report of Pedro de la Concepción, 13 January 1699; AGI, Guatemala 299, fols. 1156–61, Benito Garret y Arloví to Crown,

30 November 1711; AGI, Guatemala 455, fols. 586–91, declaration of León de Cádiz, 5 June 1724; Karl H. Offen, "El Indio Mosqueto y su Río Dorado," *Temas Nicaragüenses* 58 (2013): 19. The total Mosquito population at the end of the seventeenth century may have been between fifteen hundred and two thousand souls. For similar raiding practices in the Chesapeake, see James D. Rice, "War and Politics: Powhatan Expansionism and the Problem of Native American Warfare," *William and Mary Quarterly* 77 (2020): 27–28.

29. Mary Helms, *Ulysses' Sail: An Ethnographic Oddyssey of Power, Knowledge, and Geographical Distance* (Princeton, N.J.: Princeton University Press, 1988), 197–98.

30. It appears that Willem's father, Albert, had explored the region around 1630. From 1632 to 1638 he was employed by the company. See TNA, Colonial Office 124/1, fols. 69–70, Gilbert Gerrard to Sussex Cammock, 30 July 1634; BL, Add. Ms. 63854B, fol. 26, William Jessop to Alteus Blauvelt, 11 August 1634; TNA, Colonial Office 124/2, fol. 157, Providence Company court minutes, 31 January 1638. Willem was involved in the slave trade and operated as a privateer out of Nieuw Amsterdam after 1642. In the early 1650s he was based in Tortuga and following the English conquest also stayed in Jamaica, where Bluefields Bay is presumably named after him. See AGI, Guatemala 16, ramo 5, no. 37, declaration of Martín Hernández, Francisco Gonzáles, and Juan Díaz, 24 March 1644; AGI, Santo Domingo 58, ramo 1, no. 11, testimony of Baltazar Calderón y Espinoza, 27 March 1654.

31. Bodleian Library, University of Oxford, Ms. Rawlinson A. 347, fol. 29, list of buccaneering vessels, 1663; AGI, Guatemala 21, ramo 4, no. 51, Francisco López de Sotomayor to Crown, 16 and 18 August 1665. The men may have looted vessels that could not reach Granada because a massive earthquake in May 1663 had blocked the passage on the Río San Juan.

32. AN, Marine 3JJ 282, no. 3, memorandum of Jean de Grammont, 22 August 1679. For examples of Mosquito involvement with raiders see AGI, Panamá 93, no. 1199, fols. 54–58, testimony of Juan de Lao, 14 February 1671; AGI, Panamá 95, no. 25, testimony of Gonzalo de Guedes, 28 May 1680.

33. William Dampier, *A New Voyage Round the World* (London: James Knapton, 1697), 7–8.

34. AGI, Indiferente General 1600, no. 181, articles of agreement of Henry Morgan, 8 January 1669. The list includes a certain Ipseiorawas. The name could be composed of the adverbial particle *ip*, which means "suddenly," the middle part *siwra*, which means "just recently," and the end *was*, which means "water" both in the Ulwa and Mayangna language groups of the region. However, it looks more like a place name rather than a personal name, and Mosquitos, particularly those who were in close contact with Europeans, were known to have taken English names.

35. AGI, Guatemala 455, fols. 487–512, Diego de la Haya Fernández to Crown, 15 December 1721. Many larger canoes or pirogues were actually seized from inland groups during raids. Around the turn of the century, Sumu communities began to deliver canoes as tribute to Mosquitos. See Kendra McSweeney, "The Dugout Ca-

noe Trade in Central America's Mosquitia: Approaching Rural Livelihoods through Systems of Exchange," *Annals of the Association of American Geographers* 94 (2004): 642–44.

36. AGN, Civil 1877, exp. 4, fols. 290–99, memorandum of Antonio de Velasco, 16 August 1716.

37. AGI, Guatemala 26, ramo 3, no. 91, testimony of Domingo de Lahoya Riva Agüero, 1 February 1680; AGI, Guatemala 297, fols. 237–45, report of Pedro de la Concepción and Raymundo Barrientos, 26 August 1699. The silver was presumably used to purchase goods from Jamaican traders.

38. AGI, Guatemala 299, fols. 1156–61, Benito Garret y Arloví to Crown, 30 November 1711.

39. AGI, Guatemala 74, no. 35, Lope de Sierra Osorio to Lorenzo de Montufar, 25 November 1679; AGI, Guatemala 280, no. 72, Miguel Gómez de Lara to Crown, 4 October 1681. The timeline is confirmed in AGI, Guatemala 359, ramo 3, fols. 31–34, declaration of Juan Bonilla, 18 October 1703, but no details seem to survive about the earliest assaults. In 1699 native bands pillaged missions in Honduras, in 1702 San Pedro Sula, in 1704 cacao plantations in the Matina valley in Costa Rica, in 1704 and 1707 San Felipe de Lara near the Guatemala coast, and in 1705 settlements along the colonial frontier in Nicaragua, which subsequently receded toward the west.

40. Beinecke Rare Book and Manuscript Library, Yale University, New Haven, Conn., Osborn Shelves fb 190, vol. 3, fol. 321, Duke of Albemarle to Earl of Dartmouth, 11 February 1688; AGI, Panamá 99, no. 288, Edward Brookes to Philip Dassigny, 19 April 1688; Jamaica Archives, Spanish Town, 1B/5/3/3b, fols. 117–19, Jamaica Council minutes, 15 and 16 June 1688.

41. Nathaniel Uring, *The Voyages and Travels of Capt. Nathaniel Uring* (London: James Peele, 1726), 182.

42. Rockefeller Library, Colonial Williamsburg Foundation, William Blathwayt Papers 25, folder 5, Hender Molesworth to William Blathwayt, 9 February 1687; AGI, Indiferente General 1601, no. 5, Melchor Portocarrero y Lasso de la Vega to Crown, 31 March 1687; *London Gazette*, 19 May 1687. The published account does not mention the role the natives played when the pirates were captured. Bannister and three of his consorts were hanged on the vessel and brought back to Port Royal dangling from a yardarm.

43. TNA, Colonial Office 1/64, fols. 41–42, Duke of Albemarle to Board of Trade and Plantations, 11 February 1688. An initial alliance was probably agreed on in the mid-1630s. One of the headmen was a certain Jeremy, the son of Oldman, who was referred to as king of the Mosquitos after the visit. However, this title can be interpreted as a political myth used to legitimize weak leadership. See Mary W. Helms, "Of Kings and Contexts: Ethnohistorical Interpretation of Moskito Political Structure and Function," *American Ethnologist* 13 (1986): 508–13.

44. A captured Mosquito raider compared himself with European privateers

when he described his trade as to sail the seas as a "Cosario." See AGCA, AI (Nicaragua), leg. 77, exp. 632, fols. 9–12, declaration of Saintin, 2 May 1710.

CHAPTER 6. SHIFTING ALLIANCES ON PANAMÁ'S DARIÉN FRONTIER

1. Paul E. Hoffman, *The Spanish Crown and the Defense of the Caribbean, 1535–1585: Precedent, Patrimonialism, and Royal Parsimony* (Baton Rouge: Louisiana State University Press, 1980), 181–210. For the raids, see John Cummins, *Francis Drake: The Lives of a Hero* (London: St. Martin's Press, 1995), 44–64; Harry Kelsey, *Sir Francis Drake: The Queen's Pirate* (New Haven, Conn.: Yale University Press, 1998), 46–50. An account of the relations between the freebooters and maroons is in Ruth Pike, "The Cimarrons of Sixteenth-Century Panama," *Americas* 64 (2007): 255–66.

2. Alfredo Castillero Calvo, *Conquista, evangelización y resistencia: Triunfo o fracaso de la política indigenista?* (Panamá: Editorial Mariano Arosemena, 1995), 159–68.

3. AGI, Panamá 19, ramo 5, no. 52, Enrique Enríquez de Sotomayor to Crown, 15 July 1638; BL, Sloane Ms. 758, fol. 159, journal of Nathaniel Butler, 24 August 1639.

4. AGI, Contaduría 1480, fols. 34–36, testimonies of Domingo Rodríguez and Blas de Peralta, 11 April 1650. The Spaniards learned that the intruders, with the assistance of the indigenous population, planned to cross the isthmus and reach the South Sea. This prompted the authorities to build a small colonial outpost, El Real de Santa María, in the east of the province, which, in turn, led to a native uprising in early 1651.

5. Peter Earle, *The Sack of Panamá* (London: Norman and Hobhouse, 1981), 241–42.

6. Bodleian Library, University of Oxford, Ms. Rawlinson A. 175, fols. 313–15, James Jeniten to Samuel Pepys, 29 May 1675.

7. ANOM, Colonies C⁹ᴬ 1, fol. 130, Jacques Nepveu de Pouancey to Jean-Baptiste Colbert, 1 April 1677.

8. Longleat House, Coventry Papers 75, fols. 203–04, Charles Atkinson to Sir Thomas Lynch, 18 and 23 July 1677; AGI, Panamá 26, ramo 3, no. 42, Lucas Fernández de Piedrahita to Junta de Guerra, 1 November 1677; BL, Sloane Ms. 2724, fols. 12–13, Symon Musgrave to Earl of Carlisle, 14 November 1680.

9. AGI, Panamá 25, ramo 4, no. 25, memorandum of Luis Carrisoli de Alfaraz, 11 April 1678. This relatively small group was in frequent conflict with neighboring Cunas, Urabas, and Ogonias. The Gorgonas requested to be resettled to the Isla del Rey, but on inspection the small island was deemed uninhabitable due to a lack of food sources.

10. AGI, Panamá 37, no. 65, Juan Matías Pérez to Crown, 25 April 1677; AGI, Santa Fé 255, fols. 169–71, report of Joseph de Campos, 21 December 1677; AGI, Panamá 84, fols. 6–7, Alonso de Mercado y Villacorta to Crown, 25 December 1678.

11. AGI, Panamá 27, ramo 2, no. 10, examination of Gregorio de Ochoa, 19 September 1679; AGI, Panamá 99, no. 81, Bernardo de Madrid to Crown, 15 August 1685.

12. Ignacio J. Gallup-Diaz, *The Door of the Seas and Key to the Universe: Indian Politics and Imperial Rivalry in the Darién, 1640–1750* (New York: Columbia University Press, 2004), 25–68.

13. Mary W. Helms, *Ancient Panama: Chiefs in Search of Power* (Austin: University of Texas Press, 1979), 119–79; Carl H. Langebaek, "Cuna Long Distance Journeys: The Result of Colonial Interactions," *Ethnology* 30 (1991): 371–80.

14. William Dampier, *A New Voyage Round the World* (London: James Knapton, 1697), 181–84. Dampier suggests that this happened roughly between 1665 and 1668.

15. AGI, Panamá 27, ramo 2, no. 10, inquest of Isidro Roz del Castillo, 18 and 19 December 1679; AGI, Panamá 95, no. 19, report of Sebastián de Velasco, 18 July 1680.

16. BL, Sloane Ms. 3820, fol. 1, journal of Basil Ringrose, 23 March 1680.

17. AGI, Panamá 95, no. 24, Alonso de Mercado y Villacorta to Crown, 14 February 1680; AGI, Panamá 95, no. 21, Lucas Romero Parrilla and Juan Matías Pérez to Crown, 15 July 1680.

18. AGI, Panamá 95, no. 18, Lucas Fernández de Piedrahita to Crown, 14 July 1680. This letter gives the number of indigenous casualties as more than thirteen hundred, but this is certainly exaggerated. For the discovery of the gold deposits, see AGI, Panamá 95, no. 41, Francisco de Villafañe to Lope de Sierra Osorio, 25 June 1680; AGI, Panamá 231, libro 8, fols. 223–24, real cédula, 14 July 1681.

19. AGI, Panamá 95, no. 37, declaration of Juan de Salbatierra, 2 March 1680; BL, Sloane Ms. 2752, fols. 31–32, account of the assault on Portobelo, 1680; AGI, Escribanía de Cámara 456A, pieza 3, fols. 988–91, testimony of Joseph de Victoria, 23 June 1681.

20. BL, Sloane Ms. 2752, fols. 34–35, journal of a voyage with John Coxon, 8 to 13 March 1680; AGI, México 52, no. 10, examination of Lucas Antonio Gobea, 4 October 1680. The present-day name of Golden Island is Isla Seletupa.

21. BL, Sloane Ms. 3820, fols. 3–4, journal of Basil Ringrose, 5 April 1680; BL, Sloane Ms. 46B, fol. 3, journal of Bartholomew Sharpe, 7 April 1680. Sombrero de Oro also features prominently in Juan Francisco de Páramo y Cepeda's "Alteraciones del Dariel," completed by 1697. This epic poem essentially recounted the story of the conflict in the Darién and incorporated various references to Cuna leaders and their culture that the author became acquainted with during visits to the region. See Biblioteca Nacional, Madrid, Ms. 3971, fols. 21–32. For the background, see AGI, Panamá 95, no. 46, Lucas Fernández de Piedrahita to Alonso de Mercado y Villacorta, 9 February 1681.

22. A chief is the head of a regional group with limited social differentiation. A chief's position is hereditary and reinforced by social ranking. See Timothy K. Earle, *How Chiefs Came to Power: The Political Economy in Prehistory* (Stanford, Cal.: Stanford University Press, 1997), 4–7.

23. BL, Sloane Ms. 3820, fol. 2, journal of Basil Ringrose, 23 March 1680. Firearms do not seem to have played a role in cross-cultural exchange at this stage.

24. AGI, Panamá 37, no. 65, Juan Matías Pérez to Crown, 25 April 1677; BL,

Sloane Ms. 3236, fol. 16, Lionel Wafer's observations among the Cunas, ca. 1691. Missionaries were prohibited from trading with the natives, but a series of decrees against this practice indicates that at least some of them did. See, for example, AGI, Panamá 231, libro 7, fol. 40, real cédula, 26 November 1672; AGI, Panamá 231, libro 7, fol. 236, real cédula, 3 April 1675; AGI, Panamá 231, libro 8, fols. 42–43, real cédula, 6 December 1678.

25. BL, Sloane Ms. 3236, fol. 16, Lionel Wafer's observations among the Cunas, ca. 1691.

26. Philip Ayres, *The Voyages and Adventures of Capt. Barth. Sharp and others, in the South Sea* (London: Richard Holmes, 1684), 1. This book is based on the journal of John Cox, a participant in the foray. The raiders who later returned to England created the myth of a Cuna empire that had granted them a commission to assault Spanish possessions.

27. BL, Sloane Ms. 3820, fols. 7–8, journal of Basil Ringrose, 10 to 14 April 1680; BL, Sloane Ms. 46A, fols. 4–5, journal of Bartholomew Sharpe, 11 to 14 April 1680.

28. BL, Sloane Ms. 3820, fol. 10, journal of Basil Ringrose, 16 April 1680. It appears that the entire Cuna population consisted of not much above fifteen thousand souls. See Omar Jaén Suárez, *La población del Istmo de Panamá: Estudio de geohistoria* (Madrid: Ediciones de Cultura Hispánica, 1998), 115–19. For anthropological research about chiefs traveling to form alliances, see James Howe, *The Kuna Gathering: Contemporary Village Politics in Panama* (Austin: University of Texas Press, 1986), 72–75.

29. Magdelene College, University of Cambridge, Pepys Library PL 2349, fol. 4, journal of John Cox, 15 April 1680. The Cuna leader was also reported to have claimed that his daughter had been abducted by Spaniards and held captive in El Real de Santa María.

30. AGI, Panamá 95, no. 11, declaration of Juan de Ulloa, 28 May 1680; AGI, Panamá 38, no. 15a, memorandum of Alonso de Mercado y Villacorta, 27 September 1680. The captives were set ashore near Santa Marta, from where they got to Cartagena.

31. BL, Sloane Ms. 3236, fol. 14, Lionel Wafer's observations among the Cunas, ca. 1691.

32. Lionel Wafer, *A New Voyage and Description of the Isthmus of America* (London: James Knapton, 1699), 8–34. An outline of Jacinto de Peralta's previous activities is in AGI, Panamá 27, ramo 2, no. 10, examinations of Felipe Esteban and Gregorio de Ochoa, 19 September 1679. Wafer identified the leader as a certain Lacenta. For the medical practices of either party, see Jörg Wolfgang Helbig, *Religion und Medizinmannwesen bei den Cuna* (Hohenschäflarn: Klaus Renner, 1983), 139–71; Stephen Snelders, "Chirurgijns onder zeerovers in de 17e eeuw," *Nederlands Tijdschrift voor de Geneeskunde* 24 (2005): 2933–36.

33. Gallup-Diaz, *Door of the Seas*, 22.

34. AGI, Panamá 26, ramo 5, no. 108, declaration of Marcelo de la Quintana, 15 July 1680. It appears that, similar to the Mosquitos, some Cuna groups permanently settled near the coast to profit from ties to non-Spanish visitors. In the following year,

a vessel from New England sailed along the shoreline with a crew that was intent on capturing natives to be sold into slavery, but the known landing places in the Darién were spared from such assaults. See NA, Sociëteit van Suriname 212, fols. 88–94, interrogation of Charles Watts, 7 January 1684.

35. Mateo de Anguiano, *Vida, y virtudes de el Capuchino español, el V. siervo de Dios Fr. Francisco de Pamplona* (Madrid: Imprenta Real, 1704), 300–305.

36. AGI, Panamá 95, no. 46, Lucas Fernández de Piedrahita to Alonso de Mercado y Villacorta, 9 and 21 February 1681; AGI, Panamá 95, no. 47, Alonso de Mercado y Villacorta to Crown, 5 March 1681.

37. Rigsarkivet, København, Vestindisk-Guineisk Kompagni 79, fols. 220–21, George Coxon, Edward Cooke, and Steven Daniel to John Scott, 30 May 1682. By 1684 Golden Cap was dead, apparently killed by Spaniards, but no details are recorded.

38. AGI, Panamá 99, no. 9, Lucas Fernández de Piedrahita to Crown, 8 August 1684. At the same time as Fernández de Piedrahita visited the Darién, the Junta de Guerra began to plan a large-scale military conquest of the entire region. Due to a lack of resources, however, the scheme was never translated into action.

39. NA, Verenigde Oost-Indische Compagnie 1483, fols. 455–56, journal of a voyage with Peter Harris, 10 June 1684; AGI, Guatemala 29, ramo 2, no. 41, declaration of Gabriel Gómez de Guzmán, 29 December 1684.

40. AGI, Lima 85, no. 82, pt. 4, Melchor de Navarra y Rocafull to Pedro de Pontefranca y Llerena, 20 September 1684; AN, Marine B[4] 9, fol. 457, journal of Jérôme Raveneau de Lussan, 10 March 1685; AGI, Panamá 96, no. 137, Pedro de Pontefranca y Llerena to Crown, 5 May 1685; BnF, Nouvelles acquisitions françaises 7485, pt. 1, fols. 110–13, memorandum of Pierre-Paul Tarin de Cussy, 4 May 1688. These groups were joined by John Brandy along with his crew who had previously arrived in Panamá as contraband traders and stayed for a while among the Cunas. For his activities, see AGI, Guadalajara 26, ramo 3, no. 25, fols. 16–20, declaration of Antonio Hierro, 1 March 1686.

41. NA, Verenigde Oost-Indische Compagnie 1483, fols. 456–57, journal of a voyage with Peter Harris, 24 June 1684; AGI, Panamá 99, no. 1270, fols. 53–61, confession of John Newman, 11 July 1686; HL, Blathwayt Papers BL 327, examination of Richard Arnold, 4 August 1686.

42. AGI, Lima 85, no. 82, pt. 6, declaration of Juan Bernal Pacheco, 20 February 1685.

43. Rockefeller Library, Colonial Williamsburg Foundation, William Blathwayt Papers 25, folder 2, Hender Molesworth to William Blathwayt, 27 April 1685. Most crews that arrived on the Darién coast in 1684 and 1685 did not plan to return and burned their old vessels on the beach. This vessel had been commanded by Michel Andresson, who was deserted by most of his crew.

44. AGI, Panamá 231, libro 8, fols. 354–58, reales cédulas, 12 March 1685. There is no indication that the mine was really closed.

45. AGI, Panamá 99, no. 1270, fols. 7–11, Andrés Pérez Morrión to Juan de Panda y Estrada, 9 August 1685. The Spanish records contain various references to family ties between the chiefs. Among the chiefs who were supposed to have switched sides was a certain Jacinto, presumably Jacinto de Peralta.

46. AGI, Panamá 181, fols. 906–10, Pedro de Pontefranca y Llerena to Luis Carrisoli de Alfaraz, 30 August 1685; AGI, Panamá 167, ramo 2, no. 3, Pedro de Pontefranca y Llerena to Crown, 3 October 1685. In one instance, natives were reported to have refused to lead freebooters into an ambush.

47. TNA, Colonial Office 1/58, fols. 173–76, Hender Molesworth to William Blathwayt, 25 September 1685 (quote); Harry Ransom Center, University of Texas at Austin, Pforzheimer Ms. 103c, box 9, folder 4, Bulstrode newsletter, 14 December 1685; *Oprechte Haerlemsche Courant*, 22 November 1685.

48. AGI, Panamá 99, no. 1270, fols. 7–11, Andrés Pérez Morrión to Juan de Panda y Estrada, 9 August 1685; AGI, Panamá 167, ramo 2, no. 12, reward decree of Martín de Zevallos y la Cerda, 30 September 1688.

49. ANOM, Colonies C^{9A} 1, fols. 376–88, Pierre-Paul Tarin de Cussy to Jean-Baptiste Colbert de Seigneley, 27 August 1687; AGI, Panamá 181, fols. 811–18, merits of Luis Carrisoli de Alfaraz, 10 October 1699.

50. BnF, Nouvelles acquisitions françaises 9325, fols. 351–56, Jean-Baptiste du Casse to Louis Phélypeaux de Pontchartrin, 1 October 1697; University of Glasgow Library, Spencer Collection, Ms. Gen. 1681, fols. 218–19, journal of Robert Pennycook, 6 November 1698; ANOM, Colonies C^{9A} 4, fols. 36–41, Jean-Baptiste du Casse to Louis Phélypeaux de Pontchartrin, 5 February 1699; TNA, Admiralty 1/2033, no. 20, Richard Long to Board of Admiralty, 17 June 1700; AGI, Panamá 177, no. 13, Fernando Dávila Bravo de Lagunas to Crown, 9 June 1701. Frenchmen were reported to have provided the natives with firearms, but locals struggled to use them effectively. See Lionel Wafer, *A New Voyage and Description of the Isthmus of America* (London: James Knapton, 1704), 276. There is also a reference to a Cuna leader who had previously stayed with French freebooters in Petit-Goâve in the National Library of Scotland, Edinburgh, Advocates Ms. 83.7.4, no. 15, journal of Hugh Rose, 23 December 1698.

51. Gerhard Sandner, *Zentralamerika und der ferne karibische Westen: Konjunkturen, Krisen und Konflikte, 1503–1984* (Wiesbaden: Franz Steiner Verlag, 1985), 113.

CHAPTER 7. THE SOUTH SEA INCURSIONS

1. Glyndwr Williams, *The Great South Sea: English Voyages and Encounters, 1570–1750* (New Haven, Conn.: Yale University Press, 1997), 15–20.

2. Numerous publications outline Drake's exploits in the South Sea. See, above all, John Cummins, *Francis Drake: The Lives of a Hero* (London: Palgrave Macmillan, 1995), 87–114; Harry Kelsey, *Sir Francis Drake: The Queen's Pirate* (New Haven, Conn.: Yale University Press, 1998), 137–71; Samuel Bawlf, *The Secret Voyage of Sir Francis Drake, 1577–1580* (New York: Penguin Books, 2003), 112–64.

NOTES TO CHAPTER SEVEN

3. Carlos Valenzuela Solis de Ovando, *Piratas en el Pacífico* (Santiago: La Noria, 1993), 55–61; Richard F. Hitchcock, "Cavendish's Last Voyage: John Jane's Narrative of the Voyage of the *Desire*," *Mariner's Mirror* 89 (2003): 4–12.

4. Vibeke Roeper and Diederick Wildeman, *Ontdekkingsreizen van Nederlanders, 1590–1650* (Utrecht: Kosmos, 1993), 91–97.

5. Peter T. Bradley, *The Lure of Peru: Maritime Intrusions into the South Sea, 1598–1701* (London: Macmillan, 1989), 49–85; Pablo Álvarez and Marijke van Meurs, *Chile a la vista: Navegantes holandeses del siglo XVII* (Santiago: Dirección de Bibliotecas, Archivos y Museos, 1999), 88–91; Benjamin Schmidt, "Exotic Allies: The Dutch-Chilean Encounter and the (Failed) Conquest of America," *Renaissance Quarterly* 52 (1999): 440–68. The Dutch had a special affinity for Native Americans because both were perceived as victims of Spanish tyranny. For the last voyage, see also Henk den Heijer, *Goud en Indianen: Het journaal van Hendrick Brouwers expeditie naar Chili in 1643* (Zutphen: Walburg Pers, 2015), 38–43; Mark Meuwese, *To the Shores of Chile: The Journal and History of the Brouwer Expedition to Valdivia in 1643* (University Park: Pennsylvania State University Press, 2019), 4–15.

6. Pablo E. Pérez Mallaína Bueno and Bibiano Torres Ramírez, *Armada del Mar del Sur* (Sevilla: Escuela de Estudios Hispano-Americanos, 1987), 222–29.

7. Pierpont Morgan Library, New York, Ms. MA 3310, fols. 14–15, journal of Bartholomew Sharpe, 25 May 1680; AGI, Panamá 95, no. 38, Alonso de Mercado y Villacorta, Fernando Jiménez Panyagua, Jacinto Roldan de la Cuenca, et al. to Crown, 23 July 1680.

8. Free Library of Philadelphia, Ms. Elkins 169, fols. 16–17, William Hack, "Bartholomew Sharpe's South Sea Waggoner," ca. 1688.

9. BL, Sloane Ms. 3236, fol. 6, journal of William Dampier, 3 May 1681.

10. Juan David Montoya Guzmán, "Guerras interétnicas y anticoloniales: 'Bárbaros' y españoles en las tierras bajas del Pacífico, siglos XVI y XVII," *Historia y Espacio* 31 (2008): 61–88.

11. Magdalene College, University of Cambridge, Pepys Library PL 2349, fol. 14, journal of John Cox, 27 August 1680. The information was only entered into the journal when the main company learned of the fate of Doleman's crew.

12. Eulalia Carrasco, *El pueblo Chachi: El jeengume avanza* (Quito: Abya-Yala, 1983), 12–25. For the demography of the region, see Luis F. Calero, *Chiefdoms under Siege: Spain's Rule and Native Adaptation in the Southern Colombian Andes, 1535–1700* (Albuquerque: University of New Mexico Press, 1997), 155–61. An outline of the native contribution to mining is in Caroline A. Williams, "Resistance and Rebellion on the Spanish Frontier: Native Responses to Colonization in the Colombian Chocó, 1670–1690," *Hispanic American Historical Review* 79 (1999): 406.

13. AGI, Indiferente General 2578, no. 10, declaration of Gabriel Pérez de Leiba, 18 July 1681.

14. BL, Sloane Ms. 49, fol. 20, journal of John Cox, 28 to 30 October 1680; BL,

Sloane Ms. 3820, fols. 62–65, journal of Basil Ringrose, 28 to 31 October 1680; BL, Sloane Ms. 46A, fol. 48, journal of Bartholomew Sharpe, 2 November 1680.

15. It appears that the gold production in the late seventeenth century was at a low, but the raiders evidently did not know about this. For the background, see Augusto Millán Urzua, *Historia de la minería del oro en Chile* (Santiago: Editorial Universitaria, 2001), 88–89.

16. BL, Sloane Ms. 3820, fol. 71, journal of Basil Ringrose, 3 December 1680. According to Ringrose, a captured friar informed him that "the Spaniard had kild most of theire Chilean Slaves for fear they should run from them" at the time when the buccaneers attacked. However, the surviving Spanish sources do not contain any hint to such an atrocity. See AGI, Indiferente General 2578, no. 1b, report of Juan Enríquez, 8 April 1681. The fact that slaves were not mentioned in any official Spanish records can be explained with the *real cédula* of 12 June 1679 (AGI, Indiferente General 430, libro 42, fols. 243–46), which strictly banned indigenous slavery. In the previous decades, a series of Mapuche uprisings had provided the authorities with the justification to expand indigenous enslavement. See, for example, Walter Hanisch, "Esclavitud y libertad de los indios de Chile, 1608–1694," *Historia* 16 (1981): 26–58; Guillaume Boccara, *Guerre et ethnogenèse mapuche dans le Chili colonial: l'invention du soi* (Paris: L'Harmattan, 1998), 281–93.

17. BL, Sloane Ms. 46B, fols. 51–52, journal of Bartholomew Sharpe, 3 to 5 December 1680; BL, Sloane Ms. 3820, fols. 70–75, journal of Basil Ringrose, 3 to 6 December 1680.

18. Biblioteca Colombina, Sevilla, Capitular Manuscritos 60–1–4, fol. 61, Francisco de Peralta to Juan Enríquez, 17 December 1680. Similar to conditions in the Caribbean, marauders also abducted native sailors from prizes and forced them to perform menial tasks on their vessels. See AGI, Indiferente General 2578, no. 1, testimony of Francisco Gabriel, 18 July 1680; BL, Sloane Ms. 2752, fol. 64, journal of a voyage with John Coxon, 30 July 1681. A group of coerced "Negroes & Indians" attempted to rise against Sharpe's men by killing them in their sleep, but the plot was discovered and the ringleader, a native man from Iquique in northern Chile, swiftly executed. See BL, Sloane Ms. 3280, fol. 122, journal of Basil Ringrose, 12 August 1681; AGI, Indiferente General 2578, no. 18, declaration of Francisco Bernardo, 31 August 1682.

19. BL, Sloane Ms. 46A, fol. 85, journal of Bartholomew Sharpe, 8 May 1681.

20. Magdalene College, University of Cambridge, Pepys Library PL 2349, fol. 60, journal of John Cox, 27 October 1681.

21. AGI, Panamá 95, no. 22, account of Diego de Vallejo Aragón, 29 July 1680; AGI, Lima 81, no. 14, decree of Francisco Gutiérrez de Escalante, 28 December 1680; AGI, Indiferente General 2578, no. 3, Francisco Gutiérrez de Escalante to Crown, 2 July 1681. For the weak defenses of the region, largely due to a lack of funding, see Kris E. Lane, "Buccaneers and Coastal Defense in Late Seventeenth-Century Quito: The Case of Barbacoas," *Colonial Latin American Review* 6 (1997): 143–73; Peter T. Brad-

ley, *Spain and the Defence of Peru, 1579–1700: Royal Reluctance and Colonial Self-Reliance* (Morrisville, N.C.: Lulu, 2009), 113–20.

22. BL, Sloane Ms. 2752, fol. 62, journal of a voyage with John Coxon, 8 May 1681.

23. AGCA, A3 (Nicaragua), leg. 495, exp. 3782, fols. 11–12, declaration of Antonio de Navia Bolaños, 10 October 1686; AN, Marine B⁴ 9, fol. 506, journal of Jérôme Raveneau de Lussan, 18 April 1687. In addition to the gangs that crossed the Isthmus of Panamá, three English vessels sailed around South America to join the raiders. After 1686 a number of French vessels followed suit.

24. Lambeth Palace Library, London, Ms. 642, fol. 11, journal of William Ambrose Cowley, 30 July 1684.

25. BL, Sloane Ms. 3236, fol. 45, journal of William Dampier, 25 and 26 September 1684. A captured fisherman mentioned such an ordinance, but it does not seem to have survived in the archives. It is therefore unknown whether the locals were promised any compensation.

26. BL, Sloane Ms. 3236, fols. 159–60, journal of William Dampier, 28 December 1685; AGI, Guadalajara 26, ramo 3, no. 25, declaration of Jerónimo de Savedra, 28 February 1686.

27. BL, Sloane Ms. 3236, fols. 42–44, journal of William Dampier, 26 to 30 July 1684.

28. NA, Verenigde Oost-Indische Compagnie 1483, fols. 464–65, journal of a voyage with Peter Harris, 27 July 1684. Lacking trust in the natives, the authorities began to strengthen the local defenses shortly after this incident. See AGI, Guatemala 280, no. 5, Miguel de la Vega Valbuena and Joseph Fernández de Córdoba to Enrique Enríquez de Guzmán, 1 February 1685.

29. AGI, Guatemala 29, ramo 2, no. 41a, testimonies of Juan de Rivera and Juan Ramón, 2 September 1684; AGI, Panamá 99, no. 27, Miguel Gómez de Lara to Pedro de Pontefranca y Llerena, 15 September 1684. The accounts of the natives emphasize the poverty of the region and that the defense placed a heavy burden on its population. Almost two years after the raid, a tribute relief for one year was granted.

30. BL, Sloane Ms. 3236, fols. 65–66, journal of William Dampier, 4 to 6 November 1684.

31. AGI, Lima 281, no. 5, declarations of Antonio Rodea and Miguel Vaquín, 28 October 1684; AGI, Lima 85, no. 82, pt. 6, declaration of Pedro Rodríguez, 23 December 1684. According to Rodea, the robbers applied a widely used torture method known as *strappado*, meaning that the captive's hands were tied behind the back and suspended by a rope attached to the wrists, typically resulting in dislocated shoulders while the victim was repeatedly beaten.

32. BL, Sloane Ms. 3236, fols. 73–74, journal of William Dampier, 26 to 31 December 1684; AGI, Panamá 96, no. 137, Pedro de Pontefranca y Llerena to Crown, 5 May 1685.

33. AGI, Panamá 159, fols. 66–87, declaration of Juan de Molina, 13 May 1686; HL, Blathwayt Papers BL 327, examination of Richard Arnold, 4 August 1686. For

the poor treatment of the indigenous population, see also AGI, Panamá 99, no. 182, Tomás Felix de Argandoña to Crown, 3 December 1687. De Argandoña had previously been captured by Sharpe's gang but was released and later became governor of Tucumán in Argentina.

34. AGI, Lima 86, no. 60, Melchor de Navarra y Rocafull to Crown, 22 March 1687; AGI, Panamá 99, no. 151, Pedro de Pontefranca y Llerena to Crown, 16 August 1687.

35. AGI, Lima 335, no. 68, Diego Felipe de Cuéllar to Crown, 24 June 1686. Due to a lack of corroborating sources, it is almost impossible to evaluate this report.

36. AGI, Panamá 96, no. 258, Fernando Fajardo y Álvarez de Toledo to Crown, 9 November 1686. See also Lawrence A. Clayton, "The Maritime Trade of Peru in the Seventeenth Century," *Mariner's Mirror* 72 (1986): 168–72; Carolyn Hall and Héctor Pérez Brignoli, *Historical Atlas of Central America* (Norman: University of Oklahoma Press, 2003), 128–29.

37. AGI, Chile 24, ramo 1, no. 47, José de Garro to Crown, 10 December 1688.

38. NA, Verenigde Oost-Indische Compagnie 1483, fol. 497, journal of Francis Nelly, 9 August 1685. Some of these canoes had been obtained from Cunas and taken on the journey, while others had been built on the South Sea coast just before the raiders approached their target.

39. AGI, Guatemala 75, no. 51, Cristóbal Jacinto de Valdelomar to Crown, 2 September 1685; AGI, Panamá 96, no. 182, declaration of Pedro de la Barreda Cevallos, 16 September 1685. For the significance of the provincial capital, see Nicolás Buitrango Matus, *León: La sombra de pedrarias* (Managua: Fundación Ortiz Gurdian, 1998), 165–78; Jaime Incer Barquero, *Geografía dinámica de Nicaragua* (Managua: Editorial Hispamer, 1998), 215–19.

40. BL, Sloane Ms. 3236, fols. 123–28, journal of William Dampier, 9 to 24 August 1685; AGI, Guatemala 280, no. 44, Enrique Enríquez de Guzmán to Crown, 17 September 1685.

41. Jaime Incer, *Nicaragua: Viajes, rutas y encuentros, 1502–1838* (San José: Libro Libre, 1990), 339–42; Enrique de la Concepción Fonseca, *Breve historia de los indígenas de Sutiaba* (Managua: Instituto Nicaragüense de Investigación y Educación Popular, 1995), 28–31; Mario Rizo, *Identidad y derecho: Los títulos reales del pueblo de Sutiaba* (Managua: Instituto de Historia de Nicaragua y Centroamérica, 1999), 252. Against this background it was probably no coincidence that many native inhabitants of Sutiaba were in deep debt in the following decades. See Linda A. Newson, *Indian Survival in Colonial Nicaragua* (Norman: University of Oklahoma Press, 1987), 165.

42. AGI, Panamá 96, no. 190, Antonio de Navia Bolaños to Pedro de Pontefranca y Llerena, 2 October 1685; AN, Marine B⁴ 9, fols. 471–73, journal of Jérôme Raveneau de Lussan, 1 to 28 November 1685.

43. AGCA, A3 (Nicaragua), leg. 495, exp. 3782, fols. 2–3, petition of Marcos Díaz, Juan de Castañeda, Pedro Gutiérrez, and Diego Fabián, 2 October 1686. The governor of Nicaragua claimed that native support enabled the Frenchmen to move freely in

the region and circumvent Spanish ambuscades. During the foray an indigenous man from Guayaquil, who had been abducted months earlier, escaped from the intruders. See AGI, Panamá 99, no. 182, Enrique Enríquez de Guzmán to Pedro de Pontefranca y Llerena to Crown, 16 May 1686.

44. Archivo Histórico Nacional, Madrid, Diversos Colecciones 36, no. 2, fols. 44–46, Enrique Enríquez de Guzmán to Crown, 24 October 1686.

45. AGI, Lima 281, no. 3, declarations of Juan Leal, Rodrigo Puelman, Pedro Curilao, et al., 18 February 1684; NA, Verenigde Oost-Indische Compagnie 1483, fol. 555, journal of Francis Nelly, 1 April 1684; AGI, Chile 24, ramo 1, no. 30, José de Garro to Crown, 15 April 1686. In Spanish *derroteros*, the island is described as inhabited by warlike natives. See, for example, Society of Antiquaries, London, Ms. 221, fol. 143, "Derrotero General del Mar del Sur," 1669. In the 1684 edition, the text is removed, presumably for fear of providing hostile intruders with valuable strategic information. See Hispanic Society of America, New York, K44, fol. 142.

46. AGI, Panamá 159, fols. 66–87, declaration of Juan de Molina, 13 May 1686; AGI, Guatemala 94, no. 18, certificate for Francisco Rodríguez Varillas, 27 December 1688; Jérôme Raveneau de Lussan, *Journal du voyage fait à la mer du Sud, avec les flibustiers de l'Amérique* (Paris: Jean-Baptiste Coignard, 1689), 210.

47. BL, Sloane Ms. 3236, fols. 165–67, journal of William Dampier, 1 to 7 February 1686.

48. NA, Verenigde Oost-Indische Compagnie 1483, fols. 492–93, journal of Francis Nelly, 19 February 1686; AGI, Guadalajara 26, ramo 3, no. 25, Cristóbal Zesatte to Alonso Ceballos Villagutiérrez, 1 and 2 March 1686; William Dampier, *A New Voyage Round the World* (London: James Knapton, 1697), 270–72. It appears that the bowmen were crucial to this ambush, as the Spanish firearms were described as very old and the mulattos, who suffered most casualties, were only armed with lances.

49. María del Pilar Bernal Ruiz, *La toma del puerto de Guayaquil en 1687* (Sevilla: Escuela de Estudios Hispano-Americanos, 1979), 21–47; Sebastián I. Donoso Bustamante, *Piratas en Guayaquil: Historia del asalto de 1687* (Quito: El Universo, 2006), 259–98. After the raid one hundred natives had to support the citizens rebuilding the fortifications.

50. HL, Blathwayt Papers BL 327, examination of Richard Arnold, 4 August 1686. This group also included one Mosquito man who later returned to his community. The Spanish authorities were only able to capture part of the gang after receiving intelligence from a Cuna chief. See AGI, Panamá 99, no. 271, fols. 12–18, declaration of Ignacio Hernández, 9 July 1686.

51. AN, Marine B⁴ 9, fols. 487–88, journal of Jérôme Raveneau de Lussan, 12 August 1686.

52. AGI, Lima 88, no. 17, report of Dionisio López de Artunduaga, 4 July 1688; AGCA, A3 (Guatemala), leg. 23, exp. 399, fols. 6–7, report of Jacinto de Barrios Leal, 29 April 1694.

53. AN, Marine B⁴ 9, fols. 456–61, declaration of François Jamet, Isaac Chadeau,

Charles Boutin, et al., 4 May 1688; AGI, Guatemala 30, ramo 1, no. 31, Jacinto de Barrios Leal to Crown, 15 May 1688; ANOM, Colonies C^{9A} 1, fols. 448–51, Pierre-Paul Tarin de Cussy to Jean-Baptiste Colbert de Seignelay, 18 May 1688; AGI, MP-Guatemala 17, "Mapa de lo principal de la Provincia de Nicaragua," 1716. For the French term *piperie* and its possible Tupí-Guaraní origin, see Meyer H. Parry, *A Dictionary of the World's Watercraft* (London: Chatham, 2001), 457.

54. AGI, Panamá 99, no. 288, Edward Brookes to Philip Dassigny, 19 April 1688; AGI, Guatemala 32, ramo 1, no. 10, Jacinto de Barrios Leal to Crown, 29 September 1688. In order to find the passage through the mountains connecting the Río Coco with the Patuca watershed, the Frenchmen likely had native guides.

55. BnF, Fonds français 385, fols. 19–20, journal of Etienne Massertie, 10 September 1688. This manuscript is an authentic source written by a French privateer who had participated in a raiding voyage commanded by François Rolle, né Frantz Rools, into the South Sea that lasted from April 1687 to August 1693. Part of its contents can be corroborated with information provided by abducted sailors. See AGI, México 58, ramo 1, no. 35, declarations of Juan Díaz, Martín Casillas, and Mateo Hernández, 4 May 1689; AGI, Lima 88, no. 117, declarations of Nicolás del Via, Gabriel de Mesoia, and Pedro Flores, 20 July 1690. The latter reference recounts the stories of natives who had been seized by this gang. There do not seem to be any Spanish sources describing the skirmishes near the Río Yagüez, but the presence of the intruders is confirmed in AGN, Provincias Internas 30, fols. 36–38, memorandum of Juan de Sierra, 26 July 1689. For the background see Dora Elvia Enríquez Licón, "Cargas militares y república de indios en el noreste novohispano, siglos XVII y XVIII," *Anuario de Historia Regional y de las Fronteras* 19 (2014): 15–26.

56. Sebastián I. Donoso Bustamente, *Los últimos piratas del Pacífico* (Quito: Editorial Planeta, 2014), 57–94; Frantz Olivié and Raynald Laprise, *L'enfer de la flibuste* (Toulouse: Anacharsis, 2016), 54–121.

57. In February 1686 Bernardo de Uriarte was captured by Swan's crew on México's west coast and kept on the vessel along with four enslaved natives during the Pacific crossing. In Mindanao he managed to escape and was welcomed by the sultan, who made him a gunner of his flagship in the war against the rajah of Boyan. In January 1688 de Uriarte was sent with two envoys to Manila, where he provided the Spanish authorities with an account of his captivity and, shortly thereafter, embarked on a ship bound for Acapulco. He later served on a coast-guard vessel in search of François Rolle. In February 1693 he was detained and tried by the Santo Oficio as a heretic. See AGN, Inquisición 539, exp. 24, fols. 324–61.

58. Kevin P. McDonald, *Pirates, Merchants, Settlers, and Slaves: Colonial America and the Indo-Atlantic World* (Oakland: University of California Press, 2015), 37–60.

59. Susana Aldana Rivera, "No por la honra sino por el interés: Piratas y comerciantes a fines del siglo XVII," *Buletín del Instituto Riva-Aguero* 24 (1997): 21–30.

60. Liliane Crété, *La traite des nègres sous l'Ancien Régime: le nègre, le sucre et la toile* (Paris: Francia Perrin, 1989), 177–80; Wim Klooster, "Slavenvaart op Spaanse kusten:

De Nederlandse slavenhandel met Spaans Amerika, 1648–1701," *Tijdschrift voor Zee-geschiedenis* 16 (1997): 128–33; María Cristina Navarrete Peláez, "Da las 'malas entra-das' y las estrategias del 'buen pasaje': El contrabando de esclavos en el Caribe neogra-nadino, 1550–1690," *Historia Crítica* 34 (2007): 170–73.

61. Peter Earle, *The Wreck of the* Almiranta: *Sir William Phips and the Search for the Hispaniola Treasure* (London: Macmillan, 1980), 168–90; Peter Earle, *Treasure Hunt: Shipwreck, Diving, and the Quest for Treasure in an Age of Heroes* (London: Methuen, 2007), 62–67. Most native divers originated from Florida, but four Mosquitos were also among them.

62. AGI, Indiferente General 2578, no. 7, trial of Antoine Hedou, François Le Riche, Jean Amelin, et al., 9 to 13 February 1682. For the legal standards of pirate tri-als in the Spanish empire, see Óscar Cruz Barney, *El combate a la piratería en Indias, 1555–1700* (México: Universidad Iberoamericana, 1999), 35–36. For the legal context, see Patrick S. Werner, "El régimen legal de actividad marítima del imperio hispánico: El Libro Nueve de la Recopilación," *Nicaraguan Academic Journal* 3 (2000): 39–62.

63. Kent History and Library Centre, Maidstone, U 1590/88, petition of Jeremiah Oliver, Robert Mathews, John Reed, et al., 5 May 1693. The men claimed to have been inhumanely treated when they were held captive in native villages.

64. AGI, Panamá 96, no. 2, declaration of Francisco García, 24 February 1682; TNA, Colonial Office 1/48, fols. 157–58, Sir Henry Morgan to Sir Leoline Jenkins, 8 March 1682.

65. Michael Pawson and David Buisseret, *Port Royal, Jamaica* (Kingston: Univer-sity of the West Indies Press, 2000), 38–39; Mark G. Hanna, *Pirate Nests and the Rise of the British Empire, 1570–1740* (Chapel Hill: University of North Carolina Press, 2015), 132–33.

66. ANOM, Colonies C⁹ᴬ 1, fols. 186–93, memorandum of Pierre-Paul Tarin de Cussy, 24 August 1684.

CONCLUSION

1. It has been argued that the Mosquito Coast became a middle ground with shared cultural spaces that were neither entirely native nor European, as described by Richard White. See Claudia García, "Ambivalencia de las representaciones coloniales: Lideres indios y zambos de la costa de Mosquitos a fines del siglo XVIII," *Revista de Indias* 67 (2007): 673–94. However, the evidence for the seventeenth century does not support the application of this concept to the Mosquito Coast. This stretch of land was clearly under native control. For the wider, and often unsuccessful, application of the model. see Philip J. Deloria, "What Is the Middle Ground, Anyway?," *William and Mary Quarterly* 63 (2006): 15–22.

2. For the idea of a *pax hispanica* with further references, see, above all, Wolfgang Gabbert, "The *longue durée* of Colonial Violence in Latin America," *Historical Social Research* 37 (2012): 259–64.

3. The case of Santo Domingo where *pardos* repulsed an English invasion in April 1655 is exceptional, and the outcome of this encounter was largely due to the fact that the attackers were severely weakened by disease and mortality. See Bernardo Vega, *La derrota de los ingleses en Santo Domingo, 1655* (Santo Domingo: Academia Dominicana de la Historia, 2013), 49–78; Carla Gardina Pestana, *The English Conquest of Jamaica: Oliver Cromwell's Bid for Empire* (Cambridge, Mass.: Harvard University Press, 2017), 82–85.

4. Michel-Christian Camus, "Flibuste et pouvoir royal," *Revue de la Société haïtienne d'histoire et de géographie* 49 (1993): 11–15; Michel-Christian Camus, "Les gouverneurs français de Saint-Domingue et la flibuste," *Revue de la Société haïtienne d'histoire et de géographie* 52 (1996): 1–13; Mark G. Hanna, *Pirate Nests and the Rise of the British Empire, 1570–1740* (Chapel Hill: University of North Carolina Press, 2015), 222–50. For the larger development in the Spanish empire, see Antonio Domínguez Ortiz, *La sociedad americana y la corona española en el siglo XVII* (Madrid: Editorial Marcial Pons, 1996), 151–80.

NOTE ON SOURCES

1. Carmen Boullosa, *El médico de los piratas: Bucaneros y filibusteros en el Caribe* (Madrid: Siruela, 2002), 65–71; Stephen Snelders, *Vrijbuiters van de heelkunde: Op zoek naar medische kennis in de tropen, 1600–1800* (Amsterdam, Uitgeverij Atlas, 2012), 55–56.

2. Peter Earle, *The Sack of Panamá* (London: Norman and Hobhouse, 1981), 265–66.

3. Michel-Christian Camus, "Une note critique à propos d'Exquemelin," *Revue française d'histoire d'Outre-mer* 77 (1990): 82–89. It appears that Exquemelin left the Netherlands with Governor Jan van Erpecum toward the end of 1682 to serve as an agent of the merchant Baltasar Coymans in Curaçao. He later worked under the name Alexander Oliver in the same capacity in Jamaica, where he was involved in illegal activities.

4. Archivo General de Simancas, Estado 3958, Pedro Ronquillo to Crown, 29 June 1682. An unknown observer noted with disgust that Sharpe presented himself as an adventurer, even though he was a ruthless robber. See Colonial Williamsburg, Rockefeller Library, William Blathwayt Papers 23, folder 2, anonymous letter to Sir Thomas Lynch, 31 August 1683.

5. Derek Howse and Norman J. W. Thrower, *A Buccaneer's Atlas: Basil Ringrose's South Sea Waggoner* (Berkeley: University of California Press, 1992), 261.

6. See, for example, Anna Neill, "Buccaneer Ethnography: Nature, Culture, and Nation in the Journals of William Dampier," *Eighteenth-Century Studies* 33 (2000): 172–77; Geraldine Barnes and Adrian Mitchell, "Measuring the Marvelous: Science and the Exotic in William Dampier," *Eighteenth-Century Life* 26 (2002): 47–53; Diana Preston and Michael Preston, *A Pirate of Exquisite Mind: Explorer, Naturalist, and*

Buccaneer (London: Walker and Company, 2004), 229–49; William Hasty, "Piracy and the Production of Knowledge in the Travels of William Dampier, *c.* 1679–1688," *Journal of Historical Geography* 37 (2011): 42–54.

7. Ignacio J. Gallup-Diaz, *The Door of the Seas and Key to the Universe: Indian Politics and Imperial Rivalry in the Darién, 1640–1750* (New York: Columbia University Press, 2004), 17–25. In 1698 Wafer supported the Scottish scheme to establish a colony in Darién, and the second edition of his book, published in 1704, emphasized the feasibility of an English settlement in the region, despite the Scots' disaster.

8. BnF, Fonds français 22804, fol. 271, Michel Bégon to Esprit Cabart de Villermont, 19 October 1694. According to Bégon, Raveneau fled from the law after he had stolen belongings of his landlady in France.

9. NA, Verenigde Oost-Indische Compagnie 1483, fol. 657, daily journal of Ternate, 3 June 1689.

Index

Printed in the United States
by Baker & Taylor Publisher Services